PETER OLIVER'S ORIGIN & PROGRESS
OF THE AMERICAN REBELLION

PETER OLIVER (1713-1791), ATTRIBUTED TO JOHN SINGLETON COPLEY.
Courtesy of Andrew Oliver, New York.

PETER OLIVER'S

ORIGIN & PROGRESS OF

THE AMERICAN REBELLION

A TORY VIEW

EDITED BY

DOUGLASS ADAIR & JOHN A. SCHUTZ

STANFORD UNIVERSITY PRESS

STANFORD, CALIFORNIA

Stanford University Press
Stanford, California
© 1961 by the Henry E. Huntington
Library and Art Gallery
First Published in 1961 by the Huntington Library
Reissued 1967 by Stanford University Press
by arrangement with the Huntington Library

Printed in the United States of America
Cloth ISBN 0-8047-0599-2
Paper ISBN 0-8047-0601-8

Last figure below indicates year of this printing:
03   02   01   00   99   98   97   96   95   94

Stanford University Press publications are
distributed exclusively by Stanford University
Press within the United States, Canada, and
Mexico; they are distributed exclusively by
Cambridge University Press throughout
the rest of the world.

CONTENTS

EDITORS' NOTE, 1967

For the Stanford University Press edition, we have corrected half a dozen minor errors and added the two portraits on pp. xxiii-xxiv.

J.A.S.
D.A.

INTRODUCTION

"WHO SHALL WRITE the history of the American revolution? Who can write it? Who will ever be able to write it?"[1] These questions put by John Adams to Thomas Jefferson in July 1815, thirty-nine years after the Declaration of Independence, still have not been finally answered, one hundred and forty-five years after Adams asked them. It is easy, of course, to set down today the names of dozens of scholars and hundreds of books that have attempted to tell the story of the American Revolution, but if we examine them, we must still admit we have as yet no final answer to Adams' questions. In 1958 Edmund S. Morgan, one of the ablest students of the revolutionary era, repeated the Adams' query, noting especially the wide disagreements among scholars about the causes of the revolution.[2]

One difficulty in writing a balanced history of the American Revolution arises in part from its success as a creator of our nation and our nationalistic sentiment. The revolution is a historic event that all Americans applaud today as both necessary and desirable. Unlike our Civil War, unlike the French Revolution, the American Revolution produced no lingering social trauma in the United States. No Age of Hate or counterrevolution followed. No substantial body of American citizens nursed grievances about its consequences; both contemporaries and posterity have generally agreed that our revolution had its happy ending in the 1780's. Even the nineteenth- and twentieth-century British historians were predisposed by their Whiggish assumptions to agree with the judgment.

One of the results, however, of this happy unanimity on the desirable consequences of the civil war and revolution that began in 1775 is that the chief losers—the American Loyalists—have fared badly at the hands of historians. It was nearly a hundred years after the revolution before the extremely heterodox opinion was advanced

[1] John Adams to Thomas Jefferson and Thomas McKean, July 30, 1815, *The Adams-Jefferson Letters*, ed. Lester J. Cappon (Chapel Hill, N.C., 1959), II, 451.

[2] Edmund S. Morgan, *The American Revolution: A Review of Changing Interpretations* (Washington, D.C., 1958). Morgan's concluding sentence (p. 18) is: "We must continue to ask, for we still do not fully know, what the Revolution was."

by Lorenzo Sabine that the Loyalists were not all devils. It has only been in the last fifty years that a scattering of monographs and biographies has attempted to do justice to their position. But even today the Loyalists have not found their historian, and in most textbooks and scholarly accounts of our War of Independence, the Tories still receive only grudging understanding. Paradoxically, while it has been possible for American scholars to accept the arguments of Beer, Andrews, and Gipson that Great Britain's policies toward the unruly colonies in the 1760's are both understandable and defensible, it has been difficult for many of those same scholars to accept as reasonable the position of those Anglo-Americans of 1775 who paid the price for their loyalty in exile and expropriation.[3]

Above all, the course of American history during the last hundred and seventy-five years has made the Loyalist spokesmen of 1775 *appear* to be undependable and untrustworthy historical witnesses. Even granting disinterested motives for their loyalty to the British Empire, does not their blindness to the glorious possibilities of independence, now documented by all American history since 1776, prove that they were incapable of judging accurately the significance of the events taking place before their eyes? Contrariwise, does not the same history prove that the patriots of 1776, who were such remarkable prophets about the destiny of an independent America, are also the more to be trusted about the nature of the struggle to achieve independence than the Tories who lost?

These are dubious assumptions, but they have controlled to a large extent the use that American historians have made of contemporary Tory interpretations of the American rebellion. The pamphlets and letters of an Adams, a Jefferson, and a Dickinson explaining and justifying the revolution from the patriot position, have been printed and reprinted, while Tory interpretations have been used most gingerly—and almost with apologies because they are so "distorted" and "partisan." Thomas Hutchinson's *History of ... Massachusetts-Bay* and Samuel Seabury's *Letters of a Westchester Farmer* are almost alone among the reprints of Tory literature. The complete works of Jonathan Boucher, Daniel Leonard, and Joseph Galloway

[3]George L. Beer, *The Origins of the British Colonial System, 1578-1660* (New York, 1908) and *British Colonial Policy, 1754-1765* (New York, 1933); Charles M. Andrews, *The Colonial Period of American History*, 4 vols. (New Haven, 1934-38); Lawrence H. Gipson, *The British Empire before the American Revolution*, 10 vols. (Caldwell, Ida., and New York, 1936—).

have not been republished since the eighteenth century.[4] In a recent history of American political thought Galloway's works were not even cited.[5] These Tory writers, though important, temper their language, take long views of revolution, and argue their views from principles rejected by the majority of Americans. It is understandable, therefore, that an account of rebellion that offends patriot sensibilities as Peter Oliver's does—by attacking the hallowed traditions of the revolution, challenging the motives of the founding fathers, and depicting revolution as passion, plotting, and violence—would receive rough treatment from patriot writers and thus would not be published.

Dated 1781 (the year of Yorktown), Oliver's manuscript is significantly entitled "The Origin & Progress of the *American* Rebellion," as if to emphasize the ugly, unnatural, and unjustified nature of the movement that drove him into exile and made America independent of Britain. Moreover, there is no hesitation in Oliver's judgment of the causes of the rebellion and the methods used by the leading rebels to achieve their ends. In his eyes the revolt in Massachusetts was caused by the selfish and ignoble ambition and avarice of a relatively few demagogues, who by a completely unscrupulous linking of propaganda of the word and propaganda of the deed tricked the foolish but basically contented populace of Massachusetts into unfilial rebellion against the mother country.[6]

Any reader of Oliver's account of Massachusetts' revolutionary politics will recognize that Oliver had suffered a traumatic experience. His descriptions of the leaders of the patriot party, of their program and motives, is unforgiving and bitter. And inevitably it is partisan. But it records the impressions of one who had experienced these events, knew most of the combatants intimately, and saw the collapse of the society he had lived in. His views of the rebels were

[4]Hutchinson, *The History of the Colony and Province of Massachusetts-Bay*, ed. Lawrence Shaw Mayo, 3 vols. (Cambridge, Mass., 1936); Seabury, *Letters of a Westchester Farmer (1774-1775)*, ed. Clarence H. Vance, Publications of the Westchester County Historical Society, Vol. VIII (White Plains, N.Y., 1930); Boucher, *A View of the Causes and Consequences of the American Revolution* (London, 1797); Leonard, *Massachusettensis* (London, 1776); [Galloway], *Historical and Political Reflections on the Rise and Progress of the American Rebellion* (London, 1780).

[5]Alan Pendleton Grimes, *American Political Thought* (New York, 1960).

[6]The reader will find the bitterness joined with an irony that at first seems odd. The jokes, puns, and facetiousness on a theme that was obviously tragic to Oliver personally can perhaps be explained by his belief that "the Weapons of Reason" were to be used against reasonable opponents, but that "a red hot Zealot, without understanding, is to be attacked with Ridicule."

those of a contemporary, who judged them as associates and opponents. Unlike present historians, he observed them without the filter of time and had the advantage of historical evidence that is not available to scholars. We shall never know how much evidence was purposely destroyed by the patriots; all we know is that quantities were burned. For historians, therefore, to judge Oliver by patriot evidence is plainly unfair, though many have tried and then have used Oliver's evaluations in their narratives. If Oliver seems fair when patriot evidence supports his conclusions, why are many of his other unsupported statements branded as prejudiced? But should this matter of distortion be the primary consideration of historians in using Oliver's works? Does not the chief value lie in the impressions that Oliver has of the revolution, the explanations of its character, and the judgment of its origins? Oliver witnessed a revolution that shocked him as much as it did Adams and Jefferson. Has he anything to offer as an explanation of its origins from his vantage point as one of the half-dozen leaders of the administration in Massachusetts? A sketch of Peter Oliver's life up to 1781 explains why his history is a very important contemporary account of the origins of the revolution in Massachusetts in spite of its overpowering expression of emotion.

I

Oliver was deeply committed to the old regime replaced by the rebellion. For a quarter of a century he had been a judge in the Massachusetts courts, rising finally to be chief justice of the Superior Court. He owned extensive property at Middleborough that rivaled any in New England, with a great house on a hill, a library occupying one wing, gardens, orchards, and grain fields spreading from it, and an iron foundry that made him master of an eighteenth-century industrial complex.

Oliver was closely related to the noble families of New England, the Belchers, Bradstreets, Stoddards, Vaughans, and Partridges. Daniel Oliver, the father of Peter, had married Elizabeth, sister of Governor Jonathan Belcher. Their two sons, Andrew and Peter, succeeded to the family wealth at their deaths and tripled it by the time of the revolution. In 1728 Andrew, a graduate of Harvard College like his brother, went into business with their father and four years later married Mary Sanford.[7] Besides bringing him wealth

[7]Andrew Oliver's marriage to Mary Sanford was his second. He was married to Mary, daughter of Thomas Fitch, in 1728, and had three children by the time of her

as the daughter of a rich Rhode Island merchant, Mary was the sister-in-law of Thomas Hutchinson, soon to be the colony's most important officeholder. Peter Oliver's marriage to Mary Clarke occurred about the time of his brother's marriage, bringing him also good family ties. The brothers first associated in the shipping business, sometimes including as partners the Clarkes and Hutchinsons, but then in the war years of the 1740's Peter concentrated his efforts in the iron foundry business at Middleborough and also transferred other business activity there.

Peter was unusually successful. His heavy profits from iron (war contracts) and agriculture gave him time for politics. Besides serving in community and church positions in Middleborough, he accepted a commission as justice of the peace in 1744, then as justice of the Common Pleas Court of Plymouth in 1748, and finally as associate judge of the colony's highest court, the Superior Court, in 1756. During these years his participation in government was rivaled and surpassed by his brother's. Before 1756 Andrew had served as a member of both the lower and upper houses of the legislature, and in that year he became the secretary of the colony. Rising even higher in power was their friend Thomas Hutchinson. A councilor, a judge, and chief adviser of the governor, in 1758 Hutchinson was named the lieutenant governor of Massachusetts.

For the first time in 1759 Peter Oliver took a seat in the upper house (the Council), with his brother and Hutchinson. A year later he promoted the marriage of his son and namesake to Sara Hutchinson, daughter of the lieutenant governor, who was soon to become Oliver's colleague and chief on the Superior Court. These ties of the Olivers and Hutchinsons multiplied as they advanced in the colony's offices. When Hutchinson succeeded to the governorship, Andrew Oliver soon became the lieutenant governor, and Peter the chief justice of the Superior Court. Their sons, sons-in-law, and lesser relatives filled other important offices of government. Peter Oliver, as one of the big three in Massachusetts politics in the 1770's, served as one of the judges in the trial of the Boston Massacre soldiers, was a leading figure in the controversy over British salaries for the judges, and was an intimate adviser of governors Hutchinson and Gage.

---

death in 1732. Andrew spent most of his life in Boston, developed his father's business into a vast mercantile enterprise, and divided his energy in later life between his various businesses and his public offices. Clifford K. Shipton, *Sibley's Harvard Graduates* . . . , VII (Boston, 1945), 383-412.

When Boston was sealed off from the country by Gage's orders in 1775, Peter chose to remain in the town, serving as a Mandamus Councilor, a manager of the Loyalist Association, and a supporter of General Gage. Though Peter's health was poor and he suffered much from the shock of the revolution, sometime during the siege he became interested in preserving a record of the revolutionary crisis and began collecting evidence.

Peter Oliver wrote most of the "Origin & Progress" in the quiet of a small cottage in suburban London. "I live in a retired Part of the Town, clean, healthy & free from Noise; the Doctor and his Family with me; many of our New England Acquaintance nigh me & the rest I can see every Day. I can at once burst into the Bustle of Life or remain in a still & almost rural Retreat. The Amusements & Instructions of Life are easily entred into, or I can entertain my self, undisturbed, with my Book; every Thing is upon such an extensive Scale, that a Person must be compleatly stupid to wear out Life in Complaints of having nothing to do."[8] His few surviving letters show little bitterness, except that he was bewildered as most exiles were by the success of the revolution and by its complete overturn of their career and life expectations, and he wondered at its cause. He could see God's punishment in the later madness of Otis and Hawley, the ruined estates of Hancock, and the early deaths of Warren and others. But he could not help asking himself how the revolution occurred and why he was an exile.

II

For the actual beginning of Peter Oliver's narrative of the revolution, readers may turn to Chapter II of the "Origin & Progress." His preliminary remarks, though important in drawing the historical lines of separation between Britain and her colonies, represent the usual Tory search for an explanation of rebellion.[9] Starting in 1761 political events had an explosive quality, a volcanic pressure, which made them revolutionary. When the lava spread in succeeding years, the fire ate away the hard surface of American loyalty and institutions, and the fire of revolution soon was everywhere.

"I can see a concatenation of Incidents," he says, which ushered in

[8]Peter Oliver to Polly Watson Hutchinson, April 2, 1777, Hutchinson-Watson Papers, Massachusetts Historical Society.

[9]Oliver himself apologizes for this very long introduction. He calls it a "Porch" and notes that the reader need not enter the house by the porch but can open the door of the main building, which is attached at the "End of the Porch."

the revolution. The first was the contested appointment of Thomas Hutchinson as chief justice of the Superior Court of Massachusetts by James Otis, Jr., in behalf of his father. The high bench had long been regarded as a place of prestige in the colony, and Otis, Sr., aspired to the position as a reward for his service to governors Shirley and Pownall. Though Oliver ignores this issue of service, he sees the issue just the same as a political battle between Hutchinson and Otis and details the merits of the men, favoring his friend and relative by marriage, Thomas Hutchinson. Oliver evaluates the dispute significantly in political terms and names Otis' friends, Joseph Hawley, Samuel Adams, and John Hancock, and a chorus of clergymen who supported Otis in the pulpit as the founders of the revolutionary party. Oliver dislikes Otis because he was a political manager, whose rough-and-tumble politics in the House of Representatives were hardly fitting qualifications for the high court. Otis revealed his character when he was refused the judgeship. He spread the volcanic fire of his opposition, and Oliver notes how flaws in the character of Otis' friends then carried the lava of discontent to the masses. Oliver finds in Otis, Jr., unbridled passions, a near-fatal desire for liquor, and a defect in his armor of honor as a lawyer that made him vulnerable to revolutionary fire. Hawley, too, possessed passions that got him into trouble. His religious enthusiasm bordered on insanity and, perhaps, was an early manifestation of a nervous disorder that was later to ruin his career. Samuel Adams, Oliver observes, was said to resemble Satan, undoubtedly because he was unprincipled, associated with the lower orders of mankind, and was a bankrupt. Hancock, on the other hand, had no depth of wickedness. His mind was a "meer Tabula Rasa"; he had no genius for trade and no understanding of men; he allowed Adams to involve him in serpentine plots without realizing their significance. Hancock's weakness was the unintelligent use of his economic resources. Oliver also sees many of these same character flaws in the Congregational clergy. They were too close to the people, particularly to the Boston mob. Charles Chauncy, he notes, was bombastic, ill-tempered, and rash in his relations with others, while Jonathan Mayhew and Samuel Cooper lacked piety, judgment, and devotion to lawful government. In short, Otis' party was filled with people who permitted passion to run away with reason. Oliver's impressions may be distorted and one-sided, but the personalities are differentiated and given a character analysis of a quality too valuable to be ignored in judging politics in the 1760's.

Moreover, society had allowed violations of the law to undermine its reverence for order until its legislators, without regard for honor, were attacking Governor Francis Bernard on many issues of little real importance. They finally used the Stamp Act to convince "Government of their Influence," by inciting opposition against Thomas Hutchinson, Andrew Oliver, and the customs officers. They aroused the passions of the people, and, observes Oliver, even "pious Men seemed to be wholly absorbed in the Temper of Riot." Though mob rule was shocking, the behavior of William Pitt, who rejoiced in American resistance, was worse, because "it is more eligible to be without Laws, than to leave those that are made unexecuted & trampled upon by the dirty Foot of Rebellion or Faction."

The repeal of the Stamp Act gave the leaders proof of their power. They now struck hard at local opposition, purging the Council, defaming the governor, and exciting the people through the press. The emotion aroused by these tactics was fed by the opposition to the Townshend Acts in 1767, when the leaders employed nonimportation of British goods and increased smuggling to block the effectiveness of the law. The opposition took an emotional form: home manufacturing, substitutes for tea, and scenes of frenzy. The leaders worked the people into such a state that all government was challenged. Bernard lost control of the administration, and troops came to Boston to rescue him. Safety was restored, and the town was quieter, if for only a short time, than for years. But "nocturnal Meetings" of the leaders kept the nonimportation agreements strong, and a shift of power brought John and Samuel Adams into prominence. More able than Otis and Hawley, they directed the attack upon lawful government.

There happened at this time a scrimmage between the British troops and rowdy elements in the town, branded by the patriots as a massacre in order to whip up local emotion. Evidence was collected on its cause; the clergy denounced the army from their pulpits; but the courts freed the soldiers after a fair trial. The justices were threatened with assassination; the courtrooms of the colony were repeatedly violated by mob demonstrations; and juries were intimidated.

With this destruction of orderly government, the leaders coerced the people, using tar and feathers and "every low & dirty Art." The press defamed officials, referring to them as "limping Dog," "Tom Cod," or anything else that would ridicule them. These derisive measures still did not destroy the appearance of government, though it was long helpless in enforcing its will. Governor Hutchinson, courageous and resourceful, tried to maintain the dignity of government, but "the Feathers came through his Cushion, & made him restless." Then the Boston Tea Party destroyed the appearance of government, and the faction was faced with "Neck or Nothing": revolution had come.

Though the faction was at last successful, forces were unleashed that it could not manage. Morality was gone; respect for human dignity, family, and peace went with the Gospel when the clergy substituted politics for God. The courts were soon to be closed, while the chief justice, Peter Oliver, feared for his life. The people now formed associations and openly took government into their own hands. Boston became an armed camp, and battles between soldiers and militiamen challenged British rule.

Oliver employs symbolic figures to explain the course of revolution. The explosive character of the political disturbance is illustrated by the volcano, its eruptive quality, the lava flow, and the spreading ash. The infectious growth of the revolution is described as the Hydra of mythology. Fed by greed, passion, and violence, the beast grew its heads, and the poisoned tongues spit forth the venom. Otis' spite in 1761 started its growth; Hawley, Adams, the clergy, and the newer leaders of 1767-1769 sprouted forth; the mob actions of 1765, 1768, 1770, and 1773 were the poison; the fall of Bernard, Hutchinson, and Oliver was the food. The revolution, therefore, was the result not of new institutions but of a decline in the political leadership of Massachusetts, unchecked by the mother country and, indeed, aided by William Pitt and others.

III

To give color to his work Oliver used a variety of classical and poetical quotations. Besides their selection from many famous and once-famous authors, the most impressive thing about them is their accuracy. Most poetical lines are copied with care, observing capitalization and punctuation. Apparently Oliver based many of his statements, like incidents of tar and feathering, upon newspaper accounts, taken usually from the Boston *Weekly News-Letter*. The quotations that have been located are accurate, and the essential facts in his descriptions are handled with care. Most dates and allusions to events, when they can be checked, are accurate. One is impressed again and again by the care with which Oliver wrote his history.

Though Oliver's descriptions of the revolutionaries have been criticized as prejudiced, they should be treated differently. They were impressions; they were not intended as portraits, except to reveal the hidden weaknesses of character that produced the Hydra. They were drawn in heavy lines, to emphasize passion, lust, ignorance, and any other defect that created the revolutionary disposition. In magnifying defects, Oliver had probably not intended to violate standards of accuracy, and in one place he admitted that he was in error. He may have penetrated deeper into a patriot's character than modern historians have done. George Anderson, writing the life of Ebenezer Mackintosh, considered Oliver's evaluation of Mackintosh basically sound, in spite of an appearance of exaggeration. John C. Miller cited Oliver's manuscript many times in his *Sam Adams* in order to establish character evaluations for Otis, Cooper, Samuel Adams, and Hancock. Alice M. Baldwin accepted Oliver's judgment concerning the power of the New England clergy over the common people and the revolutionaries. Malcolm Freiberg, in his scholarly articles on Thomas Hutchinson, has frequently cited Oliver's "Origin & Progress." There are professional historians who have refrained from quoting Oliver extensively, notably Arthur M. Schlesinger in his *Prelude to Independence* and Lawrence H. Gipson in his *The Coming of the Revolution, 1763-1775*. Both historians, however, have cited the works of George Anderson and John C. Miller, who have used the Oliver manuscript. Of all modern historians Clifford K. Shipton has cited Oliver with the most approval in working out the biographical details for his character studies in *Sibley's Harvard Graduates*. It is not an exaggeration to add here that Oliver's "Origin & Progress" has been cited by most historians directly or indirectly in their accounts of the revolution and that almost every page of the manuscript has been cited somewhere, though one must hasten to add that, while this is true, most professional historians cover their use of the manuscript by denouncing its Tory partiality. No historian thus far has treated it for what it is: a Tory view of revolution in Massachusetts.

While Oliver delineated his characters too sharply, he was trying to tell an accurate story of revolution. Sometimes his intemperate language was so shocking to the patriotic sensitivities of historians that his assessments of characters were dismissed without evaluations, and thus his brilliant insights were missed. His description of James Otis, Sr., for example, as one who could captivate the "Ear of Country Jurors, who were too commonly Drovers, Horse Jockies, & of other lower Classes in Life," is remarkable. Otis was a country lawyer and merchant, whose success was well established by his enlarging business. From his papers and legislative records one sees Otis as a tradesman, who had assumed the duty of a political manager for governors Shirley and Pownall. Country lawyers, it is known, worked with uneducated people, and many of the rural folk were representatives at Boston. From his ability to manage these people Otis drew his political strength but then sacrificed the respect of Peter Oliver, who regarded Otis as a valuable instrument in manipulating political power, though hardly one to grace the high bench. Otis should have held his place, and Hutchinson was justified in accepting the Superior Court appointment, if only because of his cultivated instincts as a gentleman.

Oliver's other judgments often reflect his intimate commitment to the contemporary scene. Many times his emotional language reveals his personal involvement in an event, for in nearly every clash of politics from 1759 until the revolution some member of the family was deeply concerned. His brother Andrew suffered bitterly as the stamp distributor in the riots of 1765 and was publicly humiliated at Liberty Tree. Even Andrew's funeral in 1774 was the scene of a mob reaction that made it unsafe for Peter to attend the services. Oliver's judgments, nonetheless, are valuable because they are assessments of contemporary events, insights that come from knowing the sound, smell, and feeling of the time, and impressions of one who could not join in the revolution. It is contemporary history, and Oliver has created by selective use of evidence a portrait of revolution that mirrors the feelings of a Loyalist as he sees his society crumble. His observations are important for this feeling, for the reasons that he assigns for the collapse of Massachusetts society, and for his estimates of revolutionists and Loyalists. His two impressions of the revolution, in 1776 (reprinted on page 158) and in 1781, are basically the same, except that the 1781 "Origin & Progress" has added the "Porch," or as he calls his introduction, "the procatarctick Causes." These put him in the general stream of Tory thinking that looks for long-term causes of revolution in America's development. His judgments are also significant because of his position in Massachusetts government. As chief justice of its highest court, adviser of governors, and lifelong public servant, he is a striking example of the American leader who was replaced by the rebellion. The qualities of mind and spirit as revealed in the "Origin & Progress" show Oliver to be a sophisticated gentleman of letters, utterly devoted to his country and the public service, a man whose personal charm equaled that of any revolutionist. He was caught in a struggle that allowed him no retreat, and even in the bitter days of the Boston siege he had the curiosity to ask himself how Massachusetts, presided over by so many gentlemen of peace, got embroiled in this horrifying disturbance.

IV

Oliver used the professional historian's technique of selecting his evidence in order to establish his thesis. His omissions are as interesting and valuable to an understanding of his "Origin & Progress" as the episodes and personages that he includes in the narrative. Thomas Hutchinson, for example, is built into a tragic hero who won the love and esteem of the people until Otis' men of passion came along with their campaign of hate. Hutchinson is described as a political genius, whose judgment, training, devotion to duty, experience in government, and instincts were the most cultivated of any Massachusetts leader. He was, Oliver repeatedly reminds the reader, nearly indispensable in colonial politics and was hated by the passion-directed revolutionaries because of his political successes. But Oliver nowhere speaks of Hutchinson's love for office—that peculiar lust that made him accept office upon office without ever considering the political repercussions. Surely Hutchinson was not the only man available for the chief-justiceship in 1760. Both Hutchinson and Oliver, however, seem blinded to political realities. The collection of offices in the family was unique in prerevolutionary history and would be unique in almost any other period of American history. Oliver never considered this mania for office-collecting as one of those unhealthy passions that were affecting Massachusetts life before the revolution.

Nor does he weigh the role of Governor Bernard as a political leader, except in some general remarks on the governor's virtues. Bernard was plainly not politically astute. Unlike his predecessors Shirley and Pownall, he did not rally gentlemen of influence to him in order to lay foundations of power. Hutchinson's appointment as chief justice was an example of Bernard's inability to appreciate the need for enlarging the support of the administration. The Otises were powerful people, and his alienation of them caused James Otis, Jr., to become opposition leader in the House of Representatives, a successor for James Allen, who died in 1755. Oliver is obviously wrong in saying Bernard "lived in great Harmony" with the people, when Otis was consolidating his power by removing the colonial agent, William Bollan, and when the Anglican church was again an object of controversy, but these episodes are passed over without comment.

The treatment of Bernard's administration reflects Oliver's general impression of British rule. Except for his denunciation of William Pitt, the radicalism of former Governor Thomas Pownall, and the softness of British policies in the colonies, he says almost nothing about imperial relations. The Stamp Act is accepted as a legitimate way for Britain to remove her indebtedness, and there is no consideration of the harm this kind of taxation had upon the Massachusetts economy, although even Thomas Hutchinson condemned it as an inexpedient and burdensome tax and worked for its repeal. The occupation of Boston by British regulars is not analyzed as a question of liberty and order, and no blame is placed upon Bernard, Hutchinson, or Gage for the unhealthful condition of the city before the Boston Massacre. But Oliver admits privately in another episode that the army was capable of doing injustice.

Oliver omits any reference to American legitimate rights of self-government. He held the Lockian view of revolution as a proper means of combating oppression, but he refused to consider American grievances as a sufficient excuse for rebellion. He plainly never faced up to the problem of lawful opposition, branding every one of the episodes before the revolution as evidence of mob violence, the insanity of passion, and the selfishness of miserable men. When the colonists protested British grants of salary to the jurists, Oliver saw the issue as the ungenerous attitude of the people to their public servants. He mentions that he had spent seventeen years on the bench and contributed £2,000 more than he had received in salary to emphasize his own unselfish devotion to good government. But the high road that he took was not so high as it seems. His family made a fortune from contracts during the Seven Years' War; they were ever present at Boston to advocate policies of taxation and currency that would benefit their merchant interests; and they used patronage to establish a monopoly of positions unlike anything in England or elsewhere in America. Contemporaries like John Adams found their grasping for offices shocking and ridiculed their assertions of making a sacrifice for the public good as hypocrisy. Despite Oliver's concern for the rising opposition to Britain, he did not believe any governmental policies except those of firmness could have removed the revolutionary conditions. Revolution was plainly caused by passion and not policy. Apparently British policy had not changed, loyal leadership in the colonies had not deteriorated; only the infectious element of passion changed Americans. Unlike Galloway, Pownall, and Bernard, he did not see the solution for the revolution in a new basis of imperial government. Still, he may have been more realistic than these imperialists in holding that nothing would satisfy the revolutionists except the complete gratification of their passions.

Though Oliver will not satisfy the reader in the breadth of his political observations, his "Origin & Progress" is unique for the variety of political material it presents on Massachusetts, and especially on Oliver's own education and political norms. His blind spots as a politician may not have resulted in his Loyalism, but they explain in part why he was unable to adapt himself to the fast-changing events of American life after 1760.

V

The original manuscript of Oliver's "Origin & Progress" apparently is no longer in existence, but there is a fair copy—presumably made during his lifetime—and a second made for the family a generation later. The earlier one was purchased by the British Museum in 1887 and now is number 2671 in the Egerton Manuscripts. It is unsigned, but Peter O. Hutchinson, who sold it and other Oliver-Hutchinson papers to the British Museum, certified that family tradition always attributed its authorship to Peter Oliver. Both its watermarks and handwriting indicate that it should be dated before 1800. The other copy was purchased in 1923 by the Huntington Library from Charles J. Sawyer of London, who had bought it and some other Oliver-Hutchinson items from Edith M. Bailey, a great-granddaughter of Thomas Hutchinson, in 1916. This Huntington copy was made about 1824, by four different copyists, and now is number 550 in the Huntington Library manuscripts.

Both Oliver manuscripts are basically the same in content, except for differences in capitalization, a few changes in word order, and minor variations in paragraphing. There are about three hundred words on Israel Putnam that were crossed out in the British Museum manuscript and eliminated entirely from the Huntington Library copy; this variation has been footnoted. Since the British Museum copy is the older manuscript, it has been used in editing the "Origin & Progress." The editors appreciate the permission of the Trustees of the British Museum in allowing publication of the manuscript. Though the editors have retained as much as possible of the original form of the manuscript, including peculiarities of spelling, they have divided a few of the longer paragraphs and supplied some incidental punctuation. As an aid to the reader, the manuscript has been divided into chapters, and topical headings have been inserted.

For biographical detail the editors have relied upon Shipton's excellent life of Peter Oliver in *Sibley's Harvard Graduates*, VIII (1951), 737-763, and have consulted Andrew Oliver's *Faces of a Family* (Privately printed, 1960) for Oliver family portraits. Besides this material, they have consulted the Egerton Manuscripts in the British Museum, examining Oliver's original letters and travel diaries; they have used the Oliver papers and transcripts at the Library of Congress and Massachusetts Historical Society. Their work has been made easier by the assistance of the Huntington Library staff, which obtained for their use microfilms from Harvard University and the Massachusetts Historical Society. Their research was also expedited by the help of the Claremont Graduate School, which has added to its already vast microprint collection a file of early American newspapers. The Danforth Foundation awarded John A. Schutz a travel grant so that he could study pertinent documents in the Boston area. The editors express their appreciation to the Board of Trustees of the Huntington Library for making possible the publication of this book. They are also indebted to the Library's director, John E. Pomfret, for his valuable suggestions and to Mrs. Nancy C. English for her devoted assistance in preparing the manuscript for publication. The editors wish to thank the many librarians, scholars, and secretaries who have aided them in this project. Mr. Ray Cubberly, a graduate student now at the University of Wisconsin, was especially helpful. Mr. Andrew Oliver, of New York City, gave permission to reproduce family portraits and useful bibliographical information.

JOHN A. SCHUTZ
DOUGLASS ADAIR

April 10, 1961

PETER OLIVER, ARTIST UNKNOWN, 1781.
Courtesy of Andrew Oliver, New York, and the Frick Art Reference Library.

PETER OLIVER, ARTIST UNKNOWN, C. 1785.
Courtesy of The Henry Francis Du Pont Winterthur Museum.

THE ORIGIN & PROGRESS
OF THE AMERICAN REBELLION

I. SEEDS OF REBELLION

THE ORIGIN & PROGRESS OF THE AMERICAN REBEL-
LION TO THE YEAR 1776, IN A LETTER TO A FRIEND.[1]

London March 1t. 1781.

SIR!

The Revolt of *North America*, from their Allegiance to & Connection with the Parent State, seems to be as striking a Phaenomenon, in the political World, as hath appeared for many Ages past; & perhaps it is a *singular* one. For, by adverting to the historick Page, we shall find no Revolt of Colonies, whether under the *Roman* or any other State, but what originated from severe Oppressions, derived from the supreme Head of the State, or from those whom he had entrusted as his Substitutes to be Governors of his Provinces. In such Cases, the Elasticity of human Nature hath been exerted, to throw off the Burdens which the Subject hath groaned under; & in most of the Instances which are recorded in History, human Nature will still justify those Efforts.

But for a Colony, wch. had been nursed, in its Infancy, with the most tender Care & Attention; which had been indulged with every Gratification that the most froward Child could wish for; which had even bestowed upon it such Liberality, which its Infancy & Youth could not *think* to ask for; which had been repeatedly saved from impending Destruction, sometimes by an Aid unsought-at other times by Assistance granted to them from their own repeated humble Supplications; for such Colonies to plunge into an unnatural Rebellion, & in the Reign of a Sovereign, too, whose publick Virtues had announced him to be the Father of his Country, & whose private Virtues had distinguished him as an Ornament of ye. human Species—this surely, to an attentive Mind, must strike with some Degree of Astonishment; & such a Mind would anxiously wish for a Veil to throw over the Nakedness of human Nature.[2]

---

[1] An early version of Peter Oliver's manuscript appeared in the *Massachusetts Gazette and Boston Weekly News-Letter*, Jan. 11, 1776, and is reproduced on p. 158 of this book. This newspaper will hereafter be cited by its earlier and shorter title: Boston *Weekly News-Letter*.

[2] Tory literature often adopted this line of argument. The wording here reminds one of Galloway's *Historical and Political Reflections on . . . the American Rebellion*.

The Rebellion in *America* hath been a Subject of as great Speculation, & of as much Altercation in *great Britain*, as any Topick
whatever which hath agitated the Mind of an Englishman since the
Year *1641*; & I am perswaded that few Subjects are so little understood. Liberty is the darling Idea of an Englishman, & there is so
much Magic in the bare Sound of the Word, that the Discord of
Licentiousness very seldom vibrates on the Ear. The Distinction
between natural Liberty & civil Liberty is too seldom adverted to.
Therefore, when in the former State there seems to be an Infringe-
ment, Mankind make[s] a Party to resent the Affront offered to
an Individual; & in the latter State, an inattentive Mind, regardless
of that Distinction, is too apt to suffer the latter to be absorbed in
the former; and hence arise many Evils which Society are incident
to, and which induce Anarchy & every Species of Confusion.
Whereas, by drawing the Line between them, & casting our Eye on
each Side of it, we shall view different Prospects; & unbiassed Reason
will soon determine the Boundaries by which each of them are to be
limited.

In a State of Nature, where she unbosoms herself to all her Off-
spring, he that first seizes an Object, adapted to satiate his natural
Wants, hath as much Right to enjoy it as any other Individual of her
Creation. But as Mankind increased, her Productions lessened in Proportion; so that where there was a Deficiency in her Efforts, human
Aid stepped in, to supply them, by adding to her Fertility. It may be
said, that by extending their Researches, Mankind would have explored Territory sufficient to have satiated all their Wants—true! But
who of this Number should be obliged to migrate? Every one, in his
natural State, had an equal Right to remain on that Spot which he
had occupied; but then, if Numbers chose to reside in a Community
they would, of Course, approp[r]iate particular Soils for their own
Improvement; & as different Passions operated, they would create
to themselves artificial Wants, which they would chuse to defend as
well as supply; hence would arise Encroachments upon Property.
For, as Mankind are not constituted of like Tempers & Passions, some
who were of a more indolent & indulging Make would claim a Right
to Support, from the Labors of the more active & industrious. Consequently, such a Conduct would meet with Opposition. This Opposition would create Strife, War & Bloodshed; & these would necessarily terminate in what is, with the greatest Propriety, termed civil
Government. This hath been the Fact from the earliest Ages to the
present Æra, & the Reasons on which it is founded are too irresistable

to admit of a Doubt, that the same Causes will ever produce the same Effects. Here then a State of natural Liberty must end; & a State of civil Liberty must commence.

As to a State of natural Liberty's existing, for any Length of Duration, it is perfectly ideal; & that there is any such State of Existence now, among the human Species remains at present to be proved. If we were to search for it, the most probable Path to take would be to explore the *Wilds of America*; but here we should search in vain. For every Part, which the boldest Adventurer hath as yet explored, hath discovered no Nation but among whom the Footsteps of civil Liberty may be traced by stronger or weaker Impressions. These happy Tribes, as I chuse to term them, enjoy civil Government in certain Degrees, though different in the Modes of it. They have their Kings & wise Men of Council, their *Sachems* & *Sagamores*, on whom they rely for their Conduct; & their great Confidence in them supplys, in many Instances, the deficiency of the written Laws of more refined Nations. They have a Religion of their own, which, to the eternal Disgrace of many Nations who boast of Politeness, is more influential on their Conduct than that of those who hold them in so great Contempt. As in the earliest Ages of the World, so among those Tribes, they adhere to Tradition for their Conduct, in the more important Scenes of Life.

Since then we shall find, after the most critical Researches, that a mere State of *Natural* Liberty, amongst *Plato's* two legged rational Animals, is not at present existant, nor ever did exist for any Length of Time. Let us then advert to a State of *civil* Liberty, to which the former as naturally gravitates as heavy Bodies do to the Centre of the Earth; and we shall find, that whoever changes from the former to the latter, must part with some Priviledges, real or imaginary, which he enjoyed in *that*, in order to obtain greater Advantages in *this*. In the former Situation, he was exposed to the cruel Resentment of every one who imagined himself to be offended by him. His Hand perhaps would be against every Man, & every Mans Hand against him. His ideal Property would be unsafe; & his Life as unsafe as his Property; but, by stepping into the social State, he hath secured both. But then he must not expect to reap all the Advantages to himself, without deriving some Advantage to the Society which he hath connected himself with. He must part with that Power which he was formerly in Possession of, of approp[r]iating every Thing to his own Use wch. he may first happen to stumble upon; in Exchange for which, he is to recieve the joint Force of the Community in de-

[5]

fending him in any Property he may, now, or in future, possess agreeable to the Rules of that Community which he associates with. He must part with the Right of private Revenge which he claimed in his State of Nature, & submit it to publick Vengeance; unless, where he is drove by his Enemy, to defend his Life & Property, into such a Situation which obliges him to recur to a State of Nature for his own Security; & in this Case, the Laws of the most civilized Nations will justifie him, because he was, at that Time, in the ineligible State, of being out of their Protection.[3]

He must go further still. He must abate of that self sufficiency which he had imbibed in the simple State of Nature, of doing what was right in his own Eyes; & submit his private Opinion to the publick Judgement of the many, confiding in their united Sense, as of more Authority than the Sentiments of any Individual. Nay, he must also consent to the Opinion of the *Majority* of the Society, be it never so small a Majority. Otherwise, he may introduce a Principle on which may be founded such Dissentions as would be destructive of the very Existence of such a Society; for this Majority, be it ever so small, might have a Preponderance of Weight to resist the Force of any Opposition that might be thrown into the opposite Scale; the Consequences of which, it requires no great Sagacity to foresee. The Man, who cannot conform to this System, must either revert to his former State of Nature, where he will soon meet with Destruction from those who are united in Society, or he must, like *Lord Wharton's* Puppies, open his Eyes before he is quite drowned, & repair to Society for Protection from that Destruction, as well as from lesser Evils which may be the natural Preludes to it.[4]

[3]Oliver leans toward the Lockian concept of civil government, but every now and then in his writings passages like this reflect the influence of Thomas Hobbes's *Leviathan*. Plato described man "as a two legged animal without feathers." This description was ridiculed later by Diogenes.

[4]Oliver may have taken his story of Lord Wharton's puppies from an article in the *Gentleman's Magazine*, III (1733), 529: "The Author, after having animadverted on the Folly of those Boroughs, which re-elect the same Representatives by which they have loudly declared themselves betray'd, tells the following Story, which, he believes, is known but to few

"Some few Months before the Death of the late Queen. A[rch]. B[isho]p *Sharp* meeting the Marq. of *Wharton*, in the Court of Requests, thus address'd him,—'My Lord, I am sorry to say, that the Measures which the Ministry are pursuing at present are by no Means such as I approve,—they seem to be going [to] very unwarrantable Lengths,—I have hitherto join'd with them, while I thought they had their Country's Interest, and the Welfare of the Church at Heart; but whatever they, or your Lordship may imagine, I am no Pretender's Man, no *Jacobite* nor ever shall be one. . . . To be plain, I suspect there is some Design to bring in the Pretender—they shall never

But here steps in a Maxim; which hath had a most powerfull Operation on the Minds of some who have set out in the political Race, vizt. *"that no Man can be said to be free, who hath not a Vote in enacting the Laws by which he is to be governed, or in giving his Consent to the imposing Taxes to which he is to contribute his Share."*[5] This Maxim hath been advanced by some theoretick Writers on Government, who were an Honor to human Nature: but Theory & Practice often differ. The metaphy[si]cian often fails in his Dogmas, through want of a thorough Investigation of the human Mind. The Philosopher misses it also, at particular Times, for even that great Philosophical Luminary, *Sr. Isaac Newton*, whom, as Mr. *Pope* expresses himself, the Angelick Orders shew to each other as we lower Beings shew an Ape.[6] Even Sr. *Isaac* hath had some of his Principles controverted & disproved; & why? but because neither are infallible. For there is such a Progression in Knowledge, that the Limits of the human Mind & its Duration are too contracted, fully to investigate the Process of Nature.

Let us now see what the Consequence of the foregoing Maxim, taken strictly, must be—supposing, as in *Great Britain*, there are several Millions to be governed, & each Individual is to give his Consent

---

have my Concurrence therein . . . if your Lordship will join Forces with me, . . . We will form a Party strong enough to break all their Measures'.

"Is your Grace in earnest? said the Marquis, *I am,* reply'd the Arch-Bishop gravely—Let me beg Leave then to tell your Grace a short Story, rejoin'd the Marquis with equal Gravity—I had a Present made me of a fine Bitch, which in due Time produc'd a Litter of Whelps, and pleasing my self with the Fancy that they would prove excellent in their kind, I went every Day to see them; but when the ninth Day came, the Time that all Puppies used to see, these Whelps continued still blind; I tried them the 10th, 11th, and 12th Day, and still they continued the same. Wherefore having no Hopes of them I order'd 'em to be thrown into the Horsepond—Would your Grace believe it? Just as they were sinking their Eyes opened—Which said, he walk'd away, and left the A. Bp to apply the Story."

[5]This statement may be a composite quotation, or quotation marks were placed around the maxim to give it more emphasis. There were similar statements in the *Massachusetts Spy,* Nov. 14, 1771 ("Mucius Scævola"); Boston *Gazette,* Jan. 20, 1772 ("Candidus" and "American Solon"); and the Boston *Weekly News-Letter,* Jan. 9, 1772 ("Chronus"). See also James Otis, "The Rights of the British Colonies Asserted and Proved," in *Some Political Writings of James Otis,* ed. Charles F. Mullett, University of Missouri Studies, IV (Columbia, Mo., 1929), 73. None of the above writers, however, uses the word "vote" to express consent in approving taxes.

[6]"An Essay on Man," *The Works of Alexander Pope,* ed. Whitwell Elwin and William John Courthope (London, 1871-89), II, 378, Epistle II, ll. 32-34:

A mortal man unfold all nature's law,
Admired such wisdom in an earthly shape,
And showed a Newton, as we show an ape.

to every Vote to be passed by this collective Body. Where will be found a *Blackheath* large enough for them to assemble upon in full Synod? Or, when assembled, how long a Time must it take for the Sound of every Proposal to reverberate in its full Weight? I think it may be readily answered, that it would take such a Length of Time, that each Individual would be a Governor without having any one Subject to govern; starving at the same Time, either for Want of Bread, or for Want of Work to earn Bread with.—But it may be said, let the united Body chuse those in whom they can confide to represent them in Council, & suffer this Body, or a Majority of it, to govern the whole Community. This certainly is the only or best Method that human Wisdom hath ever yet invented, or probably ever will invent, to secure the greatest Freedom to Society; but even here, it cannot be without its Objections, according to the Strictness of the aforesaid Maxim. For if the Person, whom fifty of us should depute to act for us, should act & vote our Minds, yet, if ten more Representatives of five hundred Men should outvote the one whom the fifty deputed, & pass a Law to tax me against my Consent; or the Consent of him who may represent me, how can I be said to be free? —Or supposing that I am absent, or sick, when the Choice of a Representative may come on, so that I have lost my Vote for him, how can I be said to enjoy Freedom, when I am taxed without my Consent? Nay, even supposing that the Representative, whom I might have voted for, should have declared in publick Assembly that I ought to be taxed.[7] These, added to many similar Instances that might be adduced to prove the same Consequences, must convince a rational Mind that there is no such Object as perfect Freedom to be attained, untill the Constitution of human Nature is changed; & such a Mind will be satisfied with the Lot assigned to it by the Author of Nature, & be contented, after its strictest Researches, to sit down under the Shadow of the english System of Government, so much applauded by Foreigners.

But, even in this Government, much the greater Number are unrepresented. For in the original Deposit of the Power of making Laws for the publick Safety, it was provided, that the Major Part of those who were to establish the Laws should govern the minor Part. This major Part hath delineated the Qualifications of Voters for Representation, so that there is such a Constitution formed, which, to make Innovations upon, might endanger the whole Super-

[7] These ideas may have come from [Soame Jenyns], *The Objections to the Taxation of Our American Colonies* . . . , 2nd ed. (London, 1765).

[8]

structure. Innovations have been tried, & the Building hath fallen to Ruin, & remained in that State, untill a Set of wiser Architects hath erected the present on the Ruins of the old one—Perfection in any Thing human is not to be expected. The nearer the Approach to it is, the better—*Perfection is what ne'er was, nor is, nor e'er will be*—There is a publick Confidence due from us to our Legislators. If they err, for to err is human, & they err ignorantly, all just Allowances ought be given to them, untill we can convince them, by Reason, of what is right. If they err wilfully, it will soon be in our Power to remove them; but it is not probable, that so large a Body of the Community shou'd unite in pulling down the Building, because they must know, that on the Destruction of it, they, like Samson, must be buried in its Ruins.

Methinks Sir! I hear you ask me, why all this Introduction? Why so long a Porch before the Building is reached? Let me answer You by saying, that you desired me to give You the History of the *american Rebellion*, because You thought that I was intimately acquainted with the Rise & Progress of it; having lived there for so many Years, & been concerned in the publick Transactions of Government before the Rebellion burst its Crater. I was very willing to answer your Request. I, on my Part, must ask you to oblige me, by permitting me, in the epistolary Walks, to indulge my Fancy in the Choice of my Path. Besides, you may perhaps, in the Sequel, find some Analogy between the Porch & the Building, & that they are not two detached Structures; altho' a good Architect might have produced a better Effect, by making either or both of them a little more tasty. However, if you will excuse the *Hibernicism*, you need not enter the House by its Porch, but open the Door of the main Building which hangs at the End of the Porch, & adjoins to it.

Before I introduce you to the House, let me remind you, that I shall confine myself, chiefly, to the Transactions of the Province of the *Massachusetts Bay*, as it was this Province where I resided, & was most intimate to the Transactions of; & as it was the *Volcano* from whence issued all the Smoak, Flame & Lava which hath since enveloped the whole British american Continent, for the Length of above 1700 Miles. If I deviate into other Colonies, my Excursions will be few & short. I promise You that I will adhere most sacredly to Truth, & endeavor to steer as clear as possible from Exaggeration; although many Facts may appear to be exaggerated, to a candid Mind, which is always fond of viewing human Nature on the brightest Side of its Orb.

In the following Narrative, I think it necessary to observe some Method, in order to elucidate the Subject; & therefore shall, in the first Place, give You, what Physicians & Metaphysicians too, call the *procatarctick* Cause[8] of those Disorders which have for a long Time past subsisted, & do now reign triumphant in America; for that Maxim, *Nemo repenté fuit turpissimus*, is too well established to be controverted.[9] I shall relate *Facts*, which are not drawn, but naturally flow from such Causes. I shall give to you a Sketch of different *Characters*, who were either Objects of the Resentment of this unparralleled Rebellion, or of those who were the principal Agitators in projecting & pursuing it to its present Form; & here I shall avoid suffering my Pencil to throw one Shade, either to add a Beauty or strike out a Deformity. I shall, also, give you a few of the *Consequences* that have been attendant on the triumphant Progress of this Daemon; & if you are not satiated with your Entertainment, I will, by Way of *Appendix*, spread a *Dessert* before you, which, unlike modern Desserts that convey a Relish with them, I fear will create a Nausea; which, if it should create, you must not blame me. For I present it by way of Appendix, wch. you are under no Necessity of meddling with; but if your Curiosity should be such as to take & eat, you will be in Danger of not getting the Taste out of your Mouth very soon.

THE LONG-TERM CAUSES OF REBELLION

The Narrative runs thus—

When that nocturnal Meteor, *Popery*, burst in the British Hemisphere, by the influential Rays of that more luminous Body, the *Reformation*, it was dissipated into numberless Parts. And like the Convulsions of Nature, which generally occasion Confusion among Mankind, so this Shock, in the civil & ecclesiastical World, split itself into a great Variety of Sects & produced an Anarchy of Sentiment: & no Wonder. Since the emerging so suddenly from worse than Ægyptian Darkness, the human Mind was not strong enough to bear so sudden a Flash of Light; & must necessarily grope about to feel the regular Path to walk in. Besides, the greater Part of the People, when they had in some Degree recovered their Eyesight, &

[8]The procatarctic cause was the immediate or initial cause of a disease. Oliver accepted the larger meaning given by Thomas Tryon in *A Treatise of Dreams & Visions* (London?, 169-?), p. 256: "The truth is, *Pride* may justly be said to be the chief *Procatarick*, or remote original cause of *Madness. . . .*"

[9]"No man became completely vicious all at once."

found their Shackles were knocked off, not being able to bear so sudden a Transition, indulged themselves in their own wanton Imaginations, & claimed the Priviledge of doing what was right in their own Eyes, without subjecting themselves to any Controul. The ecclesiastical Power, at this Æra, justly thought that too great a Change from the Ceremonies of the romish Church might have an ill Effect upon the Minds of the Vulgar, which had been so long habituated to a Religion of Ceremonies. They therefore retained a Number of those which they imagined would be least exceptionable: but, on the other Hand, there were many, some from spiritual Pride & the Vanity of being distinguished, & others from Sincerity of Heart, who were averse from doing Things by Halves, imagined that if Root & Branch were not extirpated, a new *Phoenix* would rise out of the Ashes of ye. old one. Like froward Children they would have all or none. They therefore seceded from the established Church, & from each other. Some went off to different Parts of the World, & others staid behind, in order to have their Names enrolled in the Catalogue of Martyrs, provided they could not triumph in Victory—among those who went to foreign Parts was a Mr. *Robert Brown*, a young Clergyman of overheated Zeal, who preached so warmly against the Ceremonies & Discipline of the *Church* of *England*, Anno *1580*, that he was obliged to fly to *Middleburg* of *Zealand* in *Holland*; where, with some of his Disciples, he formed a Church called *Brownists*, after their Leader. But after his Zeal had boiled over so long, & discharged its more volatile Particles, he returned to *England*, recanted, took Orders, & died in the Communion of the *Church of England*, Anno *1630*.[10]

Some of these *Brownists*, who were settled in *Yarmouth* 1602, & after they thought that they had been sufficiently harassed by the ecclesiastical Power, migrated to *Holland* under the Pastorate of Mr. *John Robinson*, a young Man of rigid Principles, who preached not only against the Discipline & Ceremonies of the *Church of England*, but also the *Unlawfullness* of hearing the Preachments of the Divines of that Church, although they were never so learned & pious.[11] *Mr. Robinson* afterward, when the Ebullition of his Zeal

---

[10]Robert Browne (1550?-1633?), famous separatist and founder of the Brownists, had as unusual a career as Oliver describes.

[11]John Robinson (1576?-1625), a native of Lincolnshire and minister of the Pilgrim fathers, held strong convictions, debating at various times with William Ames and John Yates. He was opposed to the Calvinist form of church government.

[11]

had subsided, recanted his rigid Sentiments, & preached also, not only the Lawfullness but the Duty of hearing such Divisions. In this last Sentiment he was confirmed by a Controversy which he had maintained with that great & good Man *Dr. Ames*, whom he had not only wrote against, but abused; 'till the *Dr.* by his superior Judgment had cooled the Ardor of his Passions & brought him to a sober Way of thinking.[12]

Under the Government of a Republick it might be thought that they would be easy, especially [in] a *Dutch* Commonwealth, where a Man may worship the Devil if he will pay a moderate Fee for his Licence; but even here, they could not be easy for any great Length of Time. For this Republick had its established Religion too, which it would not suffer to be overborne by Novelty; so that, after a few Years, they finding that the Irritability of their Nerves had not subsided, formed a Scheme for another Emigration. There had been a *Virginia* Company, who at several Times had sent over Numbers to settle that Colony, with a View to Profit from Trade, Commerce & Mines; but in *1620* King *James 1st.* granted a Patent to settle to the Northward of the *Virginia* Company, from *40* to *48* Deg: North Latitude, by the Name of *the Plymouth Company*, as it was made to a Number called the Council of *Plymouth in Devon*. Some of those, who were of *Mr. Robinson's* Church in *Holland*, together with some others in *England* of the same Way of thinking, undertook the Voyage to *America*. Those in *Holland* pretended that the Difference of Languages, the Difficulty of Subsistence & Danger of losing their Interest in the English Nation were the Cause of their Removal. The Difficulty of Subsistence & the slender Prospect of Gain in *Holland* no Body can doubt might be a sufficient Reason; for it is not sufficient to be naturalized, but a Man must be born a Dutchman, to be a Match for a Dutchman in trade. There is a certain something in human Nature, let it be called Pride, a Fondness for Superiority, or any more moderate Term, as may strike the Fancy best, which stimulates the Mind to act as a Bell Weather to a Flock, to hand our Names down to Posterity as Leaders, either in Religion, Politicks, or some other System, as may suit our Genius best. This something discovers itself in its earliest Infancy, & continues to our latest Dotage. It is more than possible, that this, to-

---

[12]William Ames (1576-1633), of an ancient Norfolk family, was an energetic Puritan minister and professor of religion at Franeker. He supported the Calvinist party in religious controversy.

gether with a View to great Advantages from the Culture of a fertile Soil, & an extended Fishery, were the principal Causes of Emigration across an Ocean of 3000 Miles.

These Emigrants, then, embarqued with a Design to have settled on *Hudson's River*, now *New York* Government, which had been explored in *1608* by Capt. *Henry Hudson* in his Attempt to find a North West Passage to the *East Indies*. They procured a Dutchman to pilot them to this River; but it was supposed that the *Hollanders* had bribed him; for there was a small Dutch Settlement on that River; & the Pilot, instead of carrying their small Fleet thither, steered them towards *Cape Cod*; & on the *18th. December 1620* they landed at a Place which they called *New Plimouth*. After grappling with many Difficulties, & having formed theirselves into a Government, they conducted their Affairs with as much Prudence & Loyalty, as perhaps any new formed Government which had ever existed; untill they were incorporated into the *Massachusetts* Charter, *October 7th. 1692*; & from hence we may date, not only their Incorporation of Interests, but of Sentiments also.

The Council of *Plimouth*, in the County of *Devon* in *England*, having sold to a Number of Persons, a Part of their Patent, extending three Miles South of *Charles River* to three Miles North of *Merrimack River*, at the Bottom of *Massachusetts Bay. King Charles* 1st. incorporated the Grantees into a Body Politick, by a Charter dated *4th. March 1629/30*, & 4th. Year of his Reign.

As much hath been pleaded, in the present Rebellion, for an Exemption from all Taxes, from the Tenor of this Charter. It may not be amiss to make some Strictures on the Validity of such Pleas. At one Time it is said, that the Charter exempts them from any Tax whatever—at another Time, that the Charter is a Compact, & that they have fullfilled their Parts, by settling the Country, & so are exempted from any Burdens, but what they may be pleased to impose upon theirselves. As to the first Plea, a Transcription of a few Clauses of the Charter will elucidate the Subject: & as to the latter Plea, I believe it was the first Time that a Charter was ever supposed to include in it the Idea of a Compact, in legal Acceptation: but taking both Pleas to be just, the Rebellion must Vail to the Charter itself.

The Words of this Charter, as far as they relate to the present Dispute, run thus—vizt.

That the Grantees "shall, from Time to Time, & at all Times for ever hereafter, be by Virtue of these Presents one Body corporate politique in Fact & in Name, by the Name, of ye. Governor & Company of the *Massachusetts Bay in New England*—shall be capable to implead & be impleaded—to purchase any Lands, Tenements, goods or Chattells; & grant, sell & dispose of the same, as other of our leige People of this our Realm of *England*, or any other Corporation, or Body politique of the same, may lawfully do. To make Laws & Ordinances for the Good & Welfare of the said Company; so as such Laws & Ordinances be not contrary or repugnant to the Laws & Statutes of this our Realm of *England*. And for their further Encouragement, of *our especial Grace & Favor*, we yeild & grant to the said Governor & Company, their Factors & Assigns, that they shall be free & quit from all Taxes, Subsidies & Customs in *New England*, for the Space of seven Years—that they may transport any Persons, Shipping, Armour, Weapons, Ordnance, Ammunition, Powder, Shot, Corn, Victuals & all Manner of Cloathing, Implements, Furniture, Beasts, Cattle, Horses, Mares, Merchandizes, & c. without paying Custom or Subsidy, inward or outward, by the space of *seven* Years from the Day of the Date of these Presents; provided, none of the said Persons be such as shall hereafter, by special Name, be restrained by us, our Heirs, & Successors. They shall be free from all Taxes & Impositions, for the Space of *twenty one Years*, upon all Goods & Merchandize, either upon Importations thither or Exportation from thence into our Realm of *England*, or our Dominions; except only the *five p Cent* due for Custom upon such Goods as, after the said *seven Years* shall be expired, shall be imported into *England* or any of our Dominions, which *five p Cent* being paid, it shall be lawfull to export the same into foreign Parts, without any other Duty, provided such Goods be shipped within thirteen Months, after first landing in any Part of said Dominions. When any Custom or Subsidy shall be due, according to the Limitation aforesaid, the Officers of the Customs shall allow six Months Time for the Payment of one half of the same."[13]

This Extract, from the original Charter of the *Massachusetts* Colonization, will best explain the Validity or Insufficiency of the present Pleas for their Rebellion; & upon the Encouragement of this Charter the Emigration was made.

About this Time, the ecclesiastical Powers held the Reins of their Government rather tighter than was agreeable to the Temper of an

---

[13]These quotations are a loose rendition of the pertinent provisions of the charter. Oliver's date is correct. *The Charters and General Laws of the Colony and Province of Massachusetts Bay* (Boston, 1814), pp. 1-17.

English Animal. In *June 1628 Dr. William Laud* was translated to the See of *London*.[14] He had been used to ride with a Curb; & rode so long with it, 'till the Animal grew so very hard mouthed as to throw his Rider. *Dr. Laud* was a learned & pious Prelate; but neither his Learning or Piety could divest him of human Passions. The beforementioned Fondness for Superiority, inherent in Mankind, he thought, gave him, as it really did, as just a Right to the Papal Chair of *England*, as *Urban* had to that of *Rome*: hence he was off his Guard, & as there is no surer Way of propagating a Cause, especially a Religious Cause, than with the Scourge of Persecution; so some Severities that leaned this Way drove many out of the Kingdom; most of whom embarqued for the *Massachusetts Bay*, as an Asylum for enjoying their own Tenets, & for the Priviledge of taking their Trick at the Helm of Persecution. A Man of a warm Heart & a cool Head is to be urged with the Weapons of Reason only; & a red hot Zealot, without understanding, is to be attacked with Ridicule, or to be suffered to run himself out of Breath. From the ecclesiastical Severities exercised by *Dr. Laud*, he may be justly honoured as the Founder of *Massachusetts* Colony. For as the Blood of Martyrs is usually termed, the Seed of the Church; so those Severities served but as the Implements of Husbandry, to convert the *New England* Wilderness into a fruitfull Field; for, in a very few Years, several thousands transported themselves to the last mentioned Colony.

Before these new Emigrants embarked for the *Massachusetts,* they thought it necessary, as Religion was the *ostensible* Cause of their Emigration, (& Religion doubtless was the *real* Cause that swayed the Minds of many of them) they procured several Nonconformist Ministers to embark with them. Unhappily for them, they did not pitch on Men whose Sentiments of Church Government were in Unison; hence, they very soon ran into Divisions, by which Means new Emigrations were made; which occasioned the Settlements of *Connecticut* & *Rhode Island* Colonies. Among their Ministers there was one, whose black Coat, alone, could pass him under that Denomination. His name was *Blackstone*.[15] Nature had formed him for a Carman, but he had thwarted her Intention, for he removed

---

[14]William Laud (1573-1645), Anglo-Roman in religious philosophy, became bishop of London in 1628 and archbishop of Canterbury in 1633. He was responsible for a religious policy that drove large numbers of Puritans into exile.

[15]William Blackstone (1596-1675), who arrived in Massachusetts in the 1620's, was the first settler of Shawmut peninsula. Unable to harmonize his ideas with the Puritans, he went to Rhode Island.

from *Salem* where the Settlers had first landed, to a Peninsula called *Shawmut*, about 20 Miles Distance, afterwards called *Boston*. Here he rode on a Bull, preached at some Times, & at other Times ploughed his Ground by drawing his Plough by his own bodily Strength; & perhaps cultivated his own Vineyard to as great Profit as he did that of his Master's.

Amongst those who embarked in this Expedition were two Gentlemen of distinguished Note, vizt. *John Winthrop* & *Thomas Dudley* Esqrs., both of them descended from Families of high Rank. Mr. *Winthrop* was a Gentleman of Sense, of Virtue, & of an Estate of £700- p Annum. He was chosen Governor or Deputy Governor for 20 Years, with an Interruption of 3 Elections only, untill his Death in 1649. He spent his Estate in the Service of the Colony; but, like many others, who sacrifice all to the publick Welfare, met with publick Ingratitude; which is not peculiar to any Nation, & from which *Athens* alone seems to have been exempt, which Government would not suffer even an old Horse to be treated ill by that accursed Vice.[16] Mr. *Winthrop* was ill used, upon some trifling Difference in religious Opinion; but his Sense & his Virtue vindicated him thoroughly.

In *April 1629*, about 2000 Passengers embarked in 10 or 11 Ships: but, before they sailed, they published a Declaration, in Order to acquit theirselves from any Suspicion of a rigid Separation from the *Church of England*. As there is something very striking in this Declaration, considering how closely it was adhered to; & as it is a Record of very little Notoriety, and it happening to be in my Possession, I shall here insert it: it may be tedious, but I think it will be Instructive.[17] It runs thus—

"The humble Request of his Majesty's loyal Subjects, the Governor and Company late gone for *New England.*

"To the *rest* of their Brethren, in & of *the Church of England*. For the obtaining of their Prayers, & the Removal of Suspicions & Misconstructions of their Intentions.

"Reverend Fathers & Brethren!

"The general Rumor of this solemn Enterprize, wherein our

---

[16]John Winthrop (1588-1649), the son of a Suffolk landowner, was governor of Massachusetts for most of the years from his arrival in 1630 until his death. Oliver was referring to his own sacrifice in serving the public. He believed that he had sacrificed estate and health for the public good.

[17]This document was taken from Hutchinson's papers. See *History of . . . Massachusetts-Bay*, I, 408-409.

selves, with others, through the Providence of the Almighty, are engaged; as it may spare us the Labor of imparting our Occasion unto You, so it gives us the more Encouragement to strengthen our Selves by the Procurement of the Prayers & Blessings of the Lord's faithfull Servants; for which End, we are bold to have Recourse unto You, as those whom GOD hath placed nearest his Throne of Mercy; which as it affords You the more Opportunity, so it imposeth the greater Bond upon You to interceed for his People in all their Streights. We beseech You therefore, by the Mercies of the LORD JESUS, to consider us *as your Brethren*, standing in very great Need of your Help, & earnestly imploring it. And howsoever your Charity may have met with some Occasion of Discouragement, through the Misreport of our Intentions, or through ye. Disaffection or Indiscretion of some of us, or rather amongst us; for we are not of those that dream of Perfection in this World; yet we desire you would be pleased to take Notice of the Principals & Body of our Company, as those who esteem it our Honor, to call the *Church of England*, from whom we rise, *our dear Mother*, & cannot part from our Native Country, where she especially resideth, without much Sadness of Heart, & many Tears in our Eyes; ever acknowledging that such Hope & Part as we have obtained in the common Salvation, we have recieved *in her Bosom*, & sucked it *from her Breasts*. We leave it not therefore, as loathing that Milk wherewith we were once nourished there, but blessing GOD for the Parentage & Education, as Members of the same Body, shall always *rejoice* in her *Good*, & unfeignedly grieve for any Sorrow shall *ever* betide her; & while we have Breath, sincerely desire & endeavour the Continuance & Abundance of her *Welfare*, with the *Enlargment of her Bounds* in the Kingdom of *Christ Jesus*."

"Be pleased, therefore, Reverend Fathers & Brethren! to help forward this Work now in Hand; which, if it prosper, you shall be the more glorious. Howsoever, your Judgment is with the *Lord*, & your Reward with your GOD. It is an usual & laudable Exercise of your Charity, to recommend to the Prayers of your Congregations the Necessity & straights of your private Neighbours. Do the like for a *Church* springing out of your *own Bowels*. We concieve much Hope that this Remembrance of us, if it be frequent & fervent, will be a most prosperous Gale in our Sails, & provide such a Passage & Welcome for us, from the GOD of the whole Earth, as both we which shall find it, & your selves, with the rest of our Friends, who shall hear of it, shall be much enlarged to bring in such daily Returns of

Thanksgivings, as the Specialties of his Providence & Goodness may justly challenge at all our Hands. You are not ignorant, that the Spirit of GOD stirred up the Apostle *Paul* to make a continual Mention of the Church of *Philippi* (which was a Colony from *Rome*) let the same Spirit, we beseech you, put you in Mind, that are the Lord's Remembrancers, to pray for us without ceasing (who are a weak Colony from your Selves) making continual Request for us to GOD in all your Prayers."

"What we intreat of you that are the Ministers of GOD, that we also crave at the Hands of all the rest of our Brethren, that they would at no Time forget us in their private Solicitations at the Throne of Grace."

"If any there be, who through Want of clear Intelligence of our Course, or Tenderness of Affection towards us, cannot concieve so much of our Way as we could desire; we would intreat such not to despise us, nor to desert us in their Prayers & Affections; but to consider rather, that they are so much the more to express the Bowels of their Compassion towards us, remembring alway that both Nature & Grace doth ever bid us to relieve & rescue, with our utmost & speediest Power, such as are dear unto us, when we concieve them to be running uncomfortable hazards."

"What Goodness you shall extend to us, in this or [any] other Christian Kindness we your Brethren in CHRIST JESUS shall labor to repay in what Duty we are or shall be, able to Perform; promising, so far as GOD shall enable us, to give him no Rest on your behalfes, wishing our Heads & Hearts may be Fountains of Tears for your everlasting Welfare, when we shall be in our poor Cottages in the Wilderness, overshadowed with the Spirit of Supplication, through the Manifold Necessities & Tribulations which may not altogether unexpectedly, nor, we hope unprofitably befall us. And so commending you to the Grace of GOD in CHRIST we shall ever rest

Your assured Friends & Brethren

From Yarmouth
aboard the
Arabella
April 7th. 1630.

John Winthrop—Governor
Charles Fines
Richard Salstonstall
Isaac Johnson
Thomas Dudley
William Coddington
George Phillips &c.

After such an applausive Declaration, in Favor of the Established *Church of England*, & so solemn an Appeal to the GOD of Heaven for the Sincerity of their Intentions, it would be injurious to suspect their Integrity, had not their consequent Behaviour evidenced their Wrongness of Conduct. For when they arrived at their first Port, *Salem*, they soon began to differ among themselves about the Mode of Church Government, which they intermixed with their civil Government; & they soon forgot their *dear Mother, the Church of England, whose Hope & Part wch. they had obtained in the Common Salvation, they had recieved in her bosom and sucked from her Breasts*; & formed themselves into independent & congregational Churches, leaving their *dear Mother* to fight her own Battles in their native Country. And so unnatural were they, that in 3 or 4 Months after their Arrival, & when they had formed themselves into a Government, they enacted Qualifications for Freemen to vote for Magistrates; one of which was, that no one should be a Voter unless he were a Member of their Church, hereby excluding all of the established Church from this so natural Priviledge. And this Prejudice was so strongly riveted in their Successors, that I question whether a *Church of England* Man was even chosen an Assistant, Councellor, or a Member of the general Assembly, for above an hundred Years after.

But the Surprize will lessen, when it is considered, that they carried over with them several Ministers,[18] some of whom were very

[18]At this point the following harsh account of Hugh Peter was apparently added to the manuscript by the copyist: "Amongst others, who went to New England, was the infamous *Hugh Peters*, who was tried in the Year 1660, for High Treason in the Murder of *King Charles* the first; he was an itinerant Preacher & resided chiefly at *Salem*, about 20 Miles from *Boston*. It was proved, on his Trial, that he was (by his own Confession) sent by the New Englanders to old England in Order to foment the Rebellion in *England* & introduce a Common Wealth; & there met with this Reward of his Temerit[y], an Halter.

"The Prefacer of the *Trial of the Regicides* makes these Remarks, vizt.

" '*Hugh Peters* was the most notorious Incendiary of the Rebels. He was a mere Epicure, a Swine in his Morals, & a false Prophet in his Doctrine. It is reported, that, at the Time of his Execution, he was in great Amazement & Confusion, sitting upon the Hurdle Like a Sot all the Way he went, & either plucking the Straws or gnawing the Fingers of his Gloves. He ascended the Ladder, not like a Minister, but like some ignorant Atheist, not knowing what to say or how to carry himself. After he had stood stupidly for a while, he put his Hand before his Eyes & prayed for a short Time, & at last very unwillingly he was turned off the Ladder.' " See Raymond Phineas Stearns, *The Strenuous Puritan: Hugh Peter 1598-1660* (Urbana, Ill., 1954), pp. 418-419.

weak, though pious Men, & others who had suffered by a too rough handling from the rigid Measures of the established Church at home, & who now thought it came to their Turn to make Retaliation, which they judged necessary to take Time by the Forelock in making; & it must be acknowledged, that they were not negligent in doing this which they esteemed the Work of the *Lord*. For as they generally formed their Code of Laws from the Jewish Institutes, so, that Section of it, vizt: *"cursed is he that doeth the Work of the Lord negligently,"* was too legible to be passed unnoticed—& as the Clergy had the greatest Influence then in the publick Transactions, which their Successors inherit to *this* Day in the amplest Manner; little else could be expected from Minds incapable of behaving decently under such a Plenitude of Power. Another Circumstance might, possibly, & probably too, if we may judge of their subsequent Conduct, actuate their Minds; vizt., that they were three thousand Miles distant, across an infrequented Ocean, & it could not enter into their Heads that an English, *Church or State Scourge*, could be made of such a Length as to reach them. The *procul á Jove, procul á Fulmine*[19] *seemed* to be a prevailing Maxim with some of them, as it has been *professedly* so with their Descendents in the present ungrateful Rebellion.

The following Instance of which may be adduced. A *Mr. Roger Williams*, a Clergyman of Sense, but who suffered his Understanding to be carried down the Torrent of Enthusiasm, had insinuated an Opinion of his Piety into the Minds of many weak People. He had lived in the Colony of *Plimouth*, but was of so restless a Constitution that he seemed always to labor under the Hectick of Enthusiasm; which at last hurried him into a Banishment from the *Massachusetts*. One of his Disciples was *Mr. Endicot*, who had been their first Governor, & was now one of the Assistants, or Councellor. Mr. *Endicot* in 1634, in his great Fervor of Zeal, cut the *Cross* out of the military Ensign, as he took it to be a Relick of Antichrist, & this Exploit was favored by others of high Rank also.[20] But the Government fearing an Admonition from home for such an atrocious Offence, censured & degraded those who were concerned in this mad Freak, & ordered the Cross to be left, in the *Ensign at the Castle*; & permitted the several military Companies to chuse their own Ensigns. In short, there

---

[19]"The farther away from Jove, the less the fear of his lightning."

[20]John Endecott (ca. 1589-1665) and Roger Williams (1603-83) were friends, but there is doubt that Williams influenced Endecott to commit this rash deed. Ola Elizabeth Winslow, *Master Roger Williams* (New York, 1957), pp. 114-117.

was such an heterogeneous Mixture of religious Sects that the Vagaries of Enthusiasm had their full Scope; & it was carried to such a Length, that it was said, that some pious Zealots refused to Brew their Beer on Saturdays lest it should work on the Sabbath, in Defiance of the fourth Commandment.

Boston was settled about the Years *1630* or *1631*. It was so called, in Honor to the *Revd.* Mr. *John Cotton*, who was one of its Ministers, & had been Vicar of *St. Botolph's Church* in *Boston* in *Lincolnshire* in *England*. Mr. *Cotton* was a Man of Learning, Piety & Moderation; & such Deference was paid to his Judgment; that he was consulted, with other Clergymen, in most of their civil Affairs. The Government found it necessary to have a Code of criminal Law; & it seemed quite necessary, for at the first Court the Grand Jury found above an hundred Bills of Presentment. Mr. *Cotton* was desired to draw up the System, but whether he thought that the Hardness of *New England* Men's Hearts equalled that of the *Jews*, or whether he imagined that the Wilderness of *America* had as just a Claim to a theocratick Government as the Land of *Palestine*, so it was, that he exhibited a Code copied, chiefly, from the Institutes of *Moses:* one of which Laws punished the Disobedience of a Son to a Father, after proper Admonitions, with Death; but this, with some others which were too severe, were rejected.[21]

The Division in religious Sentiments, wch. prevailed in this Government, produced such Irregularities of Conduct as occasioned many Complaints to the King in Council; so that abt. the Year 1635 his Majesty issued a Commission to Arch Bishop *Laud* & several others, to take Cognizance of the Complaints; & this commission is too evidential of the Strides which ye *Arch Bishop* was making towards arbitrary Power. The unhappy Monarch was influenced to sign it, & perhaps it was the most disgracefull Paper he ever affixed his Name to, it striking at the Foundation of the english Law. This Commission impow'red any five of those mentioned in it, to take full Cognizance of *all Matters, civil & ecclesiastical*; & to punish by *Imprisonment;* or by *loss of Life or Member*. This was really carrying

---

[21]Oliver's judgment about the Judicials was not uncommon in most writers from his time to the present. Most of the provisions were taken from many sources, though of course supported by biblical quotations. See Isabel Calder, "John Cotton's 'Moses His Judicials,'" Publications of the Colonial Society of Massachusetts, XXVIII (1935), 86-94; Edmund S. Morgan, *The Puritan Dilemma: The Story of John Winthrop* (Boston, 1958), pp. 166-173; George Lee Haskins, *Law and Authority in Early Massachusetts: A Study in Tradition and Design* (New York, 1960), pp. 124-126.

the Matter further than it would bear, & had no other Effect than irritating the People.

Complaints against the Plantation being Continued, his Majesty, in *1638*, revoked the Charter; but they refused to deliver it, & assigned their Reasons of Refusal in an Address to him. At another Time, perhaps this Refusal would have been resented, but Rebellion in *England* began now to plume itself, & there was too much Work at home to pay any Attention to distant Colonies, which had now their full Swing at doing what was right in their own Eyes. And after that Catastrophe, which will ever disgrace the english Annals, there was too great a Sympathy of Soul between the Brethren of *Old* & of *New England*, for the latter to dread any Thing from the Government of the former. Indeed, their Principles so perfectly coincided, that a literary Correspondence was held between *Oliver Cromwell* & the before mentioned *Mr. Cotton*; & I have seen a Letter from the former, in his own handwriting, with this Expression, *"pray Sir! whereabouts are we in the Revelations?"*[22] *Cromwell* understood human Nature too well, not to feel the Warmth of their Attachment to his Republick; otherwise, his determined Temper would have made them feel as much of the Weight of his Authority, as *Virginia* & some of the English Islands in the *West-Indies* did; who, for their Allegiance to the royal Cause, had their Estates confiscated, by an Ordinance in 1650;–but there was no Occasion for the Exertion of his Authority in this Plantation.

ACCESSION OF CHARLES II

Upon the Accession of *King Charles 2d*; the *Massachusetts* Province, in December 1660, sent over an Address of Congratulation to him on this Occasion, in a scriptural Stile, which was answered in a most gracious Manner; & not long after, an Order was sent to them, that all Writs & Processes should be in his Majesty's Name, which 'till then they had issued in their own Name; which they complied with. It seems, by such a Conduct, that they attempted to avail themselves of as much Independence upon the Parent State as they dared to; & in another Instance they also assumed the royal Prerogative vizt. of coining Mony, which they coined at several Times, but it was all stamped, with *1652*.

[22]The exchange of letters in [Hutchinson], *A Collection of Original Papers . . .* (Boston, 1769), pp. 233-237, is probably not that referred to by Oliver, although this work would have been available to him.

When *Charles 2d.* came to the Throne, many of his Father's regicidal Judges quitted the Kingdom to avoid the Punishment of their Demerits. Some, who chose to go to Heaven in a Swing, stayed behind to enjoy the Halter. Three of them fled to *New England* as the safest Asylum, vizt. Colo. *Dixwell*, Colo. *Whaley* & Colo. *Goffe.*[23] Orders were sent to *New England* to secure them—the *Massachusetts* issued a Proclamation to take them. It is prudent in most Cases to save Appearances, but perhaps there was no surer Cities of Refuge than these Colonies; for neither of them were arrested. Colo. *Dixwell* lived for several Years in *Newhaven* in *Connecticut*, by the Name of *Davis*, & his Grave Stone was lately, if not now, standing in *Newhaven* Burying Yard, with the Letters *I. D.* inscribed upon it.

Colo. *Goffe* fled to the Skirts of *Northampton*, about 120 Miles from *Boston*, & secreted himself for a long Time in a Cavern, & was known scarcely to any but to Mr. *Russell* the Minister of that Town, who furnished him with the Necessaries of Life. It seems that he was so fond of Life, that rather than take his Chance, with some of his Brethren Regicides, in the World at large, he chose to breath away a wearisome Existence in the lonely Hermitage of a dreary Wilderness. I have seen the Diary which he kept during his Retirement; but there seemed to be more of the Enthusiast in it than of the great Man. An Anecdote relative to Colo. *Goffe* may be a Curiosity. The Indians frequently invaded the out Settlements of the Colonies; they appeared on the Skirts of *Northampton*. The Inhabitants went out armed against them. On their March, Colo. *Goffe* left his Cavern & joined them; he wore a large flapped Hat, white Locks, & a black Coat; the English thought him to be a Messenger from the other World; & the Indians took him for the Devil, whom they call *Hobbamocco*, & fled at the Sight of him; & he retired to his Secrecy.

In 1683 King *Charles 2d.* sent Orders to the *Massachusetts Bay*, to surrender their *Charter*, there having been Complaints entred against the Colony for a Disregard to the Acts of Trade, Persecution of their fellow Christians &c. By Vote of generall Assembly a Surrender was refused; in consequence of which a *quo Warranto* was entred in Chancery, Trinity Term 1684; Judgment was entred, & the charter vacated. Their Agent in *England* wrote thus to the Gover-

[23]John Dixwell, Edward Whalley, and William Goffe. Oliver's account was probably taken from Hutchinson, *History of . . . Massachusetts-Bay*, I, 185-187. Lemuel Aiken Welles, *The Regicides in Connecticut*, Tercentenary Commission of the State of Connecticut Committee on Historical Publications, No. 35 (New Haven, 1935). John Dixwell's assumed name was James Davids.

nor & Council, in May 1685. "The Breaches assigned against You are as obvious as unanswerable; so that all the Service, your Council and Friends could have done you here, would have only served to deplore, not prevent that inevitable Loss. Instead of sending Letters of Attorney, the Colony sent only an Address to the King, without Colony Seal, or any Subscription per Order, therefore it was not presented."

THE REVOLUTION AGAINST JAMES II

In King *James 2d*. Reign, 1686, Sr. *Edmund Andros* was sent over as their Governor; & he, with his Council, chiefly Strangers, executed *James's* tyrannick Orders so strictly, that Oppression now shifted Scales; so that 1689, on the bare Report of a Revolution in *England*, by the Way of *Virginia*, a grand Colony Mob appeared before the Fort where the Governor resided. He very prudently resigned, & he was confined on board Ship & sent to *England*—happy for *England* that a Revolution existed, & very happy for the Actors in this Affair that the news was confirmed, otherwise the gloomy Mind of that unhappy Monarch would have brought upon the Stage a Tragedy which would not have suffered a dry Eye in the Theatre.

In 1691, they were favored with a New Charter from K. *Wm. 3d* & *Qu: Mary*. Their Agent in *England*, Mr. *Mather*, as shrewd & as sensible a Man as any of the *Massachusetts*, in a great Measure had the modelling of it; but in about 20 Years they quarrell'd about the Meaning of some of its Clauses, which procured an Explanatory Charter from King *George 1st*.—Colo. *Samuel Shute* was their Governor in 1716.[24] He was a worthy, good natured, inoffensive Man, & he told his Assembly Men, yt. he aimed at nothing great, only to live comfortably, & he would consent to their Acts. His Salary was about £300. Sterling; he asked but for abt £50 more; they refused him: upon which, in 1722, he went home with 7 Complaints; vizt. *taking Possession of royal Masts cut into Logs; refusing the Governors Negative of a Speaker; assuming a joint Authority in appointing Fasts; adjourning themselves more than two Days at a time; dismantling Forts, & ordering the Guns & Stores into the Treasurers Custody; suspending military Officers & mulcting them of their Pay —sending a Committee of their own to muster the King's Forces.*

[24]Samuel Shute (1662-1742) served as governor of Massachusetts from 1716 until 1727, though the last four years of his term were spent in England answering charges of the House of Representatives. His administration was troubled by one dispute upon another with the legislature.

These Complaints *Elisha Cooke* Esqr., the *Catiline* of that Æra, was sent to *England* to answer.[25] He renounced all but the 2d. & 4th. Complaints, acknowledged the Errors of his Constituents, layed the Blame upon a former Assembly, & the whole was settled by the aforementioned explanatory Charter. *Colo. Shute* never returned to his Government, but was provided for in *England* by a Pension of £400. p Year. He was perfectly in the Right not to return, for they had attempted his Life; & it is not many Years since, that in one of the Apartments, in the Province House, where he generally resided, was to be seen the Hole where the Bullet entred, which sought his Life. If so good natured & inoffensive a Man as Colo. *Shute* could not sit easy in the Chair of this Government, what could others expect; who, as Governors, were to hold the Ballance to prevent the Power of the People from encroaching upon the royal Prerogative? And indeed, there was scarce a King's Governor, from that Time to the Year 1774, but who had a Task to perform which no wise Man could envy him for: Governor *Burnet*, they worried into his Grave;[26] others, they were continually adding Fuel to the Flame of Contention, which, like the Vestal Fire, they made it a Part of their Religion to keep alive. Another Governor, they demolish'd his House, at the same Time most cruelly attempting to murder him & his Family:[27] & never could any Governor meet with tolerable Quarter from them, unless he threw himself into their Hands, wch. in the cool Hour of Reflection he was ashamed of; & even such a diminutive Conduct would not always protect him from Censure.

I have been credibly informed, 20 Years ago, by an Assembly Man who was mostly concerned in the political Disputes that originated

[25]Elisha Cooke (1678-1737), the leader of Governor Shute's opposition, published a pamphlet, *Mr. Cook's Just and Seasonable Vindication* (Boston, 1720), in which he criticized British forest policies and the governor's part in enforcing them. For this he was elected speaker of the House of Representatives in 1720. Governor Shute retaliated by negating him and dissolving the house. He then represented the house in presenting a series of complaints against the governor to the British government. William Chauncey Fowler, "Local Law in Massachusetts . . . ," *New-England Historical and Genealogical Register,* XXV (1871), 351.

[26]William Burnet (1688-1729) was also worried into his grave by his adherence to British instructions, which forced him to accept a salary fixed at £1,000 sterling for the duration of his governorship instead of the annual grants. These instructions were considered a threat to legislative power.

[27]The governor mentioned here was a lieutenant governor, Thomas Hutchinson, whose home was destroyed by the Stamp Act riots of 1765. Edmund S. Morgan and Helen M. Morgan, *The Stamp Act Crisis: Prologue to Revolution* (Chapel Hill, N.C., 1953), pp. 126-129.

in Governors *Shutes* Administration, & were continued down to that Æra, that the Tavern Expences of Committee Men, in those Disputes, amounted to £9000 Sterling; & I have heard a Gentleman, who was an Assembly Man in Colo. *Shute's Time,* lament & curse the Day that he sided with *Mr. Cooke* in his Opposition. Unhappy it was for some of the Governors that they could not be supported in their Chairs, instead of being suffered to quit them & return to *England*:[28] for although they were honorably acquitted from the popular Charges alleged against them, & perhaps provided for at home; yet it gave such a Stimulus to the Itch of complaining, that it was ever in the mouths of the Demagogues, *that they could, when they pleased, remove any Governor from his Post.* And whilst that was their Opinion, there were enough of that Diabolical Genius to promote a Quarrell out of the profoundest Peace. It is much to be deplored, that the Springs of the English Government too often lost of their Elasticity; which, perhaps, had they have been in many Cases wound up, would have had Force enough to have prevented the present Rebellion.[29]

I have done Sir! with my *procatarctick Causes,* which I believe you to be as glad to be rid of as I am. I have given You already some of their Effects: more you will meet with. You will be presented with such a Detail of Villainy in all its Forms, that it will require some Fortitude to meet the Shock. You will see Religion dressed up into a Stalkinghorse, to be skulked behind, that Vice might perpetrate its most atrocious Crimes, whilst it bore so fair a Front to mislead & decieve the World around. In short, you will see every Thing, sacred & profane, twisted into all Shapes to serve the Purposes of Rebellion; & Earth & Hell ransacked for Tools to work the Fabrick with. But not to anticipate.

[28]Oliver was probably thinking of Francis Bernard and Thomas Hutchinson as the two recent governors who had left the colony for quieter days in England. Thomas Pownall, whose three-year term of office was generally peaceful, also expressed dissatisfaction over his relations with the legislature.

[29]It is strange that Oliver said nothing of the administations of Jonathan Belcher and William Shirley, especially the dispute between Shirley and Belcher that brought Belcher's removal in 1741. See John A. Schutz, "Succession Politics in Massachusetts, 1730-1741," *William and Mary Quarterly,* 3rd Ser., XV (1958), 508-520.

II. BEGINNINGS OF THE REVOLUTION

I shall, with all due Deference to those who have already given their Opinions upon the *immediate* Cause of this Rebellion, assign an earlier Date than that which hath been affixed to it. It is the Year *1761* from whence I shall begin my Progress; for as I was intimate to the Transactions of that Æra, so I imagine I can see a concatenation of Incidents, wch. conduced to the ushering in this memorable Event; which Time itself can never efface from the Records of New England perfidy.

Towards the latter End of the Year 1760, *Stephen Sewall*, Esqr., Chief Justice of the Province of *Massachusetts Bay*, died.[1] As their are generally Candidates for such Posts, so one in particular vizt. *James Otis Esqr.* claimed the Palm; pleading the Merit of Age, long Practice at the Bar, & repeated Promises of a former Governor. Mr. *Otis* was one, who in the early Part of his Life, was by Trade a Cordwainer.[2] But as the People of the Province seem to be born with litigious Constitutions, so he had Shrewdness enough to take Advantage of the general Foible, & work'd himself into a Pettifogger; which Profession he practised in, to the End of his Life. He had a certain Adroitness to captivate the Ear of Country Jurors, who were too commonly Drovers, Horse Jockies, & of other lower Classes in Life. He also, for many Years, had been a Member of the lower House of Assembly, too great an Ingredient of which Composition consisted of Innkeepers, Retailers, & yet more inferior Orders of Men. These he had a great Command of, & he ever took Care to mix the Chicane of the Lawyer with the busy Importance of the Assembly Man; by which Methods he acquired a considerable Fortune. Thus circumstanced, he put in his Claim to a Seat upon the Bench; his Son was a Lawyer of superior Genius to his Father. He was also a Member of the Assembly for the Town of *Boston*; & while the Appointment of a Judge was in Suspence, this Son, in the

[1]Stephen Sewall (1702-60) became chief justice in 1752 upon the death of Paul Dudley. Hutchinson was appointed Sewall's successor on Nov. 13, 1760.

[2]James Otis (1702-78), father of the patriot, served many years as an important member of the House of Representatives. He was a loyal member of the Shirley administration and thus associated with Thomas Hutchinson and the Olivers.

Plenitude of his own Importance, swore, *"that if his Father was not appointed a Justice of the superior Court; he would set the Province in a Flame if he died in the Attempt."*[3]

The People of the Province, in general, not coinciding with the Judgment which the Father had formed of his own Merit, & thinking, that Integrity was an essential Qualification of a Judge, expressed a jealous Fear of such an Appointment; the surviving Judges of the Bench also, not willing to have an Associate of such a Character to seat with them, applied to Mr. *Bernard*, the then Govr., who had the Nomination to that Office, asking the Favor to have such a Colleague with them, that the Harmony of the Bench might not be interrupted; & accordingly proposed Mr. *Hutchinson*, the then Lieut. Governor of the Province; Mr. *Bernard* most readily acquiesced, & had already, before requested, determined on the Appointment. Mr. *Hutchinson* was also applied to, by the Judges, to take a Seat with them; but he refused, 'till he could be informed of the general Sentiment; *that* was for him, & he was prevailed upon to accept the Office of Chief Justice: upon which the two *Otis's*, the eldest of whom had for many Years before almost idolized him, now exerted theirselves, *totis viribus*,[4] to revenge their Disappointment, in Mr. *Hutchinson's* Destruction.

In all such Cases, Tools are as necessary in erasing as in erecting a Building; & as Destruction was vowed, so an Apparatus must be provided for the Purpose. Among other Tools, a Mr. *Joseph Hawley*, an Attorny at Law in the Country, was secured;[5] & although he had had, for many Years, an high Opinion of & been favored by Mr. *Hutchinson*, yet the evil Genius, which too often attended him & at this Time was too officious at his Levee, urged him on to such Rancor

---

[3]James Otis, Jr. (1725-83), swore revenge against Hutchinson—Hutchinson to Israel Williams, Jan. 21, 1761, Mass. Hist. Soc., Williams MSS, II, 155. In his *History of . . . Massachusetts-Bay*, III, 64, Hutchinson made this later comment on the significance of Otis' anger: "From so small a spark a great fire seems to have been kindled." Otis denied ever making these threats and published a long explanation of the episode in the Boston *Gazette*, April 4, 1763. The belief that the revolution began with the Otis-Hutchinson feud is but one example of the parallel interpretations placed on the revolution by Oliver and John Adams. See the Adams letters to William Tudor in *The Works of John Adams . . .* , ed. Charles Francis Adams (Boston, 1850-56), X, 230-375 passim.

[4]"With all one's might."

[5]Joseph Hawley (1723-88) was a successful lawyer of Hampshire County, representing such important Bostonians in western Massachusetts litigation as Thomas and John Hancock and John Rowe. His clients were more frequently the tradesmen and debtors of the county.

& Enmity that Surprized his best Friends; & the only Reason which he assigned for his Enmity, was, that Mr. *Hutchinson* was too fond of Power, in suffering himself to be appointed a Chief Justice; & that he shewed too much Pride in wearing Robes on the Bench; which Robes he & the other Judges wore, in Compliance with the Desire of Gov. *Bernard*, who proposed the Dress in Honor of the Government. A disordered Optick will swell a Molehill to the Bulk of a Mountain; This Mr. *Hawley* was also a Member of the general Assembly.

There was another Person called in to aid the Opposition, who was always ready to every evil Word & Work vizt. Mr. *Samuel Adams*, who hath distinguished himself throughout the present Rebellion.

Mr. *Otis*, ye. Son, understanding the Foibles of human Nature, although he did not always practise upon that Theory, advanced one shrewd Position, which seldom fails to promote popular Commotions, vizt. *that it was necessary to secure the black Regiment*, these were his Words, & his Meaning was to engage ye. dissenting Clergy on his Side. He had laid it down as a Maxim, *in nomine Domini incipit omne malum*; & where better could he fly for aid than to the Horns of the Altar? & this Order of Men might, in a literal Sense, be stiled such, for like their Predecessors of 1641 they have been unceasingly sounding the Yell of Rebellion in the Ears of an ignorant & deluded People.

As I have introduced several Persons of the Drama, I shall begin to comply with the Promise I made, at first setting out, of giving a Sketch of their Portraits; those who have now offered to sit I shall begin with; the rest will be taken in their Turns. Perhaps these Sketches may throw some Light on the more interesting Scenes. I shall begin with the late Govr. *Hutchinson*.

THOMAS HUTCHINSON

Mr. *Hutchinson* was a Gentleman on whom Nature had conferred, what she is very sparing of, an Acumen of Genius united with a Solidity of Judgment & great Regularity of Manners.[6] He descended from Ancestors who conferred Honor on the Roll of Magistracy in the Colony & ye. Province of the *Massachusetts Bay*— so early as at 12 Years of Age he was matriculated into *Harvard College* in *Cambridge*, & here he bore the Palm of classick Learning.

[6]See Malcolm Freiberg, "Thomas Hutchinson: The First Fifty Years (1711-1761)", *William and Mary Quarterly*, 3rd Ser., XV (1958), 41-42.

After he had been graduated, he quitted a Collegiate Life, & trod the mercantile Walk; & his Steps were directed by fairness and Punctuality in Dealing & with Success in his Schemes. As his Ancestors had been so much in publick Life, so Mr. *Hutchinson* had derived great Advantages from both publick and private Papers in their Possession, wch. served him for many valuable Purposes in publick Life, and especially in compiling the best History of the *Massachusetts Bay* that hath been published; a Continuation of which, to the breaking out of the present Rebellion he left prepared for the Press; a Publication of which would be a valuable Present to the Publick, as it would be a Register of Facts, which neither the Talent of historick Writing, or Truth itself would blush to Patronize.

Mr. *Hutchinson's* Ancestors in their political Principles, were no Friends to Democracy; & he himself judged it necessary to support the Prerogative, that it might hold the ballance of Power in such Equilibrio, that it might not sink into Republicanism, upon the Verge of which many of the colonial Systems of Government were erected. Notwithstanding his Sentiments upon Government were universally known, yet his Candor, Integrity, & Capacity were so well established, that he very early caught the publick Eye; and the Town of *Boston*, his native Place, elected him into Offices for the Defence of her legal Rights, which he was unweariedly assiduous in protecting; & in some Instances, distinguish[ab]ly so from his Brethren Assistants in the same Causes. *Boston* very early chose him as one of her Representatives in general Assembly. The lower House of Assembly soon chose him to be their Speaker, in which Station he shone distinguished, as having filled the Chair with as much Honor & Dignity as it ever had been adorned with. Both Houses of Assembly then chose him into his Majesty's Council; from wch. he was dismissed, (by that Faction which hurried on the present Rebellion) in 1766; when he ended his political Life, as far as it depended upon the Sufferages of the People. During his last mentioned political Existence, in all Difficulties of State & Contests with neighbouring Governments the People of the Province repaired to him, with as much Avidity as the People of *Greece* repaired to the Oracle at *Delphi* in their Emergencies; but Mr. *Hutchinson* was so void of Duplicity of Soul, that he, unlike to the Priestess of *Apollo*, never returned an ambiguous Answer. They had employed him as their Agent in *England* on some important Services, & he did not deceive them; & after all his important Services he never reaped any lucrative Advantages for his private Fortune; but this was not to be wondred at, for it had been the uninterrupted Series of Gratitude, in this Government, to bestow upon its Benefactors *only* the pleasing Consolation of serving their Country without reward. Nay, when in the Year 1765 the Demagogues of this Province had spurred on a Banditti to demolish his Dwelling House & plunder his Property from it, to hunt after his Life & the Lives of his Children, & to persecute him with unparrall[el]ed Barbarity, he, with a Magnanimity of Soul, rather to be admired than capable of being imitated, was inquisitive what he had done to demerit such Cruelty; & pitied his Enemies: a conscious Rectitude of Soul, only, could support him under such Malevolence.[7]

Not long after, a Contest arose between the *Massachusetts* & *New York* Governments relative to their Boundaries, & Mr. *Hutchinson* was applied to by the general Assembly to undertake the Task of one [of] their Commissioners (in 1773); for here again, none understood the Nature of the Contest so well as he did. He went, & settled it beyond their Expectations. On his Return, provincial Ingratitude was so much their Characteris[tic]k, that they would not deign to thank him for his Services; but, on the other Hand, were then plotting to petition his Majesty to remove him from his Government on Account of the Letters which were stole by *Dr. Franklyn*, & for which Mr. *Hutchinson* was so honorably acquitted.

One singular Advantage he had derived to the Province, for which he merited the monumental Pillar, & for which the Blessings of those who were ready to perish came upon him, & which caused the Widows Heart to sing for Joy. Mr. *Hutchinson* had early studied the Nature of Mony, as a Medium of Commerce, & was a perfect Master of that Science, which to others, & men of Sense too, appeared as abstruse as the Disquisitions after the Philosopher's Stone; but to him were as simple as the first Rudiments of Grammar. This Advantage was a compleat Rescous from the Infatuation of a most infamous Paper Currency, which the Province had been bewildered in for nearly 60 Years; this Currency had been established on account of the *Canada* Expedition in *1690*, when *six Shillings* in Paper Bills could, by Law, command an Ounce of Silver; but the Province, enthusiastically imagining that the Possession of such a Power of making Paper Mony equal to the Possession of the Mines of *Potosi*, had made so many of those Emissions, by the Year 1745, that there was so great a Defalcation in the Value of the Paper Mony, that by

[7]The original description of Hutchinson's virtues seems to be in an article by "Verus" in the Boston *Weekly News-Letter*, May 16, 1771.

the Year 1748, *three Pounds* in those Bills, would command only one Ounce of Silver: & the Laws of the Province were so iniquitous, that the Persons, who had let Mony at Interest for many Years past, were obliged to submit to this Defalcation; by which Means, Widows, Orphans, Salary Men, & all Annuitants, were reduced to great Straits, & some to absolute Poverty. From future Evils of this Kind there was an Opening made for Extrication. The Parliament of *Great Britain,* in its great Liberality, reimbursed the Province the Sum of Mony which it had advanced in their Expedition to *Cape Breton,* & its Capture, 1745; the Mony was sent to them in 1749 in Spanish milled Dollars to the Amount of £183.649. Sterling.

Such an Opportunity as this to be delivered from an Egyptian Bondage, might be reasonably imagined, would be eagerly embraced; but the Infatuation of Attachment to the Garlick & Onions was so great, that many wished that the Mony had been sunk in the Ocean before its Arrival. Mr. *Hutchinson's* Sagacity, with Respect to the Finances of his Country, urged him to every Exertion, with his Connections, to secure his Country against every future Evil attendant upon a fallacious Paper Currency. He was so happy as to succeed; & the Province Medium was established on so solid a Basis, that its Reputation was raised to an higher Pitch of Justice than any other Colony upon the Continent; & for this publick Act of his, his Character was venerated by all who expressed a Regard for Justice & publick Faith. But even in his Exertions in performing so meritorious an Act, interested Men set the Canaille to insult him; which they did in the most open Manner in the publick Streets, threatening him not only with Words but with Sticks; but his Virtue was of so confirm'd a Texture, that he let the Insults pass unnoticed; untill Time had worn off the popular Frenzy, & he had lived to see many of those, who had insulted him with their Curses, follow him with their Blessings, for saving his Country from that Destruction which they madly endeavoured to plung[e] her into.

Mr. *Hutchinson* not only has sustained many publick Offices, dependant upon the Sufferages of the People, but he was appointed by the Crown, in 1757, Lieut. Governor; & in 1771 Governor & Commander in Chief of the Province of the *Massachusetts Bay.*[8] In the former Station, the Space to exert his Abilities in was contracted, except in being consulted by the Commanders in chief, who respectively derived great Advantages from his Advice & Counsel in

[8]Hutchinson's commission as lieutenant governor was published June 1, 1758. He took his oath as governor on March 14, 1771.

all the arduous Affairs of Government, in the latter Stations, the Sequel will open his Conduct.

He was also, where the Power of the Crown was united with the Nature of this provincial Legislature, appointed *Judge of Probate* for the County of *Suffolk*, the most important County of the Province; & afterwards, *Chief Justice* of the Province as also one of his Majesty's Council. As *Judge of Probate* he conciliated the Admiration, Esteem & Love of all who either repaired to him for Justice or appeared before him as Council for the litigant Parties. The Widow & the Orphan repaired to him as their Guardian, & the Doors of his Office, & his House also, were ever unlatched to their Petitions for Relief & Advice. His placid Temper & his invincible Patience seemed marked out by the GOD of Nature for the discharge of this most difficult Office, where Litigants appeared, who were uninstructed in all the Forms necessary to conduct their Cases, & too frequently carried them on with the Impertinence & Roughness of unpolished Nature; but his Decrees were given with so much legal judgment & undisguised Integrity, that the Lips of Envy & party Abuse were ever fast sealed against any Impeachment of his official Justice. This Office he discharged with peculiar Pleasure; for upon his once being asked by a Friend, "why he did not resign this very troublesome Office, since he sustained those of *Lieut. Governor* & *Chief Justice*, also, & as the Profits of it were very trifling?" His Reply was this, vizt. "it gives me so much Pleasure to relieve the Widow & fatherless, & direct them what Steps to take in managing their Estates; & also in reconciling contending Parties; that I would rather resign my other Offices, & discharge this alone without Fee or Reward."

In mentioning those three Offices, which Mr. *Hutchinson* sustained at the same Time, it may be noticed; that the Envy of Ambition in some, & the Envy of Avarice in others, were roused at the Possession of so many by one Man. But let it be remembered, that the pecuniary Stipends of this Province, to their Servants, were similar, in profit, to the Wages of Sin, for no Man could get a Living by them; & those three united in Mr. *Hutchinson*, although each of them were as profitable as any other Office, did not afford him a decent Support for his Family.

He was hailed to the Seat of *Chief Justice* with the Acclamations of the Province.[9] He had been, for several Years before, a Justice

---

[9]The statement is an exaggeration. Nearly every week the Boston *Gazette* in 1761 and 1763 carried attacks on Hutchinson.

of the *inferior Court of Common Pleas* for the County of *Suffolk*;
but this Department was so much a thoroughfare, only, to the
Superior Court of the Judicature, that a Man might be allowed,
almost, to spend a Life in this inferior Department, & at the Close of
it crowd all the Knowledge which he had acquired in it into a Nut-
shell. But Mr. *Hutchinson*, when he first fill'd this important Seat,
seemed to be all Intuition. The ablest Councellers at the Bar, & some
very able ones there were, seemed astonished, & would often, when
they were Antagonists in important Causes, & were divided in their
Opinions in drawing a special Verdict, refer the Draft to him. When,
in a few Minutes, he would return a legal one, to the Acceptance of
both Parties. In this Office he preesided for ten Years, & it was the
general Opinion, that as none of his Predecessors in Office excelled
him in the Knowledge of the Law & in Uprightness of Judgment,
so none of his Successors outrivalled him in the Science of Juris-
prudence.

In private Life, Mr. *Hutchinson* was the Scholar, without Ped-
antry—The polite Gentleman, without Affectation—the social Companion, without Reservedness—affable, without the least Tincture
of Pride—in Commerce, undisguised & open—in Morals, regular
without Severity—in Expression of his Sentiments, candid & void of
Guile—liberal in his Charity, without Ostentation or Partiality—
amiable in domestick Life, distinguished by conjugal Fidelity & attention, parental Affection, & an humane, tender & condescending
Behavior to his dependant Domesticks—his Religion sat gracefull on
his conduct; it was manly & free, undebased by Hypocrisy, Enthusiasm or Superstition; it embraced all Mankind.

One Instance only shall be adduced, vizt. When the *French Catholicks* were dispossessd of their Property in *Nova Scotia*, about 25
years ago by the English Nation, (which could not be justified, but
by the irresistible Principle of Necessity in Order to [aid] national
Security) they were all dispersed among the English Colonies; those
that were stationed in the *Massachusetts* Province, hearing of Mr.
Hutchinsons Humanity, frequently resorted to him as their Guardian, & were never disappointed in their Expectations of Advice or
Relief; some of them he took under his more immediate Care; for
he pitied the fatal Necessity of their Distress; & many of them wor-
shipped him almost as sincerely as they did their household Gods,
their Crucifixes. In short, in all the various Departments of Life, he
behaved with that Dignity which was ornamental to each of them; &
when he left his native Country & retired to *England*, his Character

was so fully established, that he was particularly noticed by the greatest Men in the Kingdom; & by his *Majesty* himself, who was too sensible of the Merits of his Service, not to distinguish him by particular Marks of his royal Favor.

I might have mentioned the Character he sustained as one of his *Majestys Council* for about seventeen Years (from 1749 to 1766). This Office was in the Election of the People, with the Salvo of the Governors negative; but here he held the Ballance so nicely, that he was the *instar omnium* of that Order;[10] his Judgment was too distinctive, not to vail their Opinions, in important Cases, to his thorough Knowledge of the political System of their Country; & here he continued, untill Rebellion began its gigantick Strides to tread down Government itself.

After 7 years Residence in *England*; from the Transition from a very active to an almost inactive Life; from a Reflection on the Miseries of his native Country, & from a Combination of other Causes, he sunk into a chronical Disorder which hurried him out of Life, though at a late Age; & he made his Exit suddenly; but such an Exit which every wise Man would wish to make; not being appalled by the Fear of Death, or having one retrospect uneasy Reflection upon his Conduct, to create such a Fear.

Perhaps Sir! you will ask me why I have been so diffuse upon Mr. *Hutchinson's* Character? Let me tell you then, that the Distinction of Applause which attended him, roused the Envy & Malice of the Leaders of the Faction, who dipped their shafts in more than infernal Gall, & made him the Butt to level them at. He exerted every Nerve to save his Country; they were determined to ruin him, tho' they plunged their Country & theirselves too, into absolute Destruction. It vexed them to find an Antagonist who was superior to them, with their united Understanding; but I will relieve you by several Contrasts; in which you will see human Nature in her various Attitudes, & you may then judge, whether to dwell upon her Beauties or Deformities is the most agreeable.

THE YOUNG MR. OTIS

The first Character of the Contrast which I shall exhibit will be young Mr. *Otis*, as he was the first who broke down the Barriers of Government to let in the *Hydra* of Rebellion; agreeable to the

10"Equal to all the others"—Cicero's comment on Plato.

already mentioned Stygian Oath which he had taken, of "setting the Province in a Flame."[11]

Mr. *Otis* was designed, by Nature, for a Genius; but it seemed as if, by the Impetuosity of his Passions, he had wrested himself out of her Hands before she had complemented her Work; for his Life seemed to be all Eccentricity. He passed through a Collegiate Education, & then entred upon the Study of the Law under a Gentleman who was at the Head of that Profession.[12] But his Education was of little or no Service to the World or to himself. He studied the Law, under his Preceptor, with great Attention; he made great Progress in it, & would have been of distinguishing Figure in it had he not have mistaken a contemptuous Pride for a laudable Ambition; & given too loose a Rein to the Wildness of his Passion. He seemed to have adopted that Maxim which *Milton* puts into the Mouth of one of his Devils, vizt.

"Better to reign in Hell than serve in Heaven."[13]

And his whole Life seemed to be a Comment on his Text. He carried his Malevolence to so great Length, that being often thwarted in his Opposition to Government, he took to the Course of Dram drinking, & ruined his Family, with an amiable Wife at the Head of it, who had brought him a Fortune, & who, by his bad Conduct, became disordered in her Mind—happy had it been for his Country, had he urged on his own Ruin, before he had brought on hers.[14] By drinking, & other Misconduct, he grew so frantick, that he was frequently under the Guardianship of the Law, & confined; & the last I heard of him was, that he seemed to be a living Monument of the Justice of Heaven, by his being a miserable Vagabond, rolling in the Streets & Gutters, the laughing-Stock of Boys & the Song of the Drunkard. Even in his best Estate, he was indelicate in his Man-

---

[11]The use of the word "Hydra" to describe the growing discontent was a common figure of speech. See Boston *Evening-Post*, Dec. 12, 1774: "When once despotism, a dreadful Hydra, dispensing more curses than ever issued from Pondora's box, with gygantic strides begins to stalk, the blessings of liberty are all on tip-toe."

[12]Jeremiah Gridley (1702-67) had such law students as James Otis, Oxenbridge Thacher, Benjamin Prat, and William Cushing. He represented the crown in the Superior Court battle over the Writs of Assistance. See *Sibley's Harvard Graduates*, VII (1945), 518-530.

[13]*Paradise Lost*, in *The Poetical Works of John Milton*, ed. Helen Darbishire (Oxford, 1952-55), I, Bk. I, 12, l. 263.

[14]John Adams in 1765 described James Otis as "fiery and feverous; his imagination flames, his passions blaze; he is liable to great inequalities of temper; sometimes in despondency, sometimes in a rage." *Works*, II, 163.

ners, & rough in his Conversation.[15] He was devoid of all Principle; & would, as a Lawyer, take Fees on both Sides, in which he had been detected in open Court.

A PORTRAIT OF MR. HAWLEY

Joseph Hawley Esqr. is the next whose Turn it is to sit for his Portrait. He was educated at *Yale College* in *Connecticut.* He was a Man of Sense & Learning, & unhappily for himself he was too sensible of it. He practised the Law with Reputation, had sustained several publick Offices, & been often a Member of the House of Representatives. He had been, 'till the Year 1760, a most firm Friend to Government, & a great Friend to *Mr. Hutchinson* in his private as well as his publick Station. At this Period, *Mr. Hawley,* for the aforementioned Reasons given by himself & from the Insinuations of *Mr. Otis* & his Adherents, turned inimical to Mr. *Hutchinson* & the Government. And from the general good Character of Integrity which he wore, he, like the red Dragon of the *Revelation,* drew a third part of the Stars of Heaven after him. And he carried his Enmity so far, that, not content with libelling Mr. *Hutchinson* personally, he libelled the whole *Supreme Court* of *Justice* where he preesided; for which, the only Punishment he recieved, & that owing to the too great Moderation of the Chief Justice, was, a dismission from the Bar, untill he found his interest suffer by it, when he was admitted again as a Barrister, upon the Confession of his Offence in open Court, by a Writing upon the Records of the Court.[16] He had obtained the Character of a Man of Piety & Virtue by a formal, decent Behaviour; Formality in Religion being the provincial Characteristick, & peculiarly so of the County of *Hamshire,* where he resided. But his Religion was something problematical; which a few Instances may evince. The first shall be of the droll & serious Kind, united, vizt. being in the military Line, he some years since was ordered to command a Party after a Number of Indians. He set out on his Expedition & discovered the Enemy at a Distance; but in the Heigth of his Fear or his Zeal (some say one, some say the other) he purposed the singing an Hymn before

[15]In 1771 John Adams noted (*Works,* II, 290) that Otis "was quite wild at the bar meeting; cursed the servants for not putting four candles on the table, swore he could yet afford to have four upon his own. . . ."

[16]Hawley criticized Hutchinson's judicial opinion by writing letters to the Boston *Evening-Post* and was punished with disbarment. Ernest Francis Brown, *Joseph Hawley: Colonial Radical* (New York, 1931), pp. 64-68.

the Attack; & as the more Noise the more Devotion, so the Hymn was sung with that audible Voice which reached the Ears of ye Indians & put them to Flight, thus

> He liv'd to fight another Day
> Without being forc'd to run away.[17]

The next Instance is this. He lived in the Town of *Northampton*, & in the Parish, of which the Revd. Mr. *Jona. Edwards*, the famous Metaphysician, so much noticed by Lord *Kaims*, was Minister.[18] He entered upon a religious Altercation with Mr. *Edwards*; & by his Influence ousted Mr. *Edwards*, with a large Family, of their Living. Afterwards, his religious controversial Zeal subsided into a religious Melancholy; & in the Depths of it he made a publick Confession, in the News Papers, of the Injury he had done to Mr. *Edwards*, & ask'd Pardon. But whether he ever made Restitution in any other Way, the World is silent.

A Third Instance shall be what was related to me by a Gentleman of Reputation. Mr. *Hawley* & he were appointed by the Government, on a Tour of publick Services; at that Time Mr. *Hawley* was in his Fits of Enthusiasm, & would by no means omit Morning & Evening Prayers at every Inn where they lodged. But not long after, upon another like Tour, he was taken with a Fit of Deism, & then the Prayers were not only omitted but ridiculed; thus versatile was he.

He had his full Share of the *Hauteur*, & a Stubbornness of Temper which was harder to bend than the knotted Oak. His Disposition was such, that like *Dryden's Duke of Buckingham*, he was

> So over violent or over civil
> That every Man with him was God or Devil.[19]

Such a Character as this it was dangerous to trust to; & the surest Method to secure him, was to sooth his Pride, for here he was sensible. But let me apologize for him, & throw a Vail over his Infirmities,

[17] James Ray, *A Compleat History of the Rebellion* (York, 1749), p. 54:
> He that fights and runs away,
> May turn and fight another Day.

[18] [Henry Home, Lord Kames], *Essays on the Principles of Morality and Natural Religion*, 2nd ed. (London, 1758), pp. 170-173. See also Jonathan Edwards, *Freedom of the Will*, ed. Paul Ramsey, in *The Works of Jonathan Edwards*, I (New Haven, 1957), 443-452.

[19] John Dryden, "Absalom and Achitophel," *The Works of John Dryden*, ed. George Saintsbury (Edinburgh, 1882-93), IX, 260, ll. 557-558.

which have brought on or rather promoted the many Evils which his Country now groans under; by saying, that he was so unfortunate as to have a very irritable Set of Nerves, which brought on hyp[o]-condriack Disorders. When he was under the Influence of those Disorders, he was often insane & would return to his Clients Fees which he had recieved from them, which he *then* would call exorbitant, although he was generally known to be moderate in his Demands from them: he was very unhappy in this constitutional Disorder, & the last Account of him, was, that he was confined under the Effects of them, an Object of Commiseration.[20]

MR. SAMUEL ADAMS

I shall next give you a Sketch of some of Mr. *Samuel Adam's* Features; & I do not know how to delineate them stronger, than by the Observation made by a celebrated Painter in *America*, vizt. "That if he wished to draw the Picture of the Devil, that he would get *Sam Adams* to sit for him:" & indeed, a very ordinary Physiognomist would, at a transient View of his Countenance, develope the Malignity of his Heart. He was a Person of Understanding, but it was discoverable rather by a Shrewdness than Solidity of Judgment; & he understood human Nature, in low life, so well, that he could turn the Minds of the great Vulgar as well as the small into any Course that he might chuse; perhaps he was a singular Instance in this Kind; & he never failed of employing his Abilities to the vilest Purposes. He was educated at *Harvard College*; and when he quitted that Scene of Life, he entered upon the Business of a Malster, the Profits of which afforded him but a moderate Maintenance; & his Circumstances were too well known for him to gain a pecuniary Credit with Mankind.[21]

He was so thorough a *Machiavilian*, that he divested himself of every worthy Principle, & would stick at no Crime to accomplish his Ends. He was chosen a Collector of Taxes for the Town of *Boston*; but when the Day of Account came, it was found that there was a Defalcation of about £1700. Sterling. He was apprized of it long before, & formed his Plans accordingly—he knew the Temper of the Town of *Boston*, that the most Part of them were inclined to

[20]Hawley suffered from chronic ill health, in which spells of melancholy would disrupt his work and nearly incapacitate him. Finally, in 1776, he was forced to retire to Northampton. Brown, *Joseph Hawley*, p. 170.

[21]John C. Miller, *Sam Adams: Pioneer in Propaganda* (Boston, 1936), pp. 4-10; *Sibley's Harvard Graduates*, X (1958), 420-425.

Opposition of Government, and he secured an Interest with them. This he did, by ingratiating himself with *John Hancock Esqr.*, a considerable Merchant of that Town, in the same Manner that the Devil is represented seducing *Eve*, by a constant whispering at his Ear.

Here I am almost necessarily led into a Digression upon Mr. *Hancock's* Character, who was as closely attached to the hindermost Part of Mr. *Adams* as the Rattles are affixed to the Tail of the Rattle Snake. Mr. *Hancock* was the Son of a dissenting Clergyman, whose Circumstances in Life were not above Mediocrity, but he had a rich Uncle. He was educated at *Harvard College*, was introduced into his uncles Warehouse as a Merchant, & upon his Death was the residuary Legatee of £60,000 Sterling. His understanding was of the Dwarf Size; but his Ambition, upon the Accession to so great an Estate, was upon the Gigantick. He was free from Immoralities, & Objects of Charity often felt the Effects of his Riches. His Mind was a meer *Tabula Rasa*,[22] & had he met with a good Artist he would have enstamped upon it such Character as would have made him a most usefull Member of Society. But Mr. *Adams* who was restless in endeavors to disturb ye Peace of Society, & who was ever going about seeking whom he might devour, seized upon him as his Prey, & stamped such Lessons upon his Mind, as have not as yet been erased. Sometimes, indeed, by certain Efforts of Nature, which he was insensible of the Causes of his self, he would almost disengage himself from his Assailant; but *Adams*, like the Cuddlefish, would discharge his muddy Liquid, & darken the Water to such an Hue, that the other was lost to his Way, & by his Tergiversation in the Cloudy Vortex would again be seized, & at last secured. Mr. *Hancock*, in Order to figure away as a Merchant, entered deeply into Trade; but having no Genius for it, (by monopolizing & other Misfortunes, together with his Ambition for being a Politician for which he was as little qualified as for a Merchant) he very soon reduced his Finances to a very low Ebb, & rendered it difficult for a Creditor to procure from him a small Ballance of Debt; & some Things he did, by reason of his distressed Circumstances, which were not compatible with the Rules of strict Justice.[23] Mr. *Adams*,

[22]This is a reference to Locke's concept of man's mental endowment at birth; hence Hancock had learned nothing.

[23]John Hancock (1737-93). William T. Baxter agrees that Hancock had "no genius for it [business]." *The House of Hancock: Business in Boston 1724-1775* (Cambridge, Mass., 1945), p. xxii.

after bringing him into such a Situation, could do no less than shove him up to the last Round of the Ladder, & he was præsident of the *american* Congress. Here he was at the Summit of his Ambition; but he has descended so far as to be the Governor of *Massachusetts* Province; & if the British Government should succeed in subduing the Rebellion, it requires no second Sight to foresee, that whereas he was once vain, that he would then be less than nothing & Vanity itself.

I here Drop my Digression, & return to Mr. *Adams*, when he had embezzled the publick Monies of *Boston*—in Order to extricate himself, he duped Mr. *Hancock*, by persuading him to build Houses & Wharves which would not bring him 2 p ct. Intrest for his Mony. This Work necessarily engaged a Variety of Artificers, whom *Adams* could prefer. This secured these Orders of Men in his Interest; & such Men chiefly composed the Voters of a *Boston* Town Meeting. At one of their Meetings the Town voted him a Discharge of 2/3d of his Debt, & Mr. *Hancock* & some others, into whose Graces he had insinuated his balefull Poison, subscribed to a Discharge of the other Third—thus was he set at large to commit his Ravages on Government, untill he undermined the Foundations of it, & not one Stone had been left upon another. He soon outrivalled Mr. *Otis* in popularity. His was all serpentine Cunning, Mr. *Otis* was rash, unguarded, foulmouthed, & openly spitefull; all which was disgustfull to those who piqued themselves upon their Sanctity. The other had always a religious Mask ready for his Occasions; he could transform his self into an Angel of Light with the weak Religionist; & with the abandoned he would disrobe his self & appear with his cloven Foot & in his native Blackness of Darkness—he had a good Voice, & was a Master in vocal Musick. This Genius he improved, by instituting singing Societys of Mechanicks, where he preesided; & embraced such Opportunities to ye inculcating Sedition, 'till it had ripened into Rebellion. His Power over weak Minds was truly surprizing. I have done with him for the present; you will soon hear more of him.

THE BLACK REGIMENT

It may not be amiss, now, to reconnoitre Mr. *Otis's* black Regiment, the *dissenting Clergy*, who took so active a Part in the Rebellion.[24] The congregational perswasion of Religion might be prop-

[24]The term "black regiment" was used in Oliver's article in the Boston *Weekly News-Letter*, Jan. 11, 1776. It was used earlier by "Israelite" in the Boston *Gazette*, Dec. 7, 1772.

erly termed the established Religion of the *Massachusetts*, as well as of some other of the *New England* Colonies; as the Laws were peculiarly adapted to secure ye Rights of this Sect; although all other Religions were tolerated, except the *Romish*. This Sect inherited from their Ancestors an Aversion to Episcopacy; & I much question, had it not been for the Supremacy of the British Government over them, which they dared not openly deny, whether Episcopacy itself would have been tolerated; at least it would have been more discountenanced than it was—& here I can not but remark a great Mistake of the Governors of the *Church of England*, in proposing to the Colonies to have their consent to a *Bishops* residing among them for ye purpose of Ordination. It was the direct Step to a Refusal; for all such Proposals from the Parent State, whether of a civil or a Religious Nature, were construed into Timidity by the Colonists, & were sure of meeting with a Repulse.

The Clergy of this Province were, in general, a Set of very weak Men; & it could not be expected that they should be otherwise, as many of them were just relieved, some from the Burthen of the Satchel; & others from hard Labor; & by a Transition from those Occupations to mounting a Desk, from whence they could overlook the principal Part of their Congregations, they, by that mean acquired a supreme Self Importance; which was too apparent in their Manners. Some of them were Men of Sense, and would have done Honor to a Country which shone in Literature; but there were few of these; & among these, but very few who were not strongly tinctured with Republicanism. The Town of *Boston* being the Metropolis, it was also the Metropolis of Sedition; and hence it was that their Clergy being dependent on the People for their daily Bread; by having frequent Intercourse with the People, imbibed their Principles.[25] In this Town was an annual Convention of the Clergy of the Province, the Day after the *Election* of his Majestys Charter Council; and at those Meetings were settled the religious Affairs of the Province; & as the *Boston* Clergy were esteemed by the others as an Order of Deities, so they were greatly influenced by them. There was also another annual Meeting of the Clergy at *Cambridge*, on the *Commencement* for graduating the Scholars of *Harvard College*; at these two Conventions, if much Good was effectuated, so there was much Evil. And some of the *Boston* Clergy,

[25]"Freeman" in the *Censor* for Jan. 4, 1772, p. 25, observed that the Boston clergy "have temporised, against their own judgments, in compliance with the prejudices of their people."

as they were capable of the Latter, so they missed no Opportunities of accomplishing their Purposes. Among those who were most distinguished of the *Boston* Clergy were Dr. *Charles Chauncy*, Dr. *Jonathan Mayhew* & Dr. *Samuel Cooper*;[26] & they distinguished theirselves in encouraging Seditions & Riots, untill those lesser Offences were absorbed in Rebellion.[27]

Dr. *Chauncy* was advanced in Life; he was a Man of Sense, but of exorbitant Passions.[28] He would utter Things in Conversation that bordered too near upon Blasphemy; & when such wild Expressions were noticed to him, by observing that his Sermons were free from such Extravagances, he would reply, that "in making his Sermons he always kept a Blotter by him." He was of a very resentfull, unforgiving Temper; & when he was in the Excess of his Passion, a Bystander would naturally judge that he had been educated in the Purlieus of *Bedlam*; but he was open in all his Actions. His hoary Head had great Respect paid to it by the factious & seditious, & it would really have been a Crown of Glory to him had it been found in the Way of Righteousness.

Dr. *Mayhew* was also a Man of Sense, but he was very slow in arranging & consolidating his Ideas.[29] In Conversation he was an awkard Disputant, as well as in his extempore Pulpit Effusions. Both were more like to the Water of a River dashing over the Rocks that impeded its Course, than to the smooth flowing Current. Both were so unharmonious and discordant, that they always grated upon the Ears of his Auditors; but his polemick, publick Performances, although elaborate & inelegant, showed Strength of Reason. He had too great a Share of Pride for an humble Disciple of so divine a Master, & looked with too contemptuous an Eye on all around him.

[26]Other members of the "black regiment" were Jonas Clark, of Lexington, whose wife was Hancock's cousin; Andrew Eliot, who was a correspondent of Thomas Hollis; John Lathrop, of Old North Church; and Samuel Cooke, of Arlington, who was a good friend of Jonas Clark and John Cleaveland.

[27]Samuel Cooper and his successor were accused of "sowing sedition and conspiracy among parishioners"—a practice that had gone on ever since the cornerstone of the church was laid. See Alice M. Baldwin, *The New England Clergy and the American Revolution* (Durham, N.C., 1928), p. 94, n. 34.

[28]Charles Chauncy (1705-87), son of a Boston merchant and minister of the First Church for sixty years, was the most influential minister of his time in Boston.

[29]Jonathan Mayhew (1702-66), minister of the West Church of Boston from 1747 to his death, was well known for his political views. John Adams said that Mayhew was a "transcendent genius" whose seasoned expressions of wit and satire were superior to any found in Swift or Franklin (*Works*, X, 287-288).

The late chief Justice *Sewall* was one of his Parishioners, & a Patron to him; & during *his* Life, his Behaviour was as decent as could be expected from a Man of his Temper; but when that very worthy Magistrate died, he gave a loose to his Passions & commenced a partizan in Politicks. And it was remarked, that on the day pre-ceeding the Destruction of Mr. *Hutchinson's* House, he preached so seditious a Sermon, that some of his Auditors, who were of the Mob, declared, whilst the Doctor was delivering it they could scarce contain themselves from going out of the Assembly & beginning their Work.[30] However, when the Villainy was perpetrated, he felt some severe Girds of what is vulgarly called Conscience; but he found, too late, that his Words were too hard of Digestion to be ate. Happy had it been for him, if the Doctrine of the Inefficacy of a Death Bed Repentance had had a proper Effect upon his own Mind.[31]

The last of the sacerdotal Triumvirate, whom I shall mention, is Dr. *Cooper*.[32] There were others of the Order, who were of the Faction, but they were Understrappers & Lacquies. Dr. *Cooper* was a young Man—very polite in his Manners—of a general Knowledge—not deep in his Profession, but very deep in the black Art. His be-havior in Company was very insinuating especially among the fair Sex; & many of them, of his Acquaintance, had their *Adams*. No Man could, with a better Grace, utter the Word of *God* from his Mouth, & at the same Time keep a two edged Dagger concealed in his Hand. His Tongue was Butter & Oil, but under it was the Poison of Asps. Never was a Scholar of *St. Omers*, who was a more thor-ough Proficient in Jesuitism. He could not only prevaricate with Man, but with *God* also; for when he, once, had invited a young Clergyman, who was not in Orders, to preach an afternoon Sermon for him, the factious Conspirators had recieved some disagreable News, in the Intervals of divine Service, & sent for Dr. *Cooper*,

[30]On Aug. 25, 1765, Mayhew preached "a fiery sermon on the text: 'I would they were even cut off which trouble you.' Soon after a mob destroyed Hutchinson's house and one of the ringleaders when caught, excused his actions on the ground that he was excited by the sermon, 'and thought he was doing God service.'" Frank Dean Gifford, "The Influence of the Clergy on American Politics from 1763 to 1776," *His-torical Magazine of the Protestant Episcopal Church*, X (1941), 108.

[31]Charles Chauncy, *A Discourse Occasioned by the Death of the Reverned* [sic] *Jonathan Mayhew* (Boston, 1766), p. 39: "His death, in the vigor of his days, and height of his usefulness, may justly be esteemed a great and public loss, calling for universal lamentation."

[32]Samuel Cooper (1725-83), born in Boston and graduated from Harvard College in 1743, was minister of the Brattle Street Church.

upon a Consultation. The Doctor was detained 'till the Hour for administring a Baptism approached, & he was sent for. He came, but pretended Sickness for his Absence; when it was known that he had been among the Leaders of the Faction. The Fluency of his Tongue & the Ease of his Manners atoned with some for all his Dissimulation; for his Manners were such, that he was always agreeable to the politest Company, who were unacquainted with his real Character; & he could descend from them to mix privately with the Rabble, in their nightly seditious Associations.[33]

I have done Sir! for the present, with my Portraits. If you like them, & think them ornamental for your Parlour, pray hang them up in it; for I assure You, that most of them justly demerit a *Suspension.*

[33]Gifford, "The Influence of the Clergy," p. 109: "Dr. Samuel Cooper of the Brattle Street Church in Boston was another who took a leading part in arousing his fellow-citizens at the time of the Stamp Act and later and thus was especially detested by the Tories and the British. His counsel was eagerly sought and he was the friend and intimate correspondent of men like Samuel Adams, Benjamin Franklin and Joseph Warren."

III. THE STAMP ACT

I shall now resume my other disagreeable Task, & open upon You the progressive Scenes of the Rebellion; & here I must previously inform You, that the Inhabitants of the *Massachusetts bay* were notorious in the smuggling Business, from the Capital Merchant down to the meanest Mechanick. And whereas in *England* it is dishonorable, to a Merchant of Honor, to be guilty of such base Subterfuges to increase their Estates, it is in *New England* so far from being reproachfull, that some of the greatest Fortunes there were acquired in this disgracefull Trade; & the *Prop[r]ietors* of them boast of their Method of Acquisition. Nay, some of those Smugglers have acquired so strong an Habit of Smuggling, that they have openly declared, that if they could gain more by a legal Trade they would prefer the former.

SMUGGLING AN ACCURSED VICE

So pernicious is this illicit Trade, that it not only wrongs the Society of those Dues which are the Resources for its Support, & injures the fair Dealer by lessening his Abilities to aid Society & maintain his private Family, but it naturally tends to the Destruction of all moral Sense. And it may safely be asserted, that a thorough Adept in this most balefull Science is ever ready to commit, not only the lesser Crimes, but is fit for Stratagems, Treasons & Murder. These have been the Effects of this accursed Vice in other Countries, & repeatedly so in this Province, where Sanctity is so much boasted of. In a Court of Justice, where a Smugler is a Witness, both Judge & Jury ever ought to be cautious & strict in the Examination of such a Witness, & in giving Credence to his Testimony; & the soundest Reason will justifie such a Jealousy.

As Instances of some of the Arts of their dishonest Profession, I will give one or two Anecdotes, leaving some others to the Time in wch. they were transacted. I knew a Captain of a Vessell in *Boston*, of no mean Reputation in Trade, & who was largely concerned in the contraband Trade, who publickly boasted, that when he came in from Sea, he made it his Practice, on the Morning of the Day on which he entred his Vessell, & previous to Office Hours, to go before the *Custom House,* hold up his Hand, and swear that *"what he should swear before the Custom House Officer on that Day should go for nothing"*; & afterwards would swear, before the Officer, that he had no contraband Goods on Board; when, at the same Time, the greatest Part of his Cargo was of that Sort. Another Captain boasted, "that he had evaded the Law, by writing two Manifests of his Cargo, one of which contained the contraband Goods he had on Board, & in the other Manifest those Goods were left out, he then went to the Custom House & stuck the true Manifest in the Sleeve of that Hand which he was to hold up in swearing, & deliverd the false Manifest to the Officer, & swore the Manifest to be a true one, meaning that which was in his Sleeve."[1] Such Arts as these are what is vulgarly called, *cheating* the *Devil;* but if those Adventurers can get no more by cheating him than they do by cheating their King, (& by the Way, that is a pretty round Sum too) they may, upon settling the Account Current, find theirselves in large Arrears, & not be able to smuggle off the Ballance.

As an Instance that Smugglers are lost to all Sense of Honor, I shall relate a Fact which was transacted in the *Massachusetts* Province. The Distillery of Rum was a capital Article of Business there—by the Interest of the *West India* Merchants a Duty of *six* Pence P Gallon was laid upon all foreign Melasses imported into the northern Colonies, & afterwards reduced to *four* Pence. This created great Uneasiness among the Merchants of this Province, where the smugling Business was carried on in its highest Perfection: upon which they wrote to the provincial Agent in *England,* upon the Act of Parliament. He wrote back, desiring them to consult together what Duties on Melasses they could afford to pay, as it was necessary that some Duty should be paid: upon which the capital Merchants of this Province met & agreed, that they were willing to pay *one Penny & an half* upon a Gallon, & if the Duty could be lowered to that, they would never run any foreign Melasses, as the Charge & Trouble of so doing would be greater than the Duty. The Agent, by his Interest, reduced the Duties to *one Penny* P Gallon,[2] & I have heard a Merchant who imported large Quantities of foreign Me-

---

[1] Stories of this type were commonplace in admiralty correspondence. Bollan to Admiralty, Feb. 26, 1743, *Historical Manuscripts in the Public Library of the City of Boston* (Boston, 1900-04), No. 1, pp. 3-8. Bollan repeats some similar incidents and concludes (p. 5) that "the Master appears boldly, and is ready to Swear any thing for the Good of the Voyage...."

[2] In 1766 (Oliver's footnote).

lasses, say, that by the Indulgence of the Custom House Officers the Duty amounted to but *three farthings* p Gallon.[3]

This, the Voice of Honesty would have said was favorable & reasonable; but so lost to all Sense of Honor was this Set of Men, that the smuggling Trade went on as usual, untill at last, with other Coincidents, it brought on the present Rebellion. This Business was so notable a School to teach the Art of tricking & foreswearing, that it became proverbial, "that no Jew could get his Bread in *Boston*," whereas in most of the other Provinces there were Numbers of those trading *Israelites*, & in some of them Synagogues of most elegant Structure. But, *here*, Circumcision availed nothing. The Uncircum-[ci]sion was all in all; & it was much to be wondered at, that there were no more Apostates from *Judaism*, since ye. Religion of an *Israelite* centers in the Acquisition of Gain, in all its Forms. There were two *Jews* who had settled in Trade for a short Time in *Boston*, but they were at last obliged to vail to the superior Sagacity of their Neighbours, & turned out Bankrupts.

THE PROVINCE IN FLAME

From the Year *1760* when Mr. *Hutchinson* had been appointed to the Office of Chief Justice, in Preference to Mr. *Otis*, the father, *Otis* the Son had been exerting the Abilities of his Head & the Malice of his Heart to perform the Vow he had made, of *"setting the Province in a Flame."* He accordingly engrafted his self into the Body of Smugglers, & they embraced him so close, as a Lawyer & an usefull Pleader for them, that he soon became incorporated with them. *They* were bold & daring in Defiance of Government, so was *he*. He was brutish in his Behavior, & bullyed for them, untill he had bullyed his self almost into a Mad-House. Besides, through his Opposition to Government, he was elected a Representative for *Boston*. And in this lower House of Assembly, he could rail, swear, lie & talk Treason *impunite*, & here he never failed to take Advantage of his Priviledge, so that the Assembly, in his Time, was more like a *Bedlam* than a Session of Senators. And here he had the joint Efforts

[3]Arthur M. Schlesinger, *The Colonial Merchants and the American Revolution*, 1763-1776 (New York, 1918), p. 59: "A keen observer [Richard Oswald] declared in retrospect [in 1775] . . . that the union among the colonies had derived 'its original source from no Object of a more Respectable Cast than that of a Successful practice in Illicit Trade, I say contrived, prompted and promoted by a Confederacy of Smuglers in Boston, Rhode Island and other Seaport Towns on that Coast.'" John Adams (*Works*, X, 345) observed that "I know not why we should blush to confess that molasses was an essential ingredient in American independence. Many great events have proceeded from much smaller causes."

of his disappointed Father, & of *Joseph Hawley Esqr.*, who had, both of them, great Interest with, & Sway over the Country Members, who were generally, Men of very inferior Understanding & were ever to be charmed with the Word Patriotism, which in the Dictionary of this Province, was translated, Republicanism; which, had these Drivers understood the Nature of, as well as their Horses did *their* Words of Command, the Commonwealth had never met with those Shocks from Rocks, & other Impediments, wch. the Leaders of the Faction had drove them against, in Order to gratifie their own base Purposes.

At this Time, the late Sr. *Francis Bernard* was Governor of the Province. He was a Gentleman well acquainted with the System of the British Constitution. He had his full Share of Learning & good Sense. His Integrity was incorrupt. His Firmness of Mind was invulnerable—his Virtue unimpeached—& his Honesty impregnable. Such a Governor would have made any other People happy; but he was too faithfull to his King & Country to continue long in the good Graces of Refractoriness. He had been recieved as their Governor in the Year 1759, & with great applause.[4] They had complimented him justly, according to his Merits; he lived in great Harmony with them for 3 or 4 Years; but as soon as he was called upon to exert his Abilities to defend the British Constitution, in Relation to the Stamp Act, he met, from the Assembly, with the most illiberal Treatment. However, his good Sense, & his Fidelity to his royal Master, were an Overmatch for the Rage of their Passion & the Weakness of their Reasonings. This vexed them, & they never quitted their blood thirsty Chace, untill they had, by their Pursuit, run him down in the Year 1769, by a Petition to his Majesty, crouded with Falsehoods, to remove him.[5] Mr. *Bernard* desired Leave to return to *England*; it was granted; & he so fully answered the scurrilous Libel, that he was honorably acquitted of their false Charges, & their Petition was voted by the King & Council, as *groundless, vexatious* & *scandalous.*[6]

[4]Francis Bernard (1712-79) arrived in Massachusetts in August 1760. For a brief analysis of Bernard's career, see Morgan, *The Stamp Act Crisis*, pp. 7-20.

[5]"Philanthrop" noted in the Boston *Evening-Post*, Dec. 29, 1766, that everything Governor Bernard did "whether good bad or indifferent, has been tortured to criminality."

[6]Oliver is referring to the employment of Governor Bernard's letters by the opposition in 1769. Bollan, the former agent, secured copies of these dispatches and had them sent to Boston, where they were used to destroy Bernard's remaining prestige. Malcolm Freiberg, "William Bollan, Agent of Massachusetts," *More Books*, XXIII (1948), 179-180.

Thus did the Petition meet with the lowest Degree of its Demerits; & had the Instigators of it met with the lowest Degree of theirs, an Outlawry, the Nation would not, perhaps, at this Time have had to grapple with the present Rebellion. But the Leaders of ye. Faction always boasted, that they could get rid of any Governor whom they were displeased with; & when they could find no just Allegations to urge, as they never could, they would go p[er] Nefas,[7] thro' thick without thin, to accomplish their Ends; & it must be acknowledged, that not any People were better qualified for the most dirty Jobs—to rake into Kennels is the proper Business of such political Scavengers.

THE STAMP ACT

The Preparatives of the *english Ministry* towards establishing a *Stamp Act* in *America*, together with the foregoing Incidents, are now to open a Scene which afforded Matter of Speculation for all *Europe*, & gave a Stimulus to the Passions & Designs of the Factious, in all the Colonies. But more especially to those of the *Massachusetts*, who had already begun their grand Tour. The Design of raising Monies, by Stamps in the Colonies, was in Order, that they should Contribute to the lessening that immense Debt which the british Nation had contracted in the late Wars. A very great Part of which was to secure the Colonies to *Great Britain*, & to rescue them, upon their own repeated, earnest & humble Supplications, from being subjugated by the French of *Canada*. This mode of raising Monies, must be allowed to have been as lenient as could be devised, as it would not have been sensibly felt in the collecting. It was a Right that was justifiable by the Principles of the english Constitution; and it was a Claim of Right that ought to have been asserted without yeilding to Opposition, untill it had been established. Much better had it been never to have planned it in Idea, than to have suffered it to fail in Execution—but the *British Ministry*, unacquainted with the Temper of the Colonists, were misled, by imagining that as there was a just Debt due from them to the parent State for her great Exertions in their Favor, it was therefore proposed to them by circular Letters in *1764*, to consider of *this* Method to reimburse the Revenue in part of what it had advanced for their Benefit; or to adopt some other Mode of Acknowledgement, as they might judge most

---

[7]*Perfas et nefas:* "by right or by wrong." They drove ahead disregarding consequences and troubled by no scruple.

convenient to their selves. This Proposal, to an impartial Mind, must surely be construed as indulgent & condescending; but to those who are acquainted with the Sentiments of the Colonists, must appear, not only Futile, but attended with the most fatal Consequences.

THE HYDRA

Accordingly, the *Hydra* was roused. Every factious Mouth vomited out Curses against *Great Britain*, & the Press rung its changes upon Slavery. A Mr. *Delany*,[8] a principal Lawyer of *Virginia*, wrote the first Pamphlet of Note upon the Subject; which, as soon as it reached *Boston* young *Mr. Otis*, the then *Jack Cade* of the Rebellion, expressed his Astonishment at it, as a Species of high Treason; but in a very short Time, he his self pamphletized in much higher, though not in so elegant, Terms. Agents from the colonial Legislatures were deputed, to agree in Remonstrances to the Court of *Great Britain* against the passing the Stamp Act. Lieut. Govr. *Hutchinson*, wth. some others, drew up a Memorial, for the *Massachusetts*, fraught with Decency; for, as yet, Anarchy in this Province had not mounted the Throne, tho' it had raised its self upon the first Step of it. Had the other Memorialists couched theirs in as modest Terms, & urged the same or as strong Reasons, it is much to be doubted whether the Act would have passed. But some of the other Colonies were so irritated, that they at once hung out the Flag of Defiance, with such Exasperations that the most indulgent Parent could not pass by unnoticed.

The Ministry found it in vain to expect any Deference from the Colonies, & the Act was passed in the british Senate (1765); & let it be here remembred, that Mr. *Pitt*, ye. late Lord *Chatham*, let it pass *sub silentio*. At this Time, Interest was made for the office of Stamp Master of the different Colonies. Dr. *Benjamin Franklin*, who is now the Agent in *France* of the present american Rebellion, put in for his Share of the Loaves & Fishes, & procured some of his Friends to be appointed as Stamp Masters. Some of the Colonies submitted, the others proceeded to Outrages, & prevailed over the British Nation, so as to affright them into a Repeal of the Act in 1766. May every future Politician weigh well the Consequences of

---

[8]Daniel Dulany (1722-97) of Maryland was noted for his *Considerations on the Propriety of Imposing Taxes in the British Colonies, for the Purpose of Raising a Revenue, by Act of Parliament* (Annapolis, 1765). See Aubrey C. Land, *The Dulanys of Maryland* (Baltimore, 1955), pp. 263-270.

his Projections, and remember, that it is more eligible to be without Laws, than to leave those that are made unexecuted & trampled upon by the dirty Foot of Rebellion or Faction.

In this Year *1765*, began the violent Outrages in *Boston*: and now the Effusions of Rancour from Mr. *Otis's* Heart were brought into Action. It hath been said, that he had secured the Smugglers & their Connections, as his Clients. An Opportunity now offered for them to convince Government of their Influence: as Seizure had been made by breaking open a Store, agreeable to act of Parliament; it was contested in the supreme Court, where Mr. *Hutchinson* praesided. The Seizure was adjudged legal by the whole Court.

This raised Resentment against the Judges. Mr. *Hutchinson* was the only Judge who resided in *Boston*, & he only, of the Judges, was the Victim; for in a short Time after, the Mob of *Otis* & his clients plundered Mr. *Hutchinsons* House of its full Contents, destroyed his Papers, unroofed his House, & sought his & his Children's Lives, which were saved by Flight. One of the Riotors declared, the next morning, that the first Places which they looked into were the Beds, in Order to murder the Children. All this was Joy to Mr. *Otis*, as also to some of the considerable Merchants who were smugglers, & personally active in the diabolical Scene. But a grave old Gentleman thought it more than diabolical; for upon viewing the Ruins, on the next Day, he made this Remark, vizt. "that if the Devil had been here the last Night, he would have gone back to his own Regions, ashamed of being outdone, & never more have set Foot upon the Earth." If so, what Pity that he did not take an Evening Walk, at that unhappy Crisis; for he hath often since seen himself outdone at his own outdoings.

The Mob, also, on the same Evening, broke into the Office of the Register of the *Admiralty*, & did considerable Damage there; but were prevented from an utter Destruction of it.[9] They also sought after the *Custom House* Officers; but they secreted themselves— these are some of the blessed Effects of smuggling. And so abandoned from all Virtue were the Minds of the People of *Boston*, that when the Kings Attorny examined many of them, on Oath, who were Spectators of the Scene & knew the Actors, yet they exculpated them before a Grand Jury; & others, who were Men of Reputation,

[9]William Story, the deputy register of the Vice-Admiralty Court, was visited by the mob on Aug. 26, 1765, when most of his personal and official papers and his home were damaged. Benjamin Hallowell, the comptroller of customs, suffered almost the total loss of his beautiful home.

avoided giving any Evidence, thro' Fear of the like Fate. Such was the Reign of Anarchy in *Boston*, & such the very awkward Situation in which every Friend to Government stood. Mr. *Otis* & his mirmydons, the Smugglers & the black Regiment, had instilled into the Canaille, that Mr. *Hutchinson* had promoted the *Stamp Act*; whereas, on the Contrary, he not only had drawn up the decent Memorial of the *Massachusetts* Assembly, but, previous to it, he had repeatedly wrote to his Friends in *England* to ward it off, by shewing the Inexpedience of it; & the Disadvantages that would accrue from it to the english Nation, but it was in vain to struggle against the *Law* of *Otis*, & the *Gospel* of his black Regiment. That worthy Man must be a Victim; Mr. *Otis* said so, & it was done.

Such was the Frenzy of Anarchy, that every Man was jealous of his Neighbour, & seemed to wait for his Turn of Destruction; & such was the political Enthusiasm, that the Minds of the most pious Men seemed to be wholly absorbed in the Temper of Riot.[10] One Clergyman of *Boston*, in particular, who seemed to be devoted to an Abstraction from the World, and had gone through an Existence of near 70 Years, reputedly free from both original Sin & actual Transgression, yet by the perpetuall buzzing of Incendiaries at his Ear, being inquired of, as an Oracle, what ought to be done by the People? He uttered his Decision with this laconick Answer. *"Fight up to your Knees in Blood."*[11] Never could the exclamation of *Tantaeñe animis cælestibus irae,*[12] be more just than on this Occasion.

The *Secretary* of the Province also, who was appointed a Stamp Master, was attacked, and his House much damaged.[13] He was carried to the Tree of Liberty by the Mob & a Justice of the Peace provided to swear him; & there he was obliged, on pain of Death, to

[10]Schlesinger describes the importance of colonial mobs thus: "Mass violence played a dominant role at every significant turning point of the events leading up to the War for Independence." "Political Mobs and the American Revolution, 1765-1776," in *Proceedings of the American Philosophical Society*, XCIX (1955), 244.

[11]"Letter of Rev. Jonathan Mayhew to Richard Clarke," Sept. 3, 1765, *New-England Historical and Genealogical Register*, XLVI (1892), 17: "As to the sermon itself, I own it was composed in a high strain of liberty. . . . But certain I am, that no person could, without abusing & perverting it, take encouragement from it to go to mobbing, or to commit such abominable outrages as were lately committed, in defiance of the laws of God and man. I did, in the most formal, express manner, discountenance everything of that kind." Oliver's description of the clergyman fits Chauncy, but Mayhew actually gave the sermon.

[12]"Does such anger dwell in heavenly minds?" Vergil, *Aeneid* I.11.

[13]The secretary was Peter Oliver's brother, Andrew (1706-74), who had been secretary of the colony since 1756.

take an Oath to resign his Office. This Tree stood in the Town,[14] & was consecrated as an Idol for the Mob to worship; it was properly the *Tree ordeal*, where those, whom the Rioters pitched upon as State delinquents, were carried to for Trial, or brought to as the Test of political Orthodoxy. It flourished untill the british Troops possessed *Boston*, when it was desecrated by being cut down & carried to the Fire ordeal to warm the natural Body. It would have been lucky for the Soldiery, had it continued to give a natural Warmth as long as it had communicated its political Heat; they then would not have suffered so much by the Severity of a cold Season.[15]

Governor *Bernard*, by his great Firmness & Prudence, had secured the Stamps which were sent from *England*, in *Castle William* about 3 Miles from *Boston*; otherwise, they would have been involved in the general Destruction; and Things remained in a State of Anarchy through the Year 1765. The Leaders of the Faction had hired a Shoemaker, named *Mackintosh*, as the antitype of *Massianello* of *Naples*; but he was a much cleverer Fellow. He was sensible & manly, & performed their dirty Jobs for them with great Eclat.[16] He dressed genteelly; & in Order to convince the publick of that Power with which he was invested, he paraded the Town with a Mob of 2000 Men in two Files, & passed by the Stadthouse, when the general Assembly were sitting, to display his Power. If a Whisper was heard among his Followers, the holding up his Finger hushed it in a Moment: & when he had fully displayed his Authority, he marched his Men to the first Rendevouz, & order'd them to retire peacably to their several Homes; & was punctually obeyed. This unhappy Fel-

[14]The tree, a large elm, stood on the corner of the present Essex and Washington streets of Boston, a short distance from the Commons. Schlesinger, "Liberty Tree: A Genealogy," in *New England Quarterly*, XXV (1952), 435-458.

[15]David Ramsay, *The History of the American Revolution* (Philadelphia, 1789), I, 64: "A new mode of displaying resentment against the friends of the stamp act, began in Massachusetts, and was followed by other colonies. A few gentlemen hung out, early in the morning, on the limb of a large tree, towards the enterance of Boston, two effigies, one designed for the stamp master, the other for a jack boot, with a head and horns peeping out at the top."

[16]Ebenezer Mackintosh (1737-1816). George P. Anderson has written two accounts on Mackintosh in the *Pubs. of the Colonial Soc. of Mass.*, XXVI (1927), "Ebenezer Mackintosh: Stamp Act Rioter and Patriot," 15-64, and "A Note on Ebenezer Mackintosh," 348-361. Oliver's estimate of Mackintosh, writes Anderson (p. 352), "sounds like an exaggeration, yet all the evidence from other sources shows Mackintosh to have been in supreme command of the riotous element during the Stamp Act period." Upon his retirement in 1774 Mackintosh lived in obscurity at Haverhill, N. H., until his death in 1816. Anderson (pp. 353-354) admits that Mackintosh may have taken to drink and been thrown into prison.

low was always ready for the Drudgeries of his Employers, untill by neglecting his Business, he was reduced to part with his *Last & all*, took to hard drinking, was thrown into a Jail & died. And, to the eternal Disgrace of his rich Employers, when he supplicated some of them for 2 or 3 Dollars to relieve his Distress, he was refused the small Pittance, because at that Time they had no further Service for him; & had he not possessed a Soul endowed with superior Honor to any of his Employers, he would have brought several of them to the Gallows. There are Instances of Villains, of the *small* vulgar Order, who discover Souls superior to those of many of the *great* Vulgar.

Indeed, it was not much to be wondred at, that the Colonies exulted in rioting, & defied the Authority of *Great Britain* for the rash laconick Sentence of that popular Statesman Mr. *Pitt*, in the House of Commons, namely, *"I rejoice that America hath resisted,"* was construed as the Voice of a God.[17] Like an electrick Shock it instantaneously pervaded the whole american Continent.[18] The Attributes of a Deity were ascribed to ye. popular Senator; & under his Auspices all was safe. Had he delivered the Sentence, or something of equal force, when the Stamp Act was on the Tapis, it might perhaps have saved much honor to the british Senate & the Colonies from a Series of Misrule, but perhaps the Orator thought he had a Right to chuse his own Times for Silence, & for Utterance. Be it as it may; the Sound hath not as yet died away in *american* ears; & greatly, very greatly hath it contributed to that Series of Opposition in the Colonies, which hath ever since subsisted: & doubtless it was in Part owing to that Speech, that the Stamp Act was finally repealed.

REPEAL OF THE STAMP ACT

In 1766 the Act was repealed.[19] Illuminations & Sky-rockets pro-

---

[17]William Pitt's speech of 1766 is reprinted in *The Parliamentary History of England*, ed. William Cobbett (London, 1806-20), XVI, 103-108. Charles R. Ritcheson, *British Politics and the American Revolution* (Norman, Okla., 1954), p. 54: "America had found her advocate."

[18]The editor of the Boston *Evening-Post*, May 12, 1766, said that Pitt's speech had an "electrical Shock" on the House of Commons.

[19]Ramsay, *History of the American Revolution*, I, 74: "The repeal of the stamp act, in a relative connexion with all its circumstances and consequences, was the first direct step to American independency. . . . They [Colonies] conceived that, in respect to commerce, she [Great Britain] was dependent on them. It inspired them with such high ideas of the importance of their trade, that they considered the Mother Country to be brought under greater obligations to them. . . ."

claimed the general Joy.[20] But it was not the Joy of Gratitude, but the Exultation of Triumph. *America* had now found out a Way of redressing her own Grievances, without applying to a superior Power. She felt her own Superiority, & has uninterruptedly applied the same Remedy. How far the Medicine may avail, in its present Operation, Time alone can discover. But happy had it been for both Sides of the Water, for the Stamp Act to have had a temporary Enforcement, 'till the Colonies had felt ye. Energy of the Supremacy of the British Legislature. For, at that Time, thinking Minds compared the Proceedings of the parent State to the whirligig Toy wch. plays backward & forward for meer Amusement, *Great Britain* pulling the String to turn one Way, & *America* taking its Turn to pull it back again. And to add to the Misfortune, a change of Ministry was productive of Disgrace to the Nation; for those who before had been promotive of the Stamp Act, when they were the *Inns*, reversed their Arguments for the Support of the Supremacy of the British Parliament, when they were the *Outs*: & they had their Partizans, who maintained a literary Corespondence with some of the Leaders of the Faction in *America*, especially in *Boston*, the Metropolis of Sedition.[21]

Notwithstanding the Repeal of the *Stamp Act*, the same Parliament passed an Act declarative of its Power over all the Colonies. This might be Termed, *saving of Appearances*; & that was all. It was told in *Gath* & published in the Streets of *Askalon*; even the Daughters of the *Philistines* laughed with their Lords; and ye. Daughters of the uncircumcised *Americans* cried, "*Pish! Words are but Wind*."[22] It was adding Contempt to Insult. They were swelled with their own Importance, & had felt so little from british Power, that they now hugged themselves in Security, regardless of what a Power at 3000 Miles distant could do unto them; & the pious Clergy made them to believe that; as Ambassadors of Heaven, they had secured all its Powers on their Side. A Law without Penalties, or one with Penalties not exacted, is similar to a Clock whose Machinery hath no Weight to set the Wheels in Motion, or to a Watch whose Spring hath lost its Elasticity. They are all useless to Mankind; nay, worse,

[20]The wild celebration upon the repeal of the act was described in the Boston *Evening-Post*, May 26, 1766.

[21]The bitterness of party politics, in which leaders often contradicted their past actions, is described by George H. Guttridge, *English Whiggism and the American Revolution* (Berkeley, 1942), pp. 19-24.

[22]II Samuel i.20.

they depreciate their Value. It is in Government as it is in private Life: a desultory, undetermined Conduct often induces Contempt. As an Evidence that the *Massachusetts* felt an Importance from the Success of their refractory Conduct, they now began to strike hard against every Man who wished well to the Authority of the british Government, & who dared to avow its Supremacy. The first Blow they struck, which *Otis* & his Myrmidons had for several Years past missed their Aim in, was at the Election of his Majesty's Council; when they voted out six Gentlemen who would not comply with their unconstitutional Proceedings, & chose six in their Stead who were always ready to go through thick & thin with them.[23] This Right they enjoyed by their Charter, & this Right, only, they pleaded; though in private they urged that those six were too well affected to the Principles of Loyalty. But it happened that the Governor had an equal Right by the same Charter of negativing any or all of the Council that might be chose; and he exercised *his* Right also. And although many of the Council were as obnoxious as those who were new chose, yet to avoid giving greater offence than was necessary, he only negatived six, as a ballance to those who were dismissed. Mr. *Barnard* had so great a Confidence in his own Integrity, that he was sometimes more open in his Declarations than was perhaps consistent with political Wisdom.[24] He not only pleaded his Right of a negative, but, in his Speeches to the Assembly, he urged *their* Dismission of those six Councellors as founded upon their Aims to destroy all Attachment to his Majesty's Authority; since they were, all of them, known to be well affected to Government. His Reasons were just & solid, but Truth, it is said, is not to be spoken at all Times. However, these Times were such, that it was immaterial whether the Truth was concealed or laid open, for the present ruling Powers were such, that nothing less would satisfy their Voraciousness than the swallowing down all legal Government, & substituting a Democracy in its Place.[25]

[23]Oliver was particularly angry here at the patriots because he was one of the councilors who were not returned to office. Francis G. Walett, "The Massachusetts Council, 1766-1774: The Transformation of a Conservative Institution," *William and Mary Quarterly*, 3rd Ser., VI (1949), 605-627.

[24]"Philanthrop," a writer often favorable to Francis Bernard, admitted that the governor's enthusiasm sometimes caused him to say unwise things. Boston *Evening-Post*, March 2, 1767.

[25]The maneuvers of the patriots made the "governor's negative . . . an ineffective weapon" in controlling the Council. Walett, "The Massachusetts Council," p. 608.

Now, the whole Pack opened, & *Otis* hallooing them: Rib- aldry & Scurrility were open mouthed. Such Language prevailed in the lower House of Assembly, that would have disgraced a *Billings- gate* Convention. The Press groaned under the Weight of Libels; & Governor *Barnard* was attacked from all Quarters. They published the meanest, libellous Falsehoods against the Man whom not long before they had caressed, & who had served the mercantile In- terest, by writing to *England* in favor of their Trade, in such a Man- ner which the Merchants of the greatest abilities acknowledged was superior to their Capacities. He despised their private Scurrilities; some of his Friends vindicated him against News Paper Calumnies; & his own good Sense was by much an Overmatch for their united Understanding. The Truth was great, and it prevailed. This pro- voked them. Mr. *Barnard* was invulnerable by the Force of their weak Arguments; he was firm to his Sovereign & the british Consti- tution, & they never quitted their Rancor untill 2 years after, when they signed a Petition to his Majesty to remove him, which was crowded with the most glaring Falshoods. He was tired with en- deavoring to serve so ungratefull a People, & asked Leave of Absence, wch. was granted; and he never returned to his Government; but was much happier in the Smiles of his Sovereign, who rewarded his Fidelity with a Pension of £1200 p Year.²⁶

There had been so frequent Changes in the English Ministry, that Opposition multiplied upon Opposition, and the Disputes with *America* had furnished the Minorities with sufficient Ground to take their Stand upon; hence, those in *England* supplied the *Ameri- cans* with all Sorts of Artillery to defend theirselves, & support their own Importance in Parliament. A constant literary Correspondence was carried on with both Sides of the Atlantick. Every speech in Parliament, in Favor of *America*, was the Sound of Victory; it echoed to their Shores with the Rapidity of Lightning. The Rabble tortured the Air with their *Io Pæans*, & new Forces repaired to the Field of Battle. Those two great Names, Lords *Chatham* & *Camden*, appeared in the Front of Advocates, & furnished a new invented Piece of Artillery, *the Distinction between internal & external Taxa- tion*, fabricated in the dark Regions of *Thomas Aquinas* & *Duns*

---

²⁶Oliver's figures on the Bernard family pension are correct. Sir Francis was awarded £800, and Lady Bernard the remaining £400. *The Barrington-Bernard Correspond- ence . . . 1760-1770*, ed. Edward Channing and Archibald C. Coolidge (Cambridge, Mass., 1912), p. xvii.

Scotus.[27] In the Fervor of Opposition, they lost Sight of the Distinction, & never once motioned to repeal other Acts, & the *Post Office Act* in particular, which was as much an internal Tax as the *Stamp Act* itself would have been, had it had its full Operation. Perhaps it might be as well, if all Parties would look forwards to the Ends & Consequences of their Efforts, instead of stopping at their first Onsets. It might prevent many untoward Effects, which too often arise, when Passion is substituted for sound reasoning & political Foresight. The Americans improved upon the Distinction between internal & external Taxes; & said it was a Distinction without a Difference. This was an Affront to the Understanding of those who advanced it, & Ld. *Chatham,* with Zeal was determined to support it, & spoke some severe Sentences in Parliament which disgusted his transatlantick Adorers into a Contempt of him, as a poor superannuated old Man. But notwithstanding his Age, he had Spirit enough remaining, to say in Parliament when he Delivered his Sentiments upon American Affairs, "that he believed they would raise no more Statues to him." They had raised a Statue to his Memory at *New York*, which was afterwards demolished, & they took Care to preserve no other Memory of him than his "*I rejoice that America hath resisted.*" This they held as sacred as the Jews did the Law delivered from *Mount Sinai*; but they were more obedient to it; for their hath not been one Instance of a Breach of it for above 15 Years past.

---

[27]Charles Pratt, first Earl Camden (1714-94), denounced taxation of the colonies as a breach of the constitution.

IV. THE TOWNSHEND DUTIES

I am now come to the Year 1767, a Year fraught with Occurrences, as extraordinary as 1765, but of a different Texture. Notwithstanding the Warnings that the Colonies had repeatedly given, of their determined Resolution to throw off the Supremacy of the british Parliament, yet the then Ministry chose to make another Trial of Skill; never adverting to the ill Success of former Attempts. They might have known, that the Contest had reached so great an Heighth, that the Colonists would never descend one Step untill they had first ascended the last Round of the Ladder; especially as they had already sung their *Te Deum* so lately, which they did not chuse to exchange for a *de profundis*; & more especially, as their parliamentary, & other efficient Advocates were encreased. It required no great Degree of second Sight to calculate Consequences. But the Ministry confiding in their own good Intentions, & placing too much Confidence in the Gratitude of the Colonists to the parent State (which by the Way they did not possess a Spark of, neither is it to be but seldom Expected to find it inhabit any where but in the private Breast, & too seldom there; to the Disgrace of human Nature), they procured a new Act to be passed, laying Duties upon *Tea, Glass, Paper,* & *Painters Colours.* This Act was not more unreasonable than many other Acts which had been submitted to for many Years past, & which, even at this Time, they made no Objection to. But the Colonists had succeeded in their first Experiment of Opposition, & their new Allies in Parliament increased their Importance.

As to the *Glass* in particular, the Duty was so trifling, that it would not have enhanced the Price of it to the Purchaser; for there were so many Sellers who aimed at a Market for their Commodities, & the Merchants had so great a Profit upon their Goods, that they could render ye. Duty of little or no Importance in their Sales; & this was actually the Case. For the Glass, during the Continuance of the Act, was sold at the same Price which it commanded before ye. Commencement of the Act. The true Reason of Opposition was this. The Inhabitants of the Colonies were a Race of Smugglers. They carried on an extensive Trade with the *Dutch,* not only in *Holland,* but very greatly with the Dutch Settlements in the *West*

Indies & at *Surrinam*. Tea was the objective Part of the Act; & an enormous Quantity of it was consumed on the american Continent; so great, that I have heard a Gentleman of the Custom House in *Boston*, say, that could the Duty be fairly collected, it would amount to £160,000 p. Year, i.e. at 12d p pound. In some of the Colonies, it was notorious that the smuggled Teas were carted through the Streets at Noon Day: whether owing to the Inattention or Connivance of the Custom House Officers, is not difficult to determine.

The Smugglers then, who were the prevailing Part of the Traders in the Capitals of the several Provinces, found it necessary for their Interest, to unite in defeating the Operation of the Act; & *Boston* appeared in the Front of ye. Battle. Accordingly they beat to Arms, & manœuvred in a new invented Mode. They entred into nonimportation Agreements. A Subscription Paper was handed about, enumerating a great Variety of Articles not to be imported from *England*, which they supposed would muster the Manufacturers in *England* into a national Mob to support their Interests. Among the various prohibited Articles, were *Silks, Velvets, Clocks, Watches, Coaches* & *Chariots*; & it was highly diverting, to see the names & marks, to the Subscription, of Porters & Washing Women. But every mean & dirty Art was used to compass all their bad Designs. One of those who handed about a Subscription Paper being asked, whether it could be imagined that such Tricks would effectuate their Purposes? He replyed "Yes! It would do to scare them in England:" & perhaps there never was a Nation so easy to be affrighted: witness the preceding Repeal of the Stamp Act.

NONIMPORTATION OF BRITISH GOODS

In order to effectuate their Purposes to have this Act repealed also, they formed many Plans of Operation. Associations were convened to prevent the Importation of Goods from *Great Britain*, & to oblige all those who had already sent for them, to reship them after their arrival. This was such an Attack upon the mercantile Interest, that it was necessary to use private evasive Arts to decieve the Vulgar. Accordingly, when the Goods arrived, they were to be in Warehouses, which were to be guarded by a publick Key, at the same Time the Owners of the Stores & Goods had a Key of their Own.[1]

[1]The following merchandise was prohibited by the local merchants: "Loaf Sugar, Cordage, Anchors, Coaches, Chaises and Carriages of all Sorts, Horse Furniture, Men and Womens Hatts, Mens and Womens Apparel ready made, Household Furniture, Gloves, Mens and Womens Shoes, Sole Leather, Sheathing and Deck Nails . . . ,

This amused the Rabble, whom the Merchants had set to mobbing; & such were the blessed Effects of some of those Merchants Villainy, that Bales & Trunks were disgorged of their Contents & refilled with Shavings, Brickbats, Legs of Bacon & other Things, & shipped for *England*; where some of them were opened on the King's Wharves or Quays, & the Fraud discovered. Many of those Merchants also continued to import the prohibited Goods, in Disguise; of which a bold Printer of *Boston* detected them in his publick Papers; for which they, out of Revenge, in 1768, attempted to murder him; but narrowly escaping with his Life he fled to *England*, as the civil Power of the Country was not sufficient to protect any one who was obnoxious to ye. Leaders of the Faction.[2]

Another base Art was used. Under Pretence of Œconomy, the Faction undertook to regulate Funerals, that there might be less Demand for English Manufactures. It was true indeed that the Custom of wearing expensive Mourning at Funerals, had, for many Years past, been noticed for Extravagance, & had ruined some Families of moderate Fortune; but there had been no Exertions to prevent it; 'till now, the Demagogues & their Mirmidons had taken the Government into their Hands. But what at another Time would have been deemed œconomical, was at this Time Spite & Malevolence. One Extreme was exchanged for another. A Funeral now seemed more like a Procession to a *May Fair*; and Processions were lengthned, especially by the Ladies, who figured a way, in order to exhibit their Share of Spite, & their Silk Gowns. In short, it was unhumanizing the Mind, by destroying the Solemnity of a funeral Obsequy, & substituting the Gaiety of Parade in its Stead. The vulgar Maxim, *that there is no Inconvenience without a Convenience*, now took place; for whereas, formerly, a Widow, who had been well rid of a bad Companion, could conceal her Joy under a long black Vail, she was now obliged to use what Female Arts she was mistress of, in

---

Wrought Plate of all Sorts, Diamond, Stone and Paste Ware, Snuff, Mustard, Clocks and Watches, Silversmiths and Jewellers Ware, Broad Cloaths that cost above 10s. per Yard, Muffs Furrs and Tippets, and all Sorts of Millenary Ware, Starch, Womens and Childrens Stays, Fire Engines, China Ware, Silk and Cotton Velvets, Gauze, Pewterers hollow Ware Linseed Oyl, Glue, Lawns, Cambricks, Silks of all Kinds for Garments, Malt Liquors & Cheese." Schlesinger, *The Colonial Merchants and the American Revolution*, p. 107.

[2]John Mein published a list of violators of the nonimportation agreements in his Boston *Chronicle*. Schlesinger, "Propaganda and the Boston Newspaper Press, 1767-1770," *Pubs. of the Colonial Soc. of Mass.*, XXXII (1937), 412-413.

order to transform her Joy into the Appearance of a more decent Passion, to impose upon the Croud of numerous Spectators.[3]

The Faction deluded their Followers with another Scheme to keep up the Ball of Contention, & to sooth their Hopes of Conquest. They plunged into Manufactures; &, like all other Projectors, suffered their Enthusiasm to stop their Ears against the Voice of Reason, which warned them of the ill Effects of their Projects. One of their Manufactures was to have been in *Wool*. They were advis'd against it; & informed, that all the Sheep in the Province of *Massachusetts Bay*, which most abounded in Sheep of any other Province, would not supply the Inhabitants of it with Wool to cloath their Feet; & that the Wool was of such a Staple as not to make a Cloth above 4/6 p Yard Price; & that this would always be the Case; for tho' the Soil was equal to the raising a greater Number of Sheep, yet the Severity of the wintry Climate would prevent the Farmers Profit by propagating them under so great a Disadvantage. But if they were determined to increase their Flocks, that they must practise the Method of one of their own Country Men, who said, that upon getting up early in a Morning he found half a dozen of his Sheep lying dead in his Yard, destroyed by the Wolves who had sucked their Blood & made off. He, finding them warm, used the expedient of tying an old & useless Horse, wch. he owned, to a Tree, & skinned him. He then skinned his dead Sheep, & applied their Skins to his Horse, which united well with ye. horse Flesh; & that he ever after sheared annually 40 £ Wool from his Horse. As Mankind are continually improving in the Arts and Sciences, the Factious might have as rationally tried this Experiment as they had tried that which they were now upon; they would have found old Horses enough for their Purpose, as well as another Race of Animals who most justly demerited a flaying for their Brutalities, & would have succeeded as well; for, after throwing away several hundred Pounds on their Manufactures, the residuum was a perfect *Caput mortuum*—but Advice is always thrown away upon an Enthusiast.

Mr. *Otis's* black Regiment, the dissenting Clergy, were also set to Work, to preach up Manufactures instead of Gospel. They preached

---

[3]"There's no inconvenience but has its convenience." [Samuel Richardson], *Clarissa, or the History of a Young Lady* (London, 1748), II, 106. "Fifty merchants of Boston set an example in August, 1764, by signing an agreement to discard laces and ruffles, to buy no English cloths but at a fixed price, and to forego the elaborate and expensive mourning of the times for the very simplest display." Schlesinger, *The Colonial Merchants and the American Revolution*, p. 63.

about it & about it; untill the Women & Children, both within Doors & without, set their Spinning Wheels a whirling in Defiance of *Great Britain*. The female Spinners kept on spinning for 6 Days of the Week; & on the seventh, the Parsons took their Turns, & spun out their Prayers & Sermons to a long Thread of Politicks, & to much better Profit than the other Spinners; for they generally cloathed the Parson and his Family with the Produce of their Labor. This was a new Species of Enthusiasm, & might be justly termed, the Enthusiasm of the Spinning Wheel.

An *American* is an adept in the Arts of Shrewdness. In these he is *generally* an Overmatch for a *Briton*, although he may sometimes fail in the Execution. As an Instance of each, take the following Anecdote of a Deacon of one [of] the dissenting Congregations in *Boston*, who imported large Quantities of Woolens from *England*. *Hogarth* drew his Line of Beauty for the Leg of a Chair; so this Person had sat so long in a Deacon's Seat, that the Muscles of his Face were so contracted into the Line of Sanctity, that he passed himself upon the World as a Man of great Reputation for Honesty. He was also a great Stickler for the Manufactures of *America*; & in the Heighth of his pious Zeal for the good old Cause, wrote to his Correspondent in *London* about american Grievances; & informed him, that unless they were redressed, they not only could, but they would redress them their selves by making Cloths from their own Produce. As a Proof that they could do it, he sent Patterns of fine broad Cloths, which he said were manufactured in *America*. His Correspondent was surprized on seeing the Patterns, & shewed them to the Manufacturer of whom he had bought them. He also was surprized; but, on examination, told the Merchant that those were the very Cloths he had sold him to ship to *America*—such are the blessed Effects of Cant & Hypocrisy.

The *Nail* Manufactory was also attempted, & this failed also. Thus by having so many Irons in the Fire, not only some, but all of them were burnt. Persons may pride their selves in the Possession of Sense, but if they are deficient in common Sense, they exhibit an ordinary Figure; & common Sense would have told them, that a Manufacturer who works for six Pence or eight Pence a Day can undersell him who will not work under two Shillings p Day: and this was the Case between *Great Britain* & *America*: but the, *quos Deus vult perdere, prius dementat* was the Obstacle that put a final Stop to their further Attempts.[4]

[4]"Whom God would destroy he first drives mad."

All this Struggle & Uproar arose from the selfish Designs of the Merchants. They disguised their Private Views by mouthing it for Liberty. The Magick of this Sound echoed through the interior Parts of the Country, & the deluded Vulgar were charmed with it— like the poor harmless *Squirrel* that runs into the Mouth of the *Rattlesnake*, the Fascination in the Word *Liberty* threw the People into the harpy Claws of their Destroyers; & for what? But to gratifie the artfull Smugglers in carrying on their contraband Tea Trade with the Dutch, to make their deluded Consumers purchase at their Prices who were the Venders; for the Act of Parliament had reduced the Duties upon it from 12 d. p Pound to three Pence, with a View to prevent Smugling; which would effectually have prevented it, had the Act been in Force a few Years, and would have broke up the Nests of those worse than Highway Men; who, for many Years, had kept the Province in a Ferment, & created Uneasiness in the parent State.

As for the People in general, they were like the Mobility of all Countries, perfect Machines, wound up by any Hand who might first take the Winch; they were like the poor Negro Boy, who, in the Time of the late Stamp Act, was bid by his Master, in the Evening, to fetch something from his Barn; but did not move at the Command. His Master spoke to him with Severity, & asked him why he did not go as he was bid? The poor Wretch replied, with Tears in his Eyes, "me fraid Massah Tamp Act he catch me." Thus the common People had had that Act, & all the Acts of Parliament since, dressed up by their seditious Leaders, either with raw Head & bloody Bones, or with Horns, Tails, & cloven Feet, which were sufficient to affright their weak Followers. And as for Men of Sense, who could see through the Delusion, it would have been imprudent for them to have interposed; for the Government was in the Hands of the Mob, both in Form & Substance, & it was in vain to combat a Whirlwind or a Hurricane.

About this Time, his Majesty had appointed *five Commissioners* to oversee his Revenue arising from the Customs on Trade.[5] This gave a new Alarm to the *Massachusetts* Traders; but not so to some of the other Governments. For *New York* Province, it was said, offered £10,000 to have their Residence fixed there; for they saw the Advantages wch. would accrue from it. The *Boston* Merchants began, at first, to muster; but some of them, who understood Trade

[5]These commissioners were Henry Hulton, John Temple, William Burch, Charles Paxton, and John Robinson.

better than the others, were satisfied of the beneficial Consequences which would attend upon their being fixed in *Boston*, & brought the others to acquiesce in so salutary a Measure; for the true Design of the Act was, to take Care that the Custom House Officers should do their Duty, & deliver the Monies arising to the Revenue into the Commissioners Hands. This Part the *Boston* Merchants thought would be no Injury to their Trade, as they could as well bribe a Custom House Officer now, as formerly they had done; but the Motive for Acquiescence was, the Powers with which the Commissioners were invested, of settling all Disputes between the Merchants & the Custom House Officers, which might arise; & had not been infrequent.

Those Disputes had formerly been considered & determined in *England*, at great Expence: but now they were relieved of their Burden, by a Settlement at their own Doors, at an inconsiderable Charge. This Consideration quieted for the present; but it did not last long; for, unhappily, one of the Commissioners was a Person who had been a Surveyor of the Customs for a great Part of *North America*,[6] & was removed from that Office, where he made perhaps £1000 p Year, to this office where he was seated at £500 p Year. To a Person who had certain Imperfections of Nature, which sometimes bordered upon Insanity, such a Change must be Irritating. Such a Salary was not sufficient to gratifie Pride & Extravagance; & he had a rich Father in Law to support him in Resentment.[7] He conducted his self in such a Behavior, as disrested his Bretheren Commissioners to so great a Degree as forced them to Applications which Effectuated his Removal from their Board; but he left behind him a Father in Law, whose Malice pursued them, as will be mentioned, when we arrive at the Year 1770, when the Riot against the Soldiers was perpetrated. The Board of Commissioners carried on their Business now, with too great Harmony to remain long unmolested by the Faction; & it was in a very short Time, that they were hunted with Cruelty; & the chace held on, 'till Rebellion had drove from his Country every Loyalist that could make his Escape; leaving the rest behind him to be persecuted with new invented diabolical Barbarities.

[6]John Temple (1732-98) was appointed surveyor general of customs in 1760 and lieutenant governor of New Hampshire a year later. He became one of the five commissioners in 1767. During the years he and Governor Bernard carried on a fierce battle of insult and slander that ended in Temple's recall. He was accused of favoring the American smuggler.

[7]Temple's father-in-law was James Bowdoin (1726-90), famous patriot leader and enemy of the Hutchinsons and Olivers.

We are now arrived to the Year *1768*, frought with Novelties. For a Moment the Scene will be changed, from the Mob without Doors to the Mob within. Part of the Legislature was formerly called, *his Majesty's Council*; but it was generally a convertible Term, as being elected by the People; now it is a fixed Term, *the Peoples Council*: so that the Ballance of Government was destroyed, & Governor *Barnard* was left alone to combat both foreign & domestick Enemies.[8] His Firmness to his royal Master was distinguished. He was obliged to retreat at last from the Field, but he retreated with Honor equal to a Victory. The general Assembly now was more like to a Pandæmonium than to a Convocation of Senators. Mr. *Otis* huff'd, swore, talked Treason. The rest of the House grinned horribly their ghastly Smile. The Council felt pleased, & the People loved to have it so. The House of Assembly wrote circular Letters to the other Provinces, summoning them to the *Massachusetts* Standard. Some appeared, wrote Petitions, & made Remonstrances, in which they uttered some Falshoods, alledging that no Monies had been raised upon them for the Purposes of a Revenue; whereas it was notorious, that they had paid an unscrupled Obedience to Acts of Parliament for those very Purposes, for a Century past. Some of the Provinces, indeed, did not comply, at first, with the Request made in their circular Letters; & the Minister for the *american* Department wrote also his circular Letters to the non complying Provinces, approving their Conduct. Unhappily, the Minister was not acquainted with the Temper of an *American*. Perhaps his Silence might have kept them quiet a little longer; but the Moment he made the Distinction, they considered that their Sister Colonies would make a *worse* Distinction, & directly repaired to the common Standard. It was unlucky at that Juncture; but all Wars are attended with Fatalities.

The Iron was now hot, & the lower House of the *Massachusetts* Assembly repeated their Blows in quick Succession. They wrote to the Marquiss of *Rockingham*, Ld. *Shelburne*, & some other Noblemen who had supported the Opposition in *England*, & who had also the Honor of beginning it. They thanked them for what they had already done for them; & complimented, soothed & flattered them into Perseverance; & those great Names, with some others of an in-

<hr/>

[8]Bernard to the earl of Hillsborough, Sept. 26, 1768, Houghton Library, Harvard University, Bernard Papers, VII, 62, "To speak Plain now the Council cooperate with the Opponents of Government, & they whose Business it is to advise & assist me do all they can to embarrass me; they who ought to join with me in executing the King's Commands are at the Head of those that oppose them, what can I do?"

ferior Degree, kept the Ball up with so great Dexterity, as not to suffer it once to touch the Ground. Had they suffered it to Fall, they too would have fell into the same Rank with some Others, & would have had the honor of being tarred, feathered and burnt in Effigy. This perhaps, in the Stile of the *Bathos*, would have been deemed, soaring low; but the Flames of such a Martyrdom would have shone with a more splendid Lustre than those which they had already Spread, both in *Great Britain* & *America*.

The English Minister, for the American Department, wrote to *Govr. Barnard*, that his Majesty was displeased with the circular Letters of the Assembly of his Province; & ordered the Governor to require the Assembly to rescind the Resolutions they had passed, relative thereto. This was not a Time for Compliance. The People now had arrived to their *ne plus ultra*. They bid Defiance to King, Lords & Commons; & at the same Time pleaded Duty to GOD & the *King* too; both of whom they paid as much Regard to, in their Proceedings, as they did to the Emperor of *China*. The Governor was ordered, on their Refusal of rescission, to dissolve them. The Assembly drew up a Letter to Lord *Hillsborough*, complaining of their Governors Misrepresentations of them to his Majesty, & justified their Proceedings as "having a natural Tendency to compose the Minds of his Majesty's Subjects in that and his other Colonies." This Letter & the Answer to the Governor, filled with personal Abuses of a most able & faithfull Servant of the Crown was substituted for a Rescission; upon which the Governor complied with his Sovereign's Commands, and dissolved them.

Now the Frenzy was worked up & the Town of *Boston*, by their Select Men (who are an Order of Men appointed as Guardians of their respective Towns) were determined to have more last Words with *great Britain*; & wrote their circular Letters to the other Towns of the Province, to chuse Members to meet in *Boston* at a general Convention, to petition his Majesty to interpose in their behalf against his Parliament. They met in *September*, & petitioned. The Governor seeing such an unlawfull Assembly sent to them, to inform them of the Illegality of such a Convention; & the major Part of them, being alarmed at the bold Stroke, in a few Days dissolved their selves.[9] The other Provinces were not so active; but waited, for some Time, to see whether the *Massachusetts* would burn their Fingers before they thrusted their own Hands into the Fire; but they soon

[9]Sept. 29 (Oliver's note).

found that the Heat was not high enough to scorch; & joined in some of the non Importation Agreements.

An unlucky Affair happened this Year, 1768. The aforementioned *Mr. Hancock* had imported a Cargo of wines, & attempted to smuggle off the Duties. He had always a Mob at Command; & they mustered & beat off the Custom House Officers, who attempted to make a Seizure. Among those Officers was the Collector, a Gentleman advanced in Life & of a most amiable Character. Him they beat & bruised, to the endangering of his Life. Brick bat Law is very partial, and its Decisions are very severe. The Mob also broke the Windows of the Collector, & of some others; & seized the Custom House Boat, & burnt her.[10] A Man of War, & Marines were near; but if two to one are odds, surely 100 to one will not make an Equality. The Vessell was afterwards tried as confiscable; & when the Trial came on, People's Minds had grown so callous by repeated Enormities, that the very Persons who had unloaded the Vessells, swore that they had not.[11] And the virtuous Mr. *Hancock* suffered them to foreswear themselves. This was in Fact the Case; for one of the Witnesses, who had thus sworn, was a Man of Substance & a great Smuggler, who took a great Cold on the Night that he helped to unload the Vessell, which terminated in a Consumption: wth. which he died some Time after. And on his Death Bed declared, that that Night's Work had pushed him into his Grave. Mr. *Hancock* also lost one of his best Captains of his Vessells, by overheating himself on that Night, who died with a Fever about 3 or 4 Days after. These are some of the Effects of Mr. *Hancock's* Vanity & Patriotism; & when he may view the List of his Crimes, with Rebellion bringing up the Rear, he may, possibly, blush to find that Vanity & *Sam Adams* had plunged him into Offences of so deep a Dye.

The Mob again triumphed; the day as well as the Night was now

[10]Ramsay, *History of the American Revolution*, I, 79-80: "The bad humour ... was about this time wrought up to a high pitch of resentment and violence, on occasion of the seizure of Mr. Hancock's sloop Liberty, for not having entered all the wines she had brought from Madeira. ... They [the mob] used every means in their power to interrupt the officers, in the execution of their business; and numbers swore that they would be revenged. Mr. Harrison the collector, Mr. Hallowell the comptroller, and Mr. Irwine the inspector of imports and exports, were so roughly handled, as to bring their lives in danger. ... Such was the temper and disposition of many of the inhabitants, that the commissioners of the customs thought proper to retire on board the Romney man of war; and afterwards to Castle William."

[11]The *Liberty* was seized on June 10, 1768. Both the collector and comptroller were abused—"none of them much hurt"—and the mob broke windows in the comptroller's house. Boston *Weekly News-Letter*, June 16, 1768.

their own. A Custom House Officer was obliged to skulk from Stones & Brickbats; & the Commissioners of ye. Customs were obliged to repair on board the *Romney Ship of War*; then in the Harbor, for Protection; from this Place they applied to the Governor & Council for Protection; the Governor referred the Case to the Council, formerly called, *his Majestys Council*; who replied, "that the Disorders which had happened, were occasioned by the violent & unprecedented Manner in which the Seizure had been made by the Officers of the Customs." This was the *ipse Dixit* of the Council, without assigning any Reason for it; whereas Lawyers and impartial Merchants knew, & acknowledged, that the whole Proceeding in the Seizure was strictly agreeable to the Rules of Law. Unlucky Thoughts will intrude, involuntarily, into the Mind, & the sooner it is rid of them the better; for this trusty Council's Reply to the Governor brings to Recollection a Speech of a Man in *Boston*, who was noticed for uncommon Sallies of Expression. This Man, upon hearing that the general Assembly had passed some extraordinary Votes, broke out into this Exclamation. "If the D——l don't take them Fellows we had as good have no D——l at all." Indeed, it was not to be much wondred at, that such a Resolve was passed; for Mr. *Bowdoin*, the Father in Law to the aforementioned Commissioner, bore great Sway in the Council. He was a Man, who had his full Share of Pride, Wealth & Illnature, & had been soothed, by that Son in Law, into a Perswasion of his being appointed to a Government; & his Son had differed with the other Commissioners of the Customs, & was a Favorite of the Mob; for he only could walk at large, whilst his Bretheren could be safe under the Protection of Cannon alone.

TROOPS ORDERED TO BOSTON

But the Time was approaching, which promised some Degree of Protection to those who wished for the Restoration of Government. Two Regiments were ordered from *Hallifax*. This brought the ruling Powers into a Dilemma; some of them trembled at the Rod, others bullyed, hectored, & swore that they would kill them, as they landed & passed through the Streets; & actually proposed Methods of firing at them from the Windows of the Houses. Many People expected a Fracas; but when the Hour of Attack approached, the Novelty of a military Parade served but to amuse a vast Rabble; & even some of the Leaders of the Faction, went out & saluted the commanding Officer on his Arrival Sept. 28, 1768. The Streets, & the

Doors & Windows of the Houses, were crouded with Spectators to view the Procession. It happened, that a Lady was standing at her Door to enjoy her Share of it. At that Time, a Man passing by her, who had but just before hectored and bullyed, in her presence, that the Troops should never land, & that he would fight up to his Knees in Blood to prevent it: he, seeing her eye the Parade, spake thus to her, "What do you stand there for? I would not look at them." She replied, "You are a very pretty Fellow! You said that you would fight up to your Knees in Blood, to destroy them, & you are now afraid to *look* at them."

The next Thing was, to provide the Troops with Quarters. The Town of *Boston* refused.[12] Had they been requested to furnish them with Halters, the Request would have been instantaneously complied with. These would have given the Inhabitants a full Swing at their wonted Riot. The Governor was now obliged to provide the Quarters himself, in the only Places where he could quarter them; one of which places was *Faneuil Hall*, the celebrated School for *Catalines*, & of Sedition. This was a great Shock to them. It was a Prophanation of their *Sanctum Sanctorum.* It must not be forgiven. They accordingly exorted their selves to pick Quarrells with the Soldiers; they insulted & abused them.[13]

Colo. *Dalrymple*, who was the first Officer in Command, was very prudent; & very strict in his Orders to the Troops, to bear the Insults, & not return them; & perhaps, Troops were never fortified with more Patience, or more obedient to Command. They cloathed themselves with Patience although the Dress did not become such an Order of Men so well as their old military Garb. But the new Dress soon grew thread bare & useless. Persons were imployed to provoke them, in Order to give Pretence for their Removal.

A famous Bruiser was pitched upon for the Attack. He began with a Soldier, who was quite in Peace; the Soldier reasoned with him, & asked him, "why he abused an innocent inoffensive Man?" But Reason was of no avail against a determined Insult. The Soldier was determined not to resent. The Man challenged him to fight: the

[12]A particularly impressive account of the uncertainties of life in Boston can be obtained from *Boston under Military Rule, 1768-1769,* ed. Oliver Morton Dickerson (Boston, 1936).

[13]Bernard to Hillsborough, Sept. 23 and 24, 1768, Bernard Papers, VII, 56: "I am sorry to see this Spirit get so high in the Government. It can end in Nothing else but obliging the Troops to provide their own Quarters. I cannot act in this myself: All that there is left for me to do is to give up the Manufactory House for the use of the Troops. This I will do without the Council tho I foresee it will create a Clamour."

Soldier replied, "that his Officer had given him Orders to the contrary." At the last, the Man gave such an Affront as not only a Soldier, but even human Nature could not bear. He beat his Antagonist in such a Manner, which rather more than satisfied him. At that Juncture, Colo. *Dalrymple* stepped in, & ordered the Soldier off for Punishment, for Breach of Orders; but some, even of the Faction, who were present at the beginning of the Affray, pleaded in behalf of the Soldier; that the provocation was beyond a bearing; & so saved him from the Halbords.

The Presence of two british Regiments was, at that Time a Restraint upon Riots; & the Faction could not, by all their Stratagems, effectuate the Removal of them, untill the Year 1770, when Capt. Preston's Guard fired upon the Mob & killed 5 of them; as will be more particularly related when we arrive at that memorable Æra; untill that Time, although the Interval was but short, yet it was observable, that the Town of Boston had not been so free from Disorders for several Years past. Before, there was no safety for Persons in walking the Streets at Nights, free of Insults. Now, it was the Reverse. The Soldiers were under so good Discipline, that they were peculiarly civil, when unmolested; & seemed rather to chuse to give Protection than Offence.[14]

It is never prudent to lose Time if it can be saved. The Faction left no Stone unturned, either in this Province, or by constant Correspondence with the neighbouring Provinces, to discourage the importation of british Manufactures. Some of the Merchants had already imported vast Quantities of them. They chose to monopolize, for there had been many of the Petty Shopkeepers, who formerly purchased of them, had turned Merchants theirselves, & imported their own Goods. The Merchants in *England* were so fond of getting rid of their Goods, that they gave a Credit to any who asked for it, & to many who had no Estates at all; which they were soon convinced of, either by losing all, or a great Part of their Debts. It was therefore the Art of the great Traders to ruin the lesser ones, & engross the whole of the Business to theirselves; both which they, in some Degree, effectuated; & notwithstanding of their solemn Promises & Subscriptions, they imported Goods enough for the Demand for them. Their little, low mercantile Arts would have shocked a

[14]Bernard to Hillsborough, Feb. 25, 1769, Bernard Papers, VII, 149: "I don't beleive there ever was an Instance of so large a Body of Troops (3 Regiments) quartered in a Town so licentious as this is, behaving so orderly, decently & quietly as these have done."

modest Mind unversed in such Chicanery. The Ladies too were so zealous for the Good of their Country, that they agreed to drink no Tea, except the Stock of it which they had by them; or in Case of Sickness. Indeed, they were cautious enough to lay in large Stocks before they promised; & they could be sick just as suited their Convenience or Inclination. Chocolate & Coffee were to be substituted for Tea; & it was really diverting, to see a Circle of Ladies about a Tea Table, & a Chocolate or Coffee Pot in the midst of it filled with Tea, one chusing a Dish of Chocolate, & another a Cup of Coffee.[15] Such a Finesse would not only be a laughable Scene to a Spectator, but it must be a Fund of Mirth to theirselves, who framed such an evasive Conceit.[16]

As to the other Evasion of Sickness; there were many who could not afford to purchase a Quantity of Tea in Stock. They, poor Souls! were forced to take Turns to be sick, & invite their Acquaintance[s] to visit them; & so the Sickness went on by Rotation. There were others who could afford to keep a large Stock by them; & one of them, who was very warm in her Love to her Country & to Tea, declared that she would not drink any, after her present Stock was expended; being asked, "what Stock of it she possessed"? Replied, "She had but one Chest in all"; & doubtless, if she had outlived her Stock, she would have been admitted into her Sexe's Hospital of Invalids.

The Clergy also, were faithfull Laborers in their Master's Vineyard; not only those who had worked hard from the beginning of the Day, but those who entred at the eleventh Hour. One of these pious Men, who had just came reeking hot from the publick Worship, seeing the Rabble breaking the Windows of one who had dared openly to be an Importer; he made an Halt in the Crowd, with this Exclamation, "see how those Boys fight for us."

The Garretts now were crowded with the Rabble, in full Divan,

[15]Boston *Gazette*, Feb. 12, 1770: "The wise and virtuous Part of the fair Sex in Boston and other Towns, who being at length sensible that by the Consumption of Tea, they are supporting the Commissioners and other—famous Tools of Power, have voluntarily agreed, not to give or receive any further Entertainments of that kind."

[16]Boston *Post-Boy*, Nov. 16, 1767:

Throw aside your Bohea and your Green Hyson Tea,
And all things with a new fashion duty;
Procure a good store of the choice Labradore,
For there'll soon be enough here to suit ye;
These do without fear, and to all you'll appear
Fair, Charming, true, lovely and clever;
Though the times remain darkish, young men may be sparkish,
And love you much stronger than ever.

with a Clergyman to præside; whose Part was to declaim on Politicks & Sedition, instead of propagating that Gospel of Peace, which, upon their entring into holy Orders, they had solemnly sworn to its divine Author to spend their Lives in inculcating. But they, pious Men, had learned of the aforementioned Smuggler, *to tuck the false Manifest in their Sleeve*, when the Oath was administred to them. Gracious God! Is it possible, that Men, who had so solemnly devoted themselves to thy Service, could act with such Duplicity as to disgrace even human Nature itself? Yes! it is possible, & the *New England* Clergy will be everlasting Monuments of the Disgrace.

In one of those Night Garret Meetings, the entire Structure of the *Babel* of Confusion was very near to Destruction. The serpentine *Dr. Cooper* præsided. The Crowd of factious Senators was great. Their Weight sunk the Floor; & they sunk with it—no very great Damage was done. Had the *Parson*, like *Samson*, grasped the Pillars & been buried in the Ruins with his gaping *Philistines*,[17] he would have reared a Monument to his Fame wch. perhaps would have prevented the present Rebellion, or, in such Case, he might possibly have been buried in Oblivion, instead of surviving to commit such atrocious Acts as will perpetuate his Name with indelible Infamy.

Thus, by nocturnal Meetings, Mr. *Saml. Adams's* Psalm-singing Myrmidons; Comittees of Correspondence throughout the Province; Emissaries from one Colony to another upon the Continent; non-Importation Agreements; the Ladies' new invented chymical Process, of transmuting Chocolate & Coffee into Tea; together with many other Arts, learn'd in the Schools of Folly, Madness and Rebellion, they so far accomplished their Purposes, as to intimidate the Parliament of *Great Britain* into a partial Repeal of their late Act, *of Duties upon Paper, Glass, Painters Colours & Tea*; the *Tea* Part of the Act was left unrepealed. This, the Colonies, for the present, acquiesced in. The *Inch* was given to them, and they well knew, from their former Success at rioting, that they could take the *Ell* when it best suited them. The *Tea* grew scarce, & they were not averse to an Opening for a new importation, to stock theirselves with that & with such an enormous Quantity of English Goods, as might create a Debt to the english Merchants, to insure new Allies to theirselves; & such a Debt, which many of the Importers never designed to pay. They always had their Geniusses, who (by the *Mob Whistle*, as horrid as the *Iroquois Yell* which always tingled in the Ears of every

[17] Judges xvi.26-30.

one who had once heared it) could fabricate the Structure of Rebellion from a single Straw. These were always ready for their Work; & it will nor be long before the Ædiface is erected, & such a one that the Exertions of *Great Britain* could scarcely prostrate.

I had forgot to mention one of the *Tea Substitutes*. It was a Vegetable, which the *Labradore Coast* abounds with, & which grows plenteously in the Eastern Parts of the *Massachusetts Bay*. It is a plant of an aromatick Flavor. This, the Clergy recommended: the Physicians, prudently, did not advise against it; & the People drank it—but the Fashion of drinking it, like all other Fashions, soon was changed—it brought on Disorders in Health; & among the rest a *Vertigo*, as fatal as that which they had brought upon theirselves with Respect to Liberty; & had they continued in the Use of *that*, as long as they had in their Reveries about the *other*, *Great Britain* would have had but few Colonists to contend with. Perhaps it would have been more eligible for them to have died that Way than by the Sword, & the Pestilence which was the consequent upon it: this would have saved them from the accumulated Guilt of Murder, Treason & Rebellion.

V. THE SPREADING POISON

Posterity may be astonished, that *Great Britain*, the most power-full Nation in *Europe*, should suffer the Seeds of Rebellion, so widely disseminated in her Colonies, to spring up & take such deep Root; that, when it grew up, there was no destroying the Tares, without the Destruction of the Wheat at the same Time. But let it be remembered, that, from an Unacquaintance with the Temper of the Colonists, the Lenity of the Parent aimed to subdue the Stubbornness of the Child. It ought to have been known, that manual Correction is justifiable, & then only, where Refractoriness prevails. The Parent had felt the Effects of this Temper, when it blazed out at the Stamp Act. Had the Force of Enthusiasm been well understood, & what Power the dissenting Clergy had over the Minds of the People in *America*, it would have been a great Error in Politicks not to have suppressed the Growth of such a Weed, as hath poisoned both *Old* & *New England*. But the *Americans* had secured the Friendship of so many of the Seditious in *England*, that a Mist was cast around those whose Office it was to have suppressed the present, & to have prevented any future Commotions. Many Merchants in *England*, who were of a republican Cast, from Interest rather than from Principle, abetted the *Americans* in their Opposition to Government. They never considered how easy it is to raise the D——l, & how hard to lay him. They were told by the *Americans*, that the Manufacturers in *England* would be without Employment, & consequently they theirselves would have no Business to transact. This Expedient touched them in their sensible Part; & for the temporary Saving of a 2 1/2 p Cent Commission, they urged their Correspondents on to the Subversion of Government; untill they have found, by a dear bought Experiment, that their *american* Debtors have plaid that D——l against them, which they theirselves had used their Exertions to raise.

MOCK PATRIOTS

There was another Set of Men, of no ignoble Degree, who having ate their Cake & being turned away, cried to have their Cake again; & thought, that by encouraging the Revolt in *America* they should have it. These played their Game very assiduosly. They embarrassed Government; they instigated their Clients to every Measure subvertive of it; who confiding in the Importance of their Patrons,

plunged into every Species of Crime, undeterred by any Chastise-
ment, while they had so secure a Shelter against whatever Storm
might blow. The Clients complimented & flattered, & Compliments
& Flattery were the sole Rewards the Patrons were honored with;
except the Ignominy of distressing the publick Measures, & pushing
their Country to the Verge of Destruction:

Semper honos, nomenquè tuum, laudesquè manebunt.[1]

Amongst the rest, though not equal in Dignity, was a most eccen-
trick Character, who had been a Governor of an american Province.[2]
He had signalized himself by a Routine of Metaphysical Exhibitions,
political Chicanery, & Duplicity, puerile Behavior & other Tricks of
high & low Cunning, just sufficient to render himself an Object of
universal Despicience. This Person being ousted of all Preferments,
& ever fond of running his Hands in the Fire, although he had
often burnt his Fingers with it, thought this to be a *Crisis* to exert
his Talents. He corresponded with the Faction, many of whom, during his Administration, he was personally acquainted with. One of
the Letters contained these treasonable Expressions, vizt. "this is the
important Crisis, to make a solemn, *sullen*, united & invincible Stand
against the cruel, tyrannous & ruinous System of Policy, adopted by
this Legislature, against the Rights & Freedom of *America*." Again—
"*one & all* firmly resolve to establish a solemn League & Covenant,
& under an Oath or Affirmation, not to purchase or use the Manufactures of this Country, &ca." This Man was at that Time a Member of the british Senate. It cannot then be wondered at, when that
Palladium of the Constitution harbored, within its Bosom, such vene-
mous Animals, that the whole Nation should be gnawed & poisoned
almost to Death by the Vermin.

There was another Mock Patriot (yes! another, & another too)
who corresponded with a Junto of the Faction in *Boston: John
Wilkes Esqr.*[3] He had raised his Reputation, by being drawn in his
Carriage by Asses instead of Horses; & Asses he ever after esteemed

[1]"Thy honor, thy renown, and thy praises shall be everlasting."

[2]Obviously this reference is to Thomas Pownall (1722-1805), the governor of Massachusetts from 1757 to 1760, who corresponded with many of the Sons of Liberty. He
was the brother of John Pownall, secretary of the Board of Trade and author of *The
Administration of the Colonies*, which was first published in London in 1764 and then
enlarged and revised in many editions until 1777. Schutz, *Thomas Pownall: British
Defender of American Liberty* (Glendale, Calif., 1951), pp. 181-214.

[3]John Wilkes (1727-97), who had challenged the powers of king and parliament in
the 1760's, became a symbol for Americans. Horace Bleackley, *Life of John Wilkes*
(London, 1917), pp. 243-244.

as the most noble Animal. The Correspondence wth. this Junto was supported for some Time: he training them up in the Way they should not have gone, & they praising his Virtues and giving him a faithfull Account of the Progress they made in the School of Sedition: untill, at the last, having outdone *his* Outdoings they unwarily blabbed it out to him, that they designed to establish an Independence of their own. This piqued his Pride as a *Briton*. He replied, "I never will give up the Supremacy of *Great Britain*." This Answer roused them into Contempt, & *John Wilkes Esqr.* was ever after a Scoundrel & a Rascal—*digito compesca labellum.*[4] Let this, perhaps single, meritorious Act of his, atone for a Multitude of his lesser Offenses; although some of his greater Crimes are almost inexpiable.

A certain *Dr. Lee* was another Agent for the Faction.[5] Mr. *Samuel Adams*, & some others, wrote to him a long Catalogue of false Facts; & *Dr. Lee* published them in *England*, & doubtless made his Penny by the Sale. Numbers were sent to *Boston*, & *Adams* made Presents of some of them to the Inn Keepers in the Country, to furnish their Guests with a Stimulant to eating & drinking. Bitter indeed they were, for they were wrote with a Pen dipped in the Gall of Asps. It is lucky for some Writers, that they have no Reputation to lose; if they had, even *Arthur Lee* would not have run the Risque of that small Proportion he might possess, for the Sake of gratifying the Malignity of his Correspondents.

BENJAMIN FRANKLIN

There was one Person more who might, *now*, be termed, the *instar omnium* of Rebellion. The Features of whose Soul were so minutely expressed in the Lines of his Countenance, that a Gentleman, whose Acumen was so great as to strike out a Character from a very slight View of a Face, was introduced to his Company many Years since; and upon his being asked his Opinion of the Man, he replied, "that he was calculated to set a whole Kingdom in a Flame." This was his Opinion of Dr. *Benjamin Franklin*.

This Narrative hath been frequently interrupted by ye. Description of Characters; but it seemed necessary to describe, when the Persons introduced theirselves upon the Stage. Let this suffice for Apology. It is now Dr. *Franklyn's Turn* to sit for his Portrait; & I

---

[4]"Check the lip with the finger," i.e., enough said!

[5]Arthur Lee (1740-92), essayist, agent for Massachusetts, and confrere of John Wilkes, was a propagandist who used the style of Junius to publicize American grievances.

shall endeavor to sketch the Outlines: perhaps I may catch a Feature or two as I go on with the Narrative.

Dr. *Benjamin Franklin* was a Native of *Boston* in the *Massachusetts Bay*. He was born in 1706, of very reputable Parents. His Father was a capital Tallow Chandler, & a worthy honest Man. His Brother also was a Man held in very good esteem. The Doctor himself was what is called a *Printers Devil*, but, by a Climax in Reputation, he reversed the Phrase, & taught us to read it backward, as Witches do the Lords Prayer. He worked at the Business of the Press untill he went to *England*, & continued in *London* for about two Years, to perfect himself in the Art, & black as the Art was before, he made it much blacker, by forcing the Press often to speak the Thing that was not. He published a Libel in *Boston*, for which he was obliged to quit. He fled to *Rhode Island*, the Asylum for those who had done what they ought not to have done—from thence he went to *Philadelphia*, & settled in the printing Business. The *Philadelphia* News Paper was published by him; & the Almanacks of *Poor Richard*, which he annually struck off, were interlaced with many usefull Observations in Agriculture & other Sciences.

Dr. *Franklin* (pardon the Expression) was cursed with a full Share of Understanding; he was a Man of Genius, but of so unprincipled an Heart, that the Merit of all his political & philosophical Disquisitions can never atone for the Mischiefs which he plunged Society into, by the Perversion of his Genius. He had such an Insight into human Nature, that he insinuated himself into various publick Departments in the Province of *Pennsilvania*, & at last arrived to the Office of one of the Post Masters in *America*, a Place worth 4 or £500. Sterling p Year. He was now released from the necessary Cares for a moderate Support; & was at Leisure to indulge in what might first strike his Fancy. He invented a Fire Stove, to warm Rooms in the northern Climates, & at the same Time to save Fuel; he succeeded: but, at the same Time, they were so destructive of Health that they fell into Disuse. He also invented a Chamber Urn contrived to make the Flame descend instead of rising from the Fire: upon which a young Clergyman of a poetical Turn, made the following Lines, vizt.

Like a *Newton*, sublimely he soar'd
To a Summit before unattain'd,
New Regions of Science explor'd,
And the Palm of Philosophy gain'd.

With a Spark that he caught from the Skies
  He display'd an unpararell'd Wonder,
And we saw, with Delight & Surprize,
  That his Rod would defend us from Thunder.

Oh! had he been Wise to pursue
  The Track for his Talents design'd,
What a Tribute of Praise had been due
  To the Teacher & Friend of Mankind?

But, to covet political Fame
  Was in him a degrading Ambition,
A Spark that from *Lucifer* came,
  And kindled the Blaze of Sedition.

Let Candor then write on his Urn,
  Here lies the renowned Inventor,
Whose Flame to the Skies ought to burn,
  But, inverted, descends to the Centre.[6]

Agreeable to the Hint given in the above Lines, the Doctor had
made some new Experiments in Electricity, which drew the Attention of the Literate, as well as of the great Vulgar & the Small. The
Eclat, which was spread from some new Phænomena he had discovered in this Science, introduced him into some of the first Company in *England*, whither he came, soon after he struck out these
new Scenes. Men of Science gave their Attention, and others, of no
ignoble Degree, gaped with a foolish Face of Praise; & it was this
Circumstance, lucky for him, but unlucky for *Great Britain* & her
Colonies, which gave such a Shock to Government, & brought on
such Convulsions, as the english Constitution will not be cured of
in one Century, if ever. By this Introduction, he grew into Importance with the Leaders of the Opposition in *England*. They found
him to be usefull to them, in their Attempts, to subvert the Foundations of Government, & they caught at every Circumstance that
Chance threw in their Way. They knew him to be as void of every
Principle as theirselves, & each of them play'd into the others Hands.
The Doctor play'd his Card well, & procured the Agency of some

[6]*Gentleman's Magazine*, XLVII (1777), 188. Composed by a Reverend Mr. Jonathan
Odell, an Episcopal clergyman of Brunswick, N.J.

of the Colonies; & the lower House of *Massachusetts* Assembly chose him for theirs. I have seen Letters from him to the latter, inciting them to a Revolt, at the same Time when he enjoyed the above lucrative Office from the Crown; but he was so abandoned to an utter Insensibility of Virtue or Honor, that he would not stick at any Villainy to gratifye his Pride.

When the Stamp Act was on the Tapis, he encouraged the passing of it; & procured, for one of his Friends, the Appointment of a Stamp Master.[7] He procured the Government of *New Jersies* for his Son; who hath behaved with a spirited Fidelity to his Sovereign to this Day. But his unnatural Treatment of this Son will fix upon him an indelible Reproach; for when the Son was about to imbark for his Government, he was in Arrears £100 Sterling, & could not leave *England* without discharging them. The Father refused to assist him, & a private Gentleman, out of Compassion, lent him the Mony— and this Son afterwards was harrassed for his Loyalty & kept in a Gaol as a Prisoner in *Connecticut*, where he suffered greatly his self & where he lost his Lady, through Hardships. All this he underwent, whilst his humane Father had the Control of the Congress, & never attempted his Release. This fixes a Character which a Savage would blush at.[8] Whilst he was in *England*, he travelled from one manufacturing Town to another, spreading Sedition as he went, & prognosticating the Independance of *America*; & notwithstanding all the Civilities he met with here, & the Bounties of the Crown, he afterwards boasted, in an intercepted Letter to his american Friends, of humbling *this huckstering Nation*, as he politely & gratefully termed them. Surely! his patriotick Friends in *England* must have Souls callous to every virtuous Feeling, to support a Man, whose every Exertion tends to the Ruin of his Country.

After the Destruction of Lieut. Govr. *Hutchinson's* House in 1765, Dr. *Franklin* maintained a familiar literary Correspondence with him, & condemned the Opposition of the Faction to him. Yet this very Man, a Traitor to his Friend as well as to his Country, set another abandoned Man to filch, from a Gentleman's File of Letters,

[7]Franklin did not propose the Stamp Act but did suggest a scheme for an equivalent revenue. His actions and ideas at this period of his life are still being traced by scholars.

[8]William Franklin (1731-1813), illegitimate son of Benjamin Franklin, had the political support of Lord Halifax and the earl of Bute. For a time during the American Revolution he was imprisoned at East Windsor, Conn. The elder Franklin was not in England at the time when Oliver reports this refusal to lend money. He was, in fact, pleased to hear of the appointment. Donald L. Kemmerer, *Path to Freedom: The Struggle for Self-Government in Colonial New Jersey 1703-1776* (Princeton, 1940), pp. 275-276.

left in his Custody by a deceased Brother, a Number of confidential ones wrote by Mr. *Hutchinson* to that Brother, which did Honor to the Writer; & had they been attended to by Government, would in all Probability have put a Stop to the present Rebellion. This base Theft brought on a Duel between the Thief & the Proprietor of the Letters. The Latter nearly lost his Life, being unacquainted with the Sword; but fought upon the false Principle of Honor, because he must fight; & carried off those Marks in his Back which Swordsmen pronounced of the murderous Kind. Upon a hearing of the State of this Transaction, before the King and Council, Dr. *Franklin*, with the Effrontery of that Countenance where Virtue could never raise a Blush, took the Theft upon himself; & was discarded by every Man who felt any Regard to Propriety of Character. It may, with strict Justice, be said of the Doctor, what *Churchill* says of his Hero in the Duellist,

> ——— of Virtue,
> Not one dull, dim Spark in his Soul,
> Vice, glorious Vice, possess'd the whole;
> And in her Service truly warm,
> He was in Sin, most Uniform.[9]

Pride is Dr. *Franklin's* ruling Passion, & from this Source may be traced all the Actions of his Life. He had a Contempt of Religion, of Mankind, & even of those whom he had duped; & had he viewed ye. Subject in a moral Light, he would have contemned hisself. Had *Churchill* drawn his Character, instead of saying, as he did of his Hero,

And shove his Savior from the Wall. He would have changed his Phrase into—*and shove his Savior, God & All.*[10]

He is now caressed at that perfidious Court, where it would have been Thought; further Instructions were not necessary; untill this Adept in the Science of Perfidy appeared, like a blazing Meteor, & has taught them, that all their former Knowledge was but the first Rudiments of their Grammar; & has qualified them for *Professors* in that Art which they were too well acquainted with before. This Hatred to the english Nation is so rivetted that it is no Breach of Charity to suppose, that when he makes his Exit:

> Such, in those Moments as in all the past
> *Ye Gods! let Britain sink!* will be his last.

[9]Charles Churchill, *The Duellist. A Poem* (London, 1764), p. 38, ll. 2-6.
[10]Ibid., p. 33, l. 16.

To avoid Anachronism & another Digression, I will decypher ye. Character of Mr. *John Adams*, Dr. *Franklin's* Colleague in the *Congress* Agency at the Court of *France*. Mr. *Adams* was born at a Town, not far from *Boston*, of Parentage not very distinguishable. It is generally supposed, that he & Mr. *Samuel Adams* were nearly related; but I believe, that there is no Relation, either by Affinity or Consanguinity, except in their united Endeavors in raising & supporting the present Rebellion; & here, one Soul informs both. Mr. J. *Adams* was, also, educated at *Harvard College* in *Cambridge*; & after he was graduated, was employed as a Schoolmaster to Children of both Sexes, in a Country Town.[11] This Employment is generally the Porch of Introduction to the sacred Office, in *New England*; but Mr. Adams chose to pass from this Porch by the same Way he entred & try his Genius in the Practice of the Law. He is a Man of Sense, & made a Figure at the Bar; but whether Nature had neglected him, or he had acquired, his self, an Acrimony of Temper by his *Busbyan* Discipline, which he was remarkable for; certain it is, that Acrimony settled into Rancor & Malignity—by having an absolute Authority over Children, he was determined to raise hisself to a Superiority which he had no claim to; & he unguardedly confessed, in one of his Sallies of Pride, that *"he could not bear to see anyone above him."* Whilst he was young at the Bar, he behaved with great Modesty; & as it is a general Misfortune incident to Gentlemen of the Bar, to brow beat their Inferiors, so, when any of his Seniors took Advantage of him in this Way, the chief Justice Mr. *Hutchinson* would, with his usual Humanity, support him, as well as show him other Marks of Respect, out of Court; but this Chief Justice, in a short Time, found that there is no Corner in a jealous malignant Heart for Gratitude to creep into.

Mr. *Adams*, being a sensible Lawyer, was for some Time, friendly to Government; but being in pursuit of a Commission for the Peace, Sr. *Francis Barnard*, the then Governor refused him. This Refusal touched his Pride, & from that Time, Resentment drove him into every Measure subversive of Law and of Government, & interwove him with the factious Junto.

Mr. *Otis*, the original Malecontent, had now outrun himself; & *Samuel Adams* had taken his Birth. *Otis*, by drinking, & by Passion,

[11]John Adams (1735-1826), after taking his Bachelor's degree from Harvard College, taught in Worcester, Mass., and studied law in his spare time.

had brought his Business as a Lawyer, & his Finances, to a very low Ebb.[12] Indeed, the Faction had so little Need of him, that they modestly dropped him (he was left out as a Representative in 1770), as they had done others who had served them, & of whom they stood in no further Need. They had now much abler Men, both in Policy & in Law, who could secrete the Measures which the other's open Temper was too apt to disclose. This Exchange was a great Advantage to Faction. *Otis* being piqued at this Revolution, said of his Brother *John Adams*, that "he was a d——d Fool for not taking Warning by his Fate." How prophetick this Observation may be, Time alone may discover; but Madmen have, sometimes, uttered Truths which were neglected at the Time of Utterance.

THE TRIAL OF A CUSTOMHOUSE OFFICIAL

I have now, Sir! parted with my disagreeable Company & return to my Narrative. The ludicrous Tea drinking Scene I left off at. I will introduce You to one of a serious Nature, such as will rouse the Feelings of Humanity. We have hitherto passed through the different Forms of Governments, of Democracy & Oligarchy, down to Anarchy. We are now arrived to the last Stage of all, hitherto unknown in the political World, a *Dæmonocracy*.

In the beginning of *March 1770*, a Mob was in Pursuit of a *Custom House Officer*,[13] who was obnoxious to the Smugglers.[14] He repaired to his House, as his Castle; they, at Noon Day, laid Seige to it. He being a Man of Spirit, like a true Veteran, determined to hold out to the last Extremity. He armed himself with Musket & Ball, & warned them against entring. They, regardless of his Threats & Intreaties, broke his Windows & Doors: upon which he fired at Random, & killed an innocent Boy[15] who was crossing the Street. This enraged the Mob, & they attempted to take him; but he made a gallant Defence, & refused to deliver himself to them, as being morally certain, that Death would be the immediate Consequence of his Surrender to *them*; but he, at the same Time, told them—that

[12]*Sibley's Harvard Graduates*, XI (1960), 280-282.

[13]Richardson (Oliver's note).

[14]The riot occurred on Feb. 22, 1770. Oliver's description of the riot and trial of Ebenezer Richardson checks very well with the account given in Hutchinson, *History of ... Massachusetts-Bay*, III, 193-194.

[15]Christopher Snyder (Oliver's note).

he would submit himself to a Peace Officer.[16] Peace Officers were sent for; but it was, with their utmost Exertions, that they could prevent his being murdered before they could house him in Prison. As the Term of the supreme Court was very near, and they thought that the Blood of the unhappy Youth which had been spilt would not be cold before the Court met; & as they were pretty sure that they could procure a Jury for Conviction, so some of the Leaders of the Faction chose that he should be hanged by the Forms of Law, rather than suffer the Disgrace of Hangmen theirselves.

Perhaps you may ask me, what is meant by procuring a Jury for Conviction? It requires some Explanation. Know then, that the Law of the *Massachusetts* Province pointed out the following Mode of returning Jurors, vizt. the Select Men, at certain Periods, pitched on a Number of Freeholders to serve in that Office; the inferior Order of Men were put into one Box, to serve at the inferior Courts. Another Set of Men, of superior Understandings, were put into another Box, to serve at the supreme Court. When the Terms of either Court approached, the Select Men, with a Constable, met & drew out, as in a Lottery from either Box, agreeable to the *Venire* they were served with. This Mode seems equitable, & it was unexceptionably practised, untill the late Times of Confusion: but now, a new Form of Government had been instituted in this Province. They thought it necessary that new Modes of Law should coincide with them. Accordingly, the Select Men of *Boston* would draw out of the Lottery Box; & if any popular Cause was to be before the Court, & that drawn Juror was not like to serve their Cause, they would make some Excuse for the absent Man, either that he was sick & would not be well, or he was going [on] a Journey or Voyage; & so return his Name into the Box, & draw untill they drew him who was for their Purpose. The *Regis ad Exemplum* took Place, & some other Towns followed Suit[17]—thus was the supreme Court harrassed with these political Manœuvres.

It very unluckily happened, that about a Week after the forementioned killing, the Affair of the Soldiers firing upon the Inhabitants was acted. These two Circumstances brought on the final Close of Law & Justice. The Supreme Court met on the 2d. Tuesday of

[16]Richardson was saved from the angry crowd by the interposition of "Gentlemen of influence" who arranged for his arrest. Boston *Weekly News-Letter*, March 1, 1770; *Censor*, March 28 (pp. 75-78) and April 4, 1772 (pp. 79-82).

[17]"By the example of the king." These new forms of procedure were copied by the other towns, in all the bombast of the original.

this Month, March. The Judges thought, that the present Rage of the People would preclude a fair Trial, either of the Custom House Officer or the Soldiers. They rather chose to postpone the Trials, untill there might be some Chance of Justice being uninterrupted; but it was not in their Choice; for the Madness of the People called aloud for Revenge; & had a Trial been refused, it was rather more than an equal Chance that the Prisoners would have been murdered by the Rabble; & the Judges have been exposed to Assasinations.

The Trial of the Custom House Officer came on. But the unhappy Man, though guiltless in Law, fell into the Hands of Tygers, whose tender Mercies were Cruelty. They brought him in *guilty*, tho' they were from 11 o'clock at Night untill eight of the Clock next Morning before the Verdict was settled, there hap'ning to be one cool Head among the twelve Jurors; as will be presently seen. There was a vast Concourse of Rabble at the Trial, who designed to have hanged the Prisoner as he came out of the Court House, to be returned to Prison untill the Jurors Verdict was settled; & they provided an Halter, ready at the Door of the Court Room, for the Purpose; but the Court had ordered the Sheriff, with the Peace Officers, to lock him into the Court Room, untill the Mob had dispersed; this took Effect.

Authority of Courts of Law were now of little Force. Forms were maintained without much Power: & during this Trial, whilst one of the Judges was delivering his Charge to the Jury, & declaring his Opinion, that the Case was *justifiable Homicide*, one of the Rabble broke out, "D——n that Judge, if I was nigh him, I would give it to him"; but this was not a Time, to attempt to preserve Decorum; Preservation of Life was as much as a Judge dared to aim at.

The next Morning, the Verdict was brought in, *Guilty*, but the Verdict was guilty of tenfold greater Criminality than the Prisoner. At Acquittals, there is often an Huzza of Joy in the Hall of Justice; but it is singular at a Conviction. But now, the Court Room resounded with Expressions of Pleasure; 'till, even one of the Faction, who had some of the Feelings of Humanity not quite erased, cried out, "for Shame, for shame Gentlemen!"—This hushed the clamorous Joy. The Verdict was received & recorded.[18]

A few Days after, the Jurors were inquired of the Foundation of their Verdict. The Foreman, with a sullen Pride of Revenge, replied,

[18]The *Censor*, April 4, 1772, p. 81, reported that the verdict was received with a "general *shout* and *clapping* in the Court," concluding that the reaction was partly inspired by the clergy and others who had been discoursing on the law from their pulpits.

"that he was not obliged to give any Reasons of his Conduct." The others shewed less of a Temper of sullen Revenge. One of them said, "that he should have acquitted the Prisoner, had the killing happened in the Night instead of the Day." In either Case, the Law had justified the Prisoner. Some of them acknowledged, that, as they past thro' the Mob, from the Court to their Apartment, they were called upon to bring the Prisoner in guilty. One of the Jurors declared, that he thought him innocent, & had persisted all Night in that Opinion, against the united Sentiment of the other eleven; but in the Morning, after a tedious whole Nights Fatigue, his Bretheren overperswaded him to unite with them, by urging this Argument upon him, vizt. "that the Court had delivered their Opinion, in Law, that the Prisoner was innocent, & that his Life would be saved; therefore, that it was not worth while to stand out any longer." These Arguments alone, he said, prevailed with him to join with the others in their Verdict. Upon the foregoing Reasons, the Court refused to pass the Sentence of Death, & recommended him to Mercy; when, after an Imprisonment of a twelve month, he obtained a Pardon. In the mean Time, the Judges were insolently called upon by the Faction, to order Execution; but they refused. The Pardon, at last, came from *England*; & at one of the Terms, he pleaded it, & was discharged—lucky for the Prisoner. At the Time he pleaded it, the Rabble were assembled in Town Meeting, at some Distance from the Hall of Justice. The Prisoner fled the Town immediately on his Discharge; the Rabble heard of it, & pursued him to execute their own Law upon him, but he happily escaped.

THE BOSTON RIOT

The popular Rage against this Custom House Officer was a prelude to what succeeded. The Faction insisted upon the Trial of the Soldiers at this Term. The Judges knowing the dæmonocratick Thermometer to be some Degrees above boiling Heat, refused to bring the Trial on; the Bar also advised to an Adjournment, as they theirselves, as well as the Court, had been fatigued with the Business of the Term in this County, & the Country Terms were approaching in quick Succession. The Faction, upon hearing the Design of the Court, were very restive. The Leaders of the Faction met at the House of Mr. *Temple*, a Commissioner of the Customs with 500£ p. year Salary; & from thence a Party came into the Court, & insolently insisted on an immediate Trial of Capt. *Preston* & his Soldiers.

Two of the Heads of this Faction (for poetick Fiction says that the Hydra has an hundred) appeared in the Front, *John Hancock* & *Samuel Adams*, who had just parted from that pious Divine *Dr. Cooper*. But the Judges were determined, & adjourned to *August* following.

When *August* arrived, one of the Judges, who lived at a Distance from *Boston*, & was on his Journy to Court, met with a Misfortune, by a Fall from his Horse, & could not proceed. The Peoples Expectations for Revenge were much raised, & the Heat of the then Dog Days did not tend to lower them. They urged for a Trial, but the three Judges, out of five which constituted the Court, finding that there was but a bare Quorum, & considering this Trial to be a Matter of great Importance, resolutely refused to proceed on it, & adjourned to the Month of *November*. *Massachusetts* lies in a northern Latitude. *November* is a cold Month; & when it arrived, the Thermometer had lowered much. The Trial came on & although it lasted many Days, yet the Jury took it from the Court; & after a short Retirement, for a few Minutes, for Form Sake, return'd their Verdict, *not guilty*.

This last Trial was a Matter of great Expectation throughout the Colonies, & of great Speculation in *England*. If you ask me why I am so diffuse upon these Trials I must inform You, that very much of the consequent Rebellion arose from these Incidents. The Sparks of it had been long hovering, but they were now collected into a Focus, & burst into Flame. Such an Opportunity had been long waited for, by the Faction, to rush into the Heat of Battle: and I trust you will excuse me, if I relate the Fracas of the Soldiery with some Minuteness, as it hath been too little understood, & Misrepresentations made of it; whereas, it was an Affair that had been previously planned by the Faction, & on which they relyed much for the Operation of their Measures to bring on their Independence on *Great Britain*. The Case stood thus.

The 2 Regiments from *Hallifax* had been arrived five or six Months. They were, what is vulgarly called an Eye Sore, to the Inhabitants of *Boston*. They restrained the Rabble from committing their accustomed Outrages, & this was termed a Restraint of that Liberty which *God* & *Nature* had blessed them with. The Inhabitants therefore used every Art of Irritation; & when the Soldiers were returning to their Evening Quarters, they met with repeated Abuses; untill, at last, Provocations followed so thick upon one another, that the Soldiers rightly judging that *God* & *Nature* had blessed them with as much natural Liberty as they had the Inhabitants of *Boston,* they returned Compliments for Compliments, & every Blow was answered by a Bruise. This Scheme not effectuating their Purposes, the Inhabitants combined, in great Numbers to make a general Assault & carry the Works by Storm. They provided themselves with massy Clubs, a new Manufacture of their own: Guns they imagined were Weapons of Death in the Eye of the Law, which the meanest of them was an Adept in; but Bludgeons were only Implements to beat out Brains with. When they were ready, they fixed upon the Time of Assault; & it came on thus.

The Kings Monies were lodged in the Custom House. From several Threatnings being thrown out, those Monies were thought insecure, & a Centinel was appointed to guard them. According to common Custom, when a Riot was to be brought on, the Factioneers would employ Boys & Negroes to assemble & make Bonfires in the Streets; & when all were ready, the Mob Whistle, already mentioned, with sometimes the Mob Horn in Unison, would echo through the Streets, to the great Terror of the peaceable Inhabitants. Those Boys & Negroes assembled before the Custom House, & abused ye. Centinel; he called for Aid, & a Party of eight Soldiers were sent to him. This Party was headed by a young Officer; Capt. *Preston,* an amiable, solid Officer, imagining that the other would not behave with that Prudence which the Occasion demanded, took the Command upon his self.

By this Time, there were 4 or 500 of the Rioters collected; the Rioters pelted the Soldiers with Brickbats, Ice, Oystershells & broken Glass Bottles. Capt. *Preston* behaved with great Coolness & Prudence. The Rioters calling out *"Damn You fire, fire if you dare!"* & Capt. *Preston* desiring them to be quiet, and ordering his Men *not to fire.* But at last, a Stout Fellow, of the Mob, knocked down one of the Soldiers; & endeavoring to wrest his Gun from him, the Soldier cried, *"D——n you fire,"* pulled Trigger & killed his Man.[19] The other Soldiers, in the midst of the Noise, supposing it was ye. Captain who gave the Order, discharged their Pieces, & five Persons were killed. Let me here observe, that upon the Trial great Stress was laid upon the Captain's giving the Order to fire, but there was no Proof of it; & the Doubt was not cleared up for many Months after; when the Soldier who gave the Word of Command, as men-

[19]"Case of Capt. Thomas Preston," *Massachusets-Gazette Extraordinary* (supplement to Boston *Weekly News-Letter*), June 21, 1770.

tioned above, solved the Doubt. But it was immaterial in Law, whether the Capt. gave it or not, for the Attack was so evidential of a murderous Design, that he must have been justified if he had given such Orders. The People, indeed, would not have discharged him of Guilt, for they had no other Idea of washing the Blood from their Streets, but by pouring greater Quantities on.

This Riot happened in the Evening of 5th. March. The Town of *Boston* was now all Uproar & Confusion. High & low repaired to the Council Chamber, & Colo. *Dalrymple* was sent for to them; whilst Colo. *Carr*, who commanded the other Regiment, like a true Veteran, drew up his Men to receive the next Assailents.[20]

Lieut. Govr. *Hutchinson* was then in the Chair; Sr. *Francis Bernard* having returned to *England* some Time before.[21] The Lieut. Govr. was sent for to the Council Chamber, to quiet the Tumult. As he was passing the Street through the Crowd, a Bludgeon was aimed at his Head with a, "*D——m him! I'll do his Business*," but a Person warded off the Blow, & saved him. He reached the Council Chamber. *Samuel Adams* was there to intimidate. He threatened Colol. *Dalrymple* with a large Body of Men, if he did not withdraw the Troops; the Colo. consented, but said that he had no Command of the other Regiment. He was replied to, "if he could order the Removal of one, he could of both." The Lt. Govrs. Advice was asked by the Colo., & finally gave it, to remove the Troops; and they were accordingly sent to the Castle, three Miles from the Town. Thus ended this Nights Riot, & the next Day was their own.

And now the Affidavit Men were set to Work; & a Narrative wrote & published; & said to be compiled by *James Bowdoin Esqr.*, one of his Majesty's Council.[22] It was wrote for, & sent to ye. Party in *England*, to raise Disturbance there. It was crowded with the most notorious Falsities; which answered the Purposes of the Faction,

[20]The Boston Massacre took place in the evening of March 5, 1770. Ramsay, *History of the American Revolution*, I, 90-91, describes the mob scene in this way: "The soldiers, when under arms, were pressed upon, insulted and pelted by a mob armed with clubs, sticks, and snowballs covering stones. They were also dared to fire. In this situation, one of the soldiers who had received a blow, in resentment fired at the supposed aggressor. This was followed by a single discharge from six others. Three of the inhabitants were killed, and five were dangerously wounded. . . . The captain, and six of the men, were acquitted. Two were brought in guilty of man-slaughter. . . . It was also proved, that only seven guns were fired by the eight prisoners."

[21]1769 (Oliver's note).

[22]John Adams (*Works*, I, 110-111) said that the *Narrative* was the "testimony of heated individuals. . . . Much of the testimony in the 'Narrative' now looked extravagant, and some was positively perjured."

untill the Trials at Law unravelled their Mysteries and developed such Rancor & Perjury, as was disgracefull to human Nature.

There was so much Malevolence against the Commissioners of the Customs & their under Officers, that Persons were tampered with to swear, that four of those Officers fired, or were accessory to the firing from the Custom House, upon the Inhabitants; particular[l]y a french Boy, Servant to one of the Officers, who swore that his Master ordered him to fire a Gun, & fired one himself. The Officers were indicted & committed, but upon their demanding Bail, the Judges of the supreme Court, upon Examination, found so little Cause of Commitment that they granted Bail; & when their Trial came on, it was rather farcical than serious: & the Jury instantaneously, without moving from their Seats, acquitted them; for it was proved, that the french Boy, the principal Evidence against them, was neither present himself, nor his Master. The *Alibi* thus proved, the french Boy was indicted for Perjury, tried, & convicted; & Part of the Punishment to be inflicted, was to be publickly whipped; but the Faction would not suffer the Sheriff to inflict it: in such State were governmental Affairs after the Withdrawall of the Soldiers from the Town; & so unhappy were the Commissioners of the Customs, that they were all, except Mr. *Temple*, forced to repair to the Castle, under military Protection.

The Clergy, both before & after the Trials of the Custom Officer & the Soldiers, were by no means guilty of doing their Work negligently. *Before* the Trials, the Pulpits rung their Chimes upon blood Guiltiness, in Order to incite the People, some of whom were to be Jurors, to Revenge, in cleansing the Land of the Blood which had been Shed; & doubtless, if they had been the Scavengers, they would have fertilized the Land with a Torrent from the Veins of those who were the Friends of Government; but happily their Arm was short'ned, & they could do little more than cry aloud, which they did not spare to do, in blowing up the Coals of Sedition.

One of those zealous Divines, Dr. *Chauncy*, who was the Head Master of the School of the Prophets, had heard that a Gentleman was wounded, on that unhappy Night when the Soldiers had fired. He waited upon the Gentleman, & asked him, whether he did not design to prosecute Capt. *Preston* in damages? The Gentleman replied, "No Sir! It will be of no Advantage. Capt. *Preston* is to be tried for his Life. If he should be convicted he will suffer Death, & then I cannot recover any Damages; & if he is acquitted I shall be in the same Circumstances": to which this hoary headed Divine, in the true Spirit of the Inquisition, said—"if I was to be one of the Jury upon his Trial, I would bring him in guilty; *evidence or no Evidence.*" What a noble Instance this of Divinity, Zeal, Rancor & Revenge, jumbled together into one Mass! But he had imbibed more of the Temper of *James* & *Peter*, than of that of his & their Master. He was always for calling down Fire from Heaven to destroy his political Opposers.

VI. ASSAULTS ON GOVERNMENT

After the Trials were over, & the Clergy & Populace were disappointed in being gratified with the Procession of an Execution, the Pulpits rung their Peals of Malice against the Courts of Justice, for not indulging them in their Wishes for the Condemnation of innocent Men. Prayers & Sermons were interlaced with Scandal against the Law & the Government. Ye. Clergy had forgot the Errand their divine Master had sent them upon, & had listed into the Service of new Masters; & to them, were most faithfull Servants:— in this Service they have continued to this Day, with Fidelity irreproachable.

Government was now pretty thoroughly dissolved. The lower House of Assembly coincided with the Measures of the Faction out of Doors. His Majesty's Council, some from Timidity, & the most Part from Inclination, coincided with the House; & the Clergy had changed their usual Form of Prayer, & prayed for the ruling Powers; & the Governor was left alone to fill up the Gap against any further Inundation.[1] Indeed, the supreme Court of Justice shewed a decent Firmness in their Department, but it was at the Risque of their Lives. One of the Councellors Sons posted up a Bill on the Door of the House of Assembly, calling upon the People to Assasinate the Judges of the supreme Court. For Forms Sake, a Proclamation was issued by the Governor and Council, offering a Reward to discover the Author; but this was not a Time to punish any of the Faction; & it was buried in Silence.

TARRING AND FEATHERING

About this Time was invented the Art of Tarring & feathering; & the Invention was reserved for the Genius of *New England*.[2] *Milton*

[1]Henry Hulton and William Burch to the duke of Grafton, April 3, 1770, quoted by O. M. Dickerson, "The Commissioners of Customs and the 'Boston Massacre,'" *New England Quarterly*, XXVII (1954), 323: "After the troops were withdrawn the town was kept quiet but the power was entirely in the hands of the leaders of the people and every one's security depended on their caprice."

[2]To the contrary, "tarring and feathering was an ancient . . . practice" (R. S. Longley, "Mob Activities in Revolutionary Massachusetts," *New England Quarterly*, VI [1933], 112). Revolutionary violence is described by an anonymous pamphleteer, believed to be James Hawkes, in *A Retrospect of the Boston Tea-Party with a Memoir of George R. T. Hewes, a Survivor* . . . (New York, 1834), pp. 33-35, 40-44.

says, that Gunpowder & Cannon were first invented at a Pandæmonium of his Devils; but this Art they had not the Sagacity of
hinting at, untill it was discovered to them by these their modern
Disciples.[3] The Town of *Salem*, about twenty Miles from *Boston*,
hath the Honor of this Invention, as well as that of Witchcraft in
the Year 1692, when many innocent Persons suffered Death by
judicial Processes.

The following is the Recipe for an effectual Operation. "First,
strip a Person naked, then heat the Tar untill it is thin, & pour it upon
the naked Flesh, or rub it over with a Tar Brush, *quantum sufficit.*
After which, sprinkle decently upon the Tar, whilst it is yet warm,
as many Feathers as will stick to it. Then hold a lighted Candle to
the Feathers, & try to set it all on Fire; if it will burn so much the
better. But as the Experiment is often made in cold Weather; it will
not then succeed—take also an Halter, & put it round the Person's
Neck, & then cart him the Rounds." This is the Method, according to
the first Invention. And I knew an honest Man, of 60 Years of Age,
who was thus disciplined in the cold Month of *March*, from nine
o'clock at Night untill one o'clock the next Morning, untill Life was
near expiring. And after a Prosecution for ye. Torture, a *Boston* Jury
would not give £20 Damages.[4]

I know no other Origin of this modern Punishment, by the Rabble, of their State Criminals, than this; namely, that the first Book
that *New England* Children are taught to read in, is called the *New
England Primer*. In the Front of it is depicted the *Pope*, stuck
around with Darts. The sight & memory of this creates and keeps
up an Aversion to Popery; & it had this Effect, untill the honorable
Congress wrote to the *popish Canadians*, that *God* & Nature had
given them a Right to worship according to their Consciences. Then,
indeed, they quitted their Aversions; & when the Congress went to
Mass Worship, all Distinctions ceased. Before these, they uniformly
practised the exhibiting a Pageant on every *5th of November*, representing the *Pope* & the *Devil* upon a Stage; sometimes both of them
tarred & feathered, but it was generally the Devils Luck to be
singular, untill he bought the Rabble off, to confer that Honor upon
their fellow Men. This is the only Clue I can find to lead me to the
Origin of this Invention. In Order to keep in Memory the Soldiers

[3]*Paradise Lost*, ed. Darbishire, I, Bk. VI, 136-137, ll. 469-536.

[4]Oliver's recipe for tarring is quoted, and other evidence of violence given, in Carl
Ubbelohde, *The Vice-Admiralty Courts and the American Revolution* (Chapel Hill,
N.C., 1960), pp. 117-118.

firing, on the Night of the *5th March*, they instituted an Anniversary Oration, upon what they called *the Massacre*; at which **Dr.** *Cooper* & some others of the Faction, displayed their Oratory in Succession. This kept the Minds of the Rabble in constant Irritation; there being enough thrown out, at one Oration, to keep the Flame alive untill the next Orator blowed his Bellows to make it Rage with greater Fury; & thus was the Fire of Contention fed with constant Fuel, untill the town of Boston was evacuated of the Filth of Sedition in 1775.

About this Time, the general Assembly of the Massachusetts was guilty of one of the Sins of Omission which, by the Way, are at some Times as inclusive of Criminality as Sins of Commission, & left out of their Code of Laws one which was of equal Importance to any of the others. It was this. It had been their Practice for a long Series of Years, to pass & renew a *Riot Act*. This Act was inserted among their Temporary Laws, which, at certain Periods, they revised, & renewed according to particular Circumstances. This Act was founded on the British Riot Act, excepting in making the Crime to be Felony. It had hitherto been deemed a salutary Law; but now, the publick moral Sense was so vitiated, that they erased this Act from their System of Laws. This Omission was so strong an Evidence of verging towards Anarchy that every one who had the least Attachment to Government viewed the Omission in such a Point of View, as to calculate, without a second Sight, Events which in their natural Consequences must be destructive of all Government; & they were not disappointed in their Calculations.

INSULTS OF THE MOB

In the Year *1770*, it was reported, that Lt. Govr. *Hutchinson* was to be the Commander in chief of *Massachusetts* Government. This provoked the Leaders of the Faction; they pretended to laugh [at] it as a mere Chimæra of his Friends. They depended so much on the Interest of their noble Friends in *England*, as to give out, that it never would happen; but in the Spring of 1771 his Commission arrived, & the *acheronta movebo* was now exemplified, to increase Dissensions.[5] Happily, for some Time they were disappointed in bringing their Attempts into Execution, & were forced to gnash

---

[5]*Flectere si nequeo superos, Acheronta movebo:* "If I cannot influence the Gods of Heaven, I will stir up Acheron itself." Vergil, *Aeneid* VII.312.

their Teeth in sullen Silence; for Mr. *Hutchinsons* Character was so well established through the Province, from the many essential Services he had performed for them, that the Orders of Men, of every Denomination, addressed him with their Congratulations on his Promotion.

The Clergy were much cooler in theirs, than any other Order; owing to the Influence of Dr. *Chauncy* & some others; but the Body of them had not so divested themselves of all Sense of Gratitude, as quite to forget past Obligations; but they were so influenced by some of their *Boston* Brethren, that *their* Address had a great Proportion of that fœtid Smell of the Lamp, which generally evaporated from their Pulpit Discourses. Be it remembred, that this Govr. had been a distinguished Friend of the Clergy.

It was in the Year *1770*, that the arch Incendiary, Dr. *Franklin* procured the before mention'd Gentleman's File of Letters to be filch'd of Govr. *Hutchinson's* confidential ones; & *Franklin*, being then Agent of the lower House of *Massachusetts* Assembly, sent them to *Boston*. The Faction secreted them for some Time, to answer the following Purpose, vizt. There was a Dispute between *New York* & *Massachusetts* Governments, with Respect to their Boundaries. The Province was sensible that no one was so capable of defending their Rights as Mr. *Hutchinson*. They therefore begged the Favor of him to act as one of the Commissioners; he readily undertook to serve them. Messrs. *Hancock* & *Hawley* were two more of the Commissioners; the former of whom was quite ignorant of the Purposes of his Embassy; but he was not ignorant that those stolen Letters were in his Possession; & accordingly treated the Govr. with uncommon Complaisance, untill ye. Commission ended to the Advantage of the *Massachusetts*; When, upon the Return of the Commission, the Letters were divulged, & a new Scene of Confusion opened, which ended in the aforementioned Exculpation of the Governor, before the King & Council.

Adams, Hawley, & some others, of the legislative Faction, were unwearied in their Arts of Calumny, & Assasination of Characters which stood in ye. Way of their Views of Independence. They used every low & dirty Art, from Mouth & Press, to stigmatize those who would not coincide with their Measures; such Arts as an Oyster Wench disdains to lower her Reputation to. They knew that the Whole Rabble must have a Tub to play with, & they knew also, that the Nightmans Tub would answer the Purpose as well as any; & this they often employed. If a Man, in publick Office, was advanced

in Life; he was an old wizzled Face Dog. If he had met with a Misfortune, by breaking a Leg, he was a limping Dog; & so on.

Even Govr. *Barnard* could not escape their pitifull Insults: he happened to be fond of a delicate Fish, called *Tom Cod*, which the Harbor of *Boston* abounded with & which the common People often regaled upon.[6] He often ate of them, & Boys were employed to cry *Tom Cod* before his Door & as he passed the Streets, even the scribling Patriots would stuff their News Papers with *Tom Cod* Paragraphs to render him contemptible to the Publick. These were part of the Weapons of their Warfare. They were vociferated in the Streets, & echoed back from that Press which the Faction had consecrated to such Purposes, & which was rather too often hovered round by that worthy Divine Dr. *Cooper*, & others of the same Cloth—from the Labors of their Brain would often issue a Bonfire, a Mob, & a tarring & feathering.

Disorders continued in this State for a long Time, & nothing else could be expected; for the military Protection had been removed. The upper & lower House consisted of Men generally devoted to the Interest of the Faction. The Foundations of Government were subverted; & every Loyalist was obliged to submit to be swept away by the Torrent. Protection was not afforded to them; this rendered their Situation most disagreeable. Some indeed dared to say that their Souls were their own; but no one could call his Body his own; for that was at the Mercy of the Mob, who like the Inquisition Coach, would call a Man out of his Bed, & he must step in whether he liked the Conveyance or not.

1772

In the Year 1772, they continued their laudable Custom of Tar & Feathers; even the fair Sex threw off their Delicacy, and adopted this new Fashion. Had it been imported from *France* it might have been indulged to them; but as it was imported from a Region where Delicacy is not much encouraged, it was a great Pity that they did not consult their own Characters, before they adopted it. The Feather Part indeed suited the Softness of the Sex; but when the Idea of Feathers, united with Tar, started into the Imagination, it was

[6]Thomas Hutchinson was called a variety of names in the newspapers, like "pensioner," "Tom Long," and "monster." There was also a general shift of terminology during this time. The "town house" became the "state house"; "provincial laws" became "laws of the land," etc. Lawrence H. Gipson, *The Coming of the Revolution, 1763-1775* (New York, 1954), p. 203.

rather disgustfull—yet one of those Ladys of Fashion was so complaisant; as to throw her Pillows out of Window, as the Mob passed by with their Criminal, in Order to help forwards the Diversion. *When a Woman throws aside her Modesty, Virtue drops a Tear.*

In the Winter of this Year, the ruling Powers seized upon a Custom House Officer for Execution.[7] They stripped him, tarred, feathered, & haltered him, carried him to the Gallows, & whipped him with great Barbarity, in the Presence of thousands, & some of them Members of the general Court. Like the Negro Drivers in the *West Indies*, if you grumbled at so wholesome a Discipline, you had Iniquity added to Transgression, & Lash succeeded Lash; & there was but one Way of escaping, which was, to feign yourself dead if you was not already so; for in that Case you would be left to yourself to come to Life again as well as you could; they being afraid of such dead Men, lest they theirselves should die after them, sooner or later. One Custom House Officer they left so for dead; but some Persons of Humanity stepped into his Relief & saved him.[8]

The *Lues Infernalis*,[9] which spread through great Part of the *Massachusetts*, & had *over*spread the Town of *Boston* was of the confluent Sort. It was so contagious, that the infection was caught by the neighboring Colonies. *Rhode Island*, some years before, in a most riotous Manner had rifled the Houses & hunted after the Lives of several Gentlemen, who were obnoxious by their Attachment to Government. In this Year, the Mob burnt his Majesty's Schooner *Gaspee*, on the *Narraganset* Shore, about 20 Miles from *Newport*. This made some Noise in *England*—from a Misrepresentation of Facts, a Commission was sent over, impowering the Govr. of *Rhode Island*, the Chief Justices of *Massachusetts, New York* & *New Jersies*, & the Judge of the Vice Admiralty Court of *Massachusetts*, to inquire into the Facts. The People of that Colony were so closely connected; & so disaffected, from the Nature of their Government, to British Legislation, that it was perfectly futile to make an Inquiry; & the Matter ended, without any other Effect from the Commission, than an Encouragement to those Colonists to play the same Game again, upon the first Opportunity.

[7]John Malcolm (Oliver's note).

[8]This incident occurred in January 1774. See the Boston *Weekly News-Letter*, Jan. 27, 1774, and the Boston *Gazette*, Jan. 31, 1774. Malcolm was tarred and feathered earlier and was not totally innocent in his conduct on this occasion. Nonetheless, the brutality of his treatment follows Oliver's description closely.

[9]"Plague of Hell"—hellish calamity.

If those who had committed the Treason of burning the *Gaspee* had been discovered, they & the Witnesses of the Fact were to be sent to *England*, that the Trial of the Offence might be had there, according to ye. Act of Parliament 32d. of *Henry the 8th*. The Commissioners Part was in the Nature of a Grand Jury, to inquire & find a Bill, & the Magistrates of the Colony were to send them over for Trial. Had it come to this Test, not a Magistrate would have been willing, much less would he have dared to execute a Process of that Nature; for this Government was so republican, that it was more abhorrent to their Constitution than to that of some other of the Colonies, that it would not have been submitted to, for there was no Protection to any Magistrate, in the legal Discharge of his Office, contrary to the Minds of the Populace. Indeed, the whole Continent was alarmed; & upon such an Attempt, they would have rushed into Rebellion 3 Years before they did.[10] Perhaps it would have been better they had done so; they might have been less prepared for it, & a decent Firmness might have more easily, & at less Cost, have subdued it, than it is probable a Subdual will be effectuated.

By the Time Govr. *Hutchinson* had been tolerably well seated in his Chair, the Feathers came through his Cushion, & made him restless; for in this Year *1772*, the aforementioned stolen Letters were published. The general Assembly entered into warm Altercations with him on their Charter Rights, & their Rights of Nature. He was an Overmatch for them—that vexed them. They wasted a great Deal of Time in their Replies—he took no Time in his Answers; it was all Amusement. They were pushed so hard, that they dared not to confide in their own consolidated Understanding, but sent an Express, 400 Miles, to a noted Lawyer of *Virginia*, to draw an Answer to one of the Govrs. Speeches. That Lawyer would not undertake it, & they were forced to return such an one as the two *Adams's*, *Hawley*, & the Junto could patch up; but it was mere Diversion to the Governor to Close upon them; & I have known him to write his Answers & converse in Company, at the same Time—nothing was more provoking to the *Massachusets* Faction than to suffer under the good Sense of a Governor: a weak one they could overcome by artfull Disputation; but a Man of solid Sense they chose to treat with ye. *argumentum baculinum;* & here they knew no Superior.[11]

The last Year, the General Court, by Orders from *England*, had

10See letter by "X" in which the writer also complains that law and order had broken down, Boston *Weekly News-Letter*, Dec. 24, 1772.

11"Club law"—the argument of the stick.

[99]

been removed from *Boston* to *Cambridge*, abt. 3 Miles distant. The Order was founded in great Wisdom; for the Members of the general Assembly were so dinnered & supper'd by the Faction in *Boston*, that they were made willing to comply with any Measures destructive of Government; and at *Cambridge* they were in some Degree out of the Danger of being led into Temptation; although, even there, they were scouted by Emissaries who had some Influence over them. Had the Geography of the Country & the Temper of the People been well understood in *England*, no less than 40 Miles Distance from *Boston* would have been thought sufficient for ye. Session of an Assembly of Malecontents. They were continually buzzing about the Governor, Like a swarm of Gad Bees, complaining of the unconstitutional Measure of removing them from the Metropolis, whereas it was a well known Fact; & agreeable to the Charter, that such Removal had been frequently made in Times past. The true Cause of Complaint was: that the Faction had not so good Opportunities of influencing the Members of the Assembly, & the Country Members had not so good a Chance of transacting their trading Business, & of saving Expence, by being treated & caressed, at *Cambridge*, as at *Boston*.

It was the Unhappiness of the Governor, that his own Mind was of so candid a Cast, that he was loth to think that every other Man's was not formed in the same Mold: hence, he wrote home for Liberty to return the Assembly to *Boston*. He had Leave, & adjourned them from *Cambridge*; but he soon found himself mistaken, & that the Swell of the political Sea rowled in with greater Rapidity. Their Demands increased, & their Insults on the british Legislature increased with them; they openly disclaimed any Authority, but their own Government. They complained that they had no Representation in the british Parliament, therefore could not be taxed by them, & in the same Breath declared, that they could not be represented there, & disavowed their Inclination to it.

BOSTON TEA PARTY

Thus Things went on untill *1773*, when the Design of the Parliament was announced, of sending over the *East India* Company's Tea.[12] The Decks were now cleared for an Engagement, & all Hands were ready. Some of the Merchants crowded over as many Goods as

[12]Oliver was personally involved in this Tea Party. Both his son-in-law and brother-in-law were consignees of the tea. Richard Clarke, the brother-in-law, and his son, Jonathan Clarke, were threatened and abused and their property destroyed. For many months in 1774 the Clarkes took refuge at Castle William.

they could, against a Time of Market; & many of them with a Design never to make Remittance. The English Ministry imagined, that it would prevent the smuggling of Tea from the *Dutch*, to send a sufficient Supply, that the Price might be so lowered as to discourage the illicit Trade; & the Condition of Sales was to be at publick Auction, to the highest Bidder. If the Scheme had succeeded, the Consumption, in the *Massachusetts* only, would have been a saving to that Province of £2000 Sterlg. p. Year. This Scheme was founded upon a lenient Principle of the british Government, in Order to avoid any Force in restraining so pernicious a Trade.

The Objection made to it, by the Colonists was, yt. the Duty was to be paid in the Colonies, instead of being paid in *England*; but the Futility of such a Plea must be evident to a very low Understanding, at first Blush; for the Consignees of the *East India* Company were to pay the Duties theirselves, on the Arrival of the Teas; whereas had the Duties been paid in *England* & the Teas been lost in their Passage, the Duties would have been lost also to that Company. It is true, that, in such Case, the Company only would have made the Saving; but it would have brought no Injury to the Colonies, neither any Advantage. The Case of the Colonies with *great Britain*, at this Time, was similar to that Reverend & zealous Divine, Dr. *Chauncy*, his Expression relative to Govr. *Hutchinson*; upon its being said to him by a Friend, "that he did not doubt that the Govr. would be the Savior of his Country," the Doctor replied, that "he had rather the Country should perish than be saved by him;" these were his Words, or very similar to them. Thus, the Colonies have acted; & they now find that their Perdition draweth nigh, whether they sink or swim, their Case being something analogous to our English *Solomon's* Mode of trying Witches. If the poor old Wretch who was thrown into the Horse Pond happened to sink under the Water, she was only drowned; but if her Emptiness should cause her to float on the surface, she was haltered & hanged.

Notwithstanding the british Parliament's good & kind Intention to the Colonies in the above Scheme: yet they never considered that the smuggling Business was so universal, & that the Smugglers Interest had engrossed so great a Power; for it was absolutely necessary, if they meaned to land the Tea, to have sent ten Soldiers, to every Chest of it, in Order to have guarded it; whereas the Mob had drove off the military three Years before—to guard against Probabilities, & even against Possibilities, is a good Maxim in all Parts of Life.

The Teas at last arrived, in the latter End of Autumn, & now

Committee Men & Mob Men were buzzing about in Swarms, like Bees, with every one their Sting. They applied first to the Consignees, to compel them to ship the Teas back again. The Mob collected with their great Men in Front. They attacked the Stores & dwelling Houses of the Consignees, but they found them too firm to flinch from their Duty; the Mob insisted that the Teas should be sent to *England*. The Consignees would not take such a Risque upon theirselves, for had the Teas been lost, they must have been the Losers. At last, the Rage of the Mob, urged on by the Smugglers & the Heads of the Faction, was increased to such an Heighth, that the Consignees were obliged to fly for Protection to the *Castle*; as the King's Ship in the Harbor, which was ordered to give them Protection, refused it to them. There was no Authority to defend any Man from Injury.

The Faction did what was right in their own Eyes; they accordingly planned their Manoeuvre, & procured some of the Inhabitants of the neighboring Towns to assist them; this they did, in Order to diffuse the Odium of the Action among their Neighbors. The Mob had, partly, Indian Dresses procured for them, & that the Action they were about to perpetrate might be sanctified in a peculiar Manner, *Adams, Hancock* & the Leaders of the Faction, assembled the Rabble in the largest Dissenting Meeting House in the Town, where they had frequently assembled to pronounce their Annual Orations upon their Massacre, & to perpetrate their most atrocious Acts of Treason & Rebellion—thus, literally, "turning the House of God into a Den of Thieves."[13]

Thus assembled, on December 14th. they whiled away the Time in Speech-making, hissing & clapping, cursing & swearing untill it grew near to Darkness; & then the signal was given, to act their Deeds of Darkness. They crowded down to the Wharves where the Tea Ships lay, & began to unlade. They then burst the Chests of Tea, when many Persons filled their Bags & their Pockets with it; & made a Tea Pot of the Harbor of *Boston* with the Remainder; & it required a large Tea Pot for several hundred Chests of Tea to be poured into, at one Time. Had they have been prudent enough to have poured it into fresh Water instead of Salt Water, they & their

[13]Leaders of the patriots met in Benjamin Edes' home in the afternoon of Dec. 16 and remained there until dusk when they went dressed like Indians to the wharves. Others attended a meeting at Old South Church and then went to the offices of the Boston *Gazette*, where they dressed for their activities at the wharves. Peter Edes to Benjamin C. Edes, Feb. 16, 1836, *Proceedings of the Mass. Hist. Soc.*, XII (1873), 174-176.

Wives, & their Children; & their little ones, might have regaled upon it, at free Cost, for a twelve Month; but now the Fish had the whole Regale to theirselves. Whether it suited the Constitution of a Fish is not said; but it is said, that some of the Inhabitants of *Boston* would not eat of Fish caught in their Harbor, because they had drank of the *East India Tea*.[14]

After the Affair was over, the town of *Boston*, finding that it was generally condemned, said it was done by a Crew of Mohawk Indians; but it was the Rule of Faction to make their Agents first look like the Devil, in Order to make them Act like the Devil. This villainous Act soon grew into serious Consideration. Some of the Country Towns, as well as some of the Inhabitants of *Boston*, thought, that Justice demanded Indemnification to the owners of the Tea; but the Faction was great; & it prevailed; it had so repeated Success, in Impunity, from their other Disorders, that the Power of *Great Britain* did not weigh a Feather in their Consideration: but it at last shut up their Port; & deprived them of some other Priviledges, as the Sequel will relate.

In the other Colonies, to which the Tea was sent, they behaved with more Prudence; the Tea was secured for the *East India* Company; but it must be considered, that in those Colonies there was a little sprinkling of the *Power* of Government, with its *Form*; whereas in this, both Form & Power were annihilated, or, which is worse, the formal Part was drawn into the Vortex of Faction; & as the other Colonies were generally at Enmity with this, they chose to have her brought into Disgrace, that they might plume themselves in a Superiority over her. However, this was not of long Continuance; for the *Massachusetts* had too much of the Cunning of the Serpent, to leave any Insinuation unapplied to bring the rest of her Sisters into the same Condemnation with herself, & involving them in the Guilt of the same Rebellion, & the already fatal Consequences of it.[15]

After the Destruction of the Tea, the *Massachusetts* Faction found they had past the *Rubicon*; it was now, Neck or Nothing. They

[14]The colonists "viewed the tea as the vehicle of an unconstitutional tax, and as inseparably associated with it. To avoid the one, they resolved to destroy the other. About seventeen persons, dressed as Indians, repaired to the tea ships, broke open 342 chests of tea, and without doing any other damage, discharged their contents into the water." Ramsay, *History of the American Revolution*, I, 100.

[15]While Oliver's language seems hard, he was justified in stressing the violence of the Massachusetts opposition. Schlesinger, *Prelude to Independence: The Newspaper War on Britain 1764-1776* (New York, 1958), p. 182, notes that the violence at Boston received a "stunned silence" in other important colonial centers.

therefore went upon Committees of Correspondence & drew up what they called a Solemn League & Covenant, whereto every one was to subscribe, not to import from *England*, nor to deal with any that did, & to renounce all Connection with those who sold *English* Goods. This was a truely infernal Scheme; it was setting the nearest Relations & most intimate Friends at irreconcilable Variance; & it had that most accursed Effect, of raising a most unnatural Enmity between Parents & Children & Husbands & Wives. This Scheme was formed & executed by *Saml. Adams* & his Myrmidons who were an Overmatch for a whole Conclave of Arch Dæmons, at any Thing that was subversive of the Foundations of moral Virtue, or that tended to the Destruction of the Creation of the supreme Being. Hand Bills were sent, from the Select Men & Committees of *Boston*, to all the Country Towns, to come into this Scheme, & there was such a Connection of Trade between those Towns & *Boston*, that few dared to refuse the Invitation.

The dissenting Hierarchy lent their Aid to sanctifie the Treason, & I knew a Clergyman, of some Note, in a Country Town, who went to the Meeting House where ye. Inhabitants usually assembled upon their civil Affairs, & took his Seat at the Communion Table; & in the Plenitude of priestly Power, declared to the Assembly then convened on the solemn League & Covenant that whoever would not subscribe to it was not fit to approach that Table to commemorate the Death & Sufferings of the Savior of Mankind. This was truly making a League with the Devil, and a Covenant with Hell. The Faction were so imbittered against all the Friends of Government, & they had so wheedled the Clergy into their Measures, that those pious Men were as saucy to the supreme Being, in their publick Prayers, that a Bystander would imagine that he was only their Executioner.

They arrogated to theirselves the Power of the Keys, & could let in & shut out whom they pleased: but they were more fond of the Key of the bottomless Pit, & dealt their Curses pretty illiberally; for one of that sacred Order used this Expression in his publick Prayers, vizt. "O Lord! Bind up all the Tories on this and the other Side of the Water, into one Bundle, & cast them into the bottomless Pit, & let the Smoke of their Torment ascend forever & ever." This was expressive of great Illnature. He would have been less inexcusable, if he had imitated the Candor of his Brother Clergyman of *Scotland*, who, praying against the *Pretender*, only desired "the *Lord* to take him up, & shake him over the bottomless Pit; but not to let him fall in." Such a Petition could have discovered less of Inhumanity, if it had

had no Tincture of Christianity in it: but what is not Zeal without Knowledge capable of saying and doing, in any Thing improper to be said or done? As to their Pulpits, many of them were converted into Gutters of Sedition, the Torrent bore down all before them, like [after] a City Shower, Dead Cats & Turnip Tops come tumbling with the Flood. The Clergy had quite unlearned the Gospel, & substituted Politicks in its Stead; they had broken the two Tables of Stone, as well as the Comment upon that moral Law comprized in the excellent Sermon upon the Mount. One of those Preachers, with the Reputation of Learning, preaching upon the sixth Commandment to his large Parish, declared to them, that *it was no Sin to kill the Tories*. Such a laudable Pattern was surely worth Imitation; and it was followed in one Sense or other very punctually, among all the parochial Officers, down to the Sexton, for he sometimes would ring the Bell to raise the Mob.

I knew a Deacon who had as much Sense & Virtue as Deacons generally have. I had known him for 30 Years of an irreproachable moral Character; but being seduced by the Madness of the Times, had entered into the Spirit of them. This Man entered into a Conversation with one of his Neighbors, upon the prevailing Extravagances; his Neighbor told him that the depriving People of their Properties, by Riots, was unjustifiable. He replied, "that it was all right, it being in a good Cause." His neighbor said, "it could not be right, for it was against the Word of God"; to which this holy Man answered, "that they had laid aside the Bible for the present." To enumerate any more Instances might be tedious; & would be holding a Mirror to the Deformity of human Nature; which is disgustfull to view, too minutely. Such Actions are too picturesque of the Character of those

Who serve God as if the Devil was in them.

Thus tarring & feathering, solemn Leagues & Covenants, & Riots, reigned uncontroled. The Liberty of the Press was restrained by the very Men who, for Years past, had been hallooing for Liberty herself; those Printers, who were inclined to support Government, were threatened, & greatly discouraged. So that the People were deprived of the Means of Information; & the Faction had engrossed the Press, which now groaned with all the Falsities that seditious Brains could invent, which were crammed down the Credulity of the Vulgar.

One most atrocious Falsity, in particular, was published in the *Philadelphia* Paper, said to be, & generally believed to be, fabricated by that great Patriot Dr. *Franklin*, & was republished in some other of the Colonies News Papers. *Boston* made particular Advantages of it, & spread it through the *Massachusets*. The Purport of the Paragraph was this, vizt: "that the Parliament of *Great Britain* had in Contemplation a Bill, for its next Session, imposing a Tax upon the Colonists of £50 for every Marriage; of £20 for every Birth; with License to murder the illegitimate Children." At almost any other Time, the *credat Judaeus apella*[16] would have been *à propos*, & it would have been a subject of ridicule only; but, now, the Frenzy was worked up so high, that the most incredible Tales were the most readily assented to; & if the Faction had told their deluded Followers, that an Army of 30,000 Men were crossing the Atlantick in Egg Shells, with a Design to roast the Inhabitants alive & eat them afterwards, the People would have first stared, & swallowed down the Tale, whole.

It was astonishing with what Avidity it was listened to; & even some of the Clergy, who are the Oracles of their Parishes, hugged the Delusion; & the People would have rather suffered their Brains to be beat out of their Heads, than to have their Faith in this Absurdity beat out of their Brains. To attempt to undeceive them was talking to a Whirlwind; & a Man ran the risque of having his own Brains knocked out, who undertook the Task; & very few, that had any would dare to do it. *Mad Tom* of *Bedlam* thought all the World were mad but himself.

About this Time some of the Clergy, at 2 or 300 Miles Distance, undertook their Pilgrimages to the *new Jerusalem, Boston*, to consult Measures for the Conduct of the sacerdotal Order; & some of the *Boston* Clergy took their Airings into the Country Towns, to creep into Houses & lead silly Men & Women captive; & they cannot be denyed the everlasting Honor of being as industrious in the Cause of Sedition as the first Martyrs were in the Cause of Christianity; but, perhaps, they would not have been equally faithfull to Death, in any cause. Mr. *Otis* was prophetically right, at his first Outset, with Respect to his black Regiment; neither their Cloaths, their Shoes, or their Throats are as yet worn out. The Faction deceived them; they have helped to deceive the People; & when the Time may come that the People like Ld. *Wharton's* Puppies, may open their eyes before drowning, the Curses of the deluded Sufferers will alight upon their Heads, to their irrecoverable Contempt, without *Benefit of the Clergy*. Never was a Circumstance more seriously laughable, than what happened at the Conclusion of the Trial of

---

[16]"Let the Jew Apella believe that! (not I)."

Capt. *Preston's* Soldiers in *Boston*; one of them, who was brought in guilty of Manslaughter, standing at the Bar, was asked by the chief Justice, what Objection he had to offer why sentence of Death should not be passed upon him? The simple Fellow did not know what to say. A Bystander whispered to him, to *pray the Benefit of the Clergy*.[17] The Man not understanding the whole of the Direction, bawled out with an audible Voice, "may it please your Honors! I pray the *Death* of the Clergy"—& many present nodded their *Amen*.

SALARY FOR THE JUDGES

An Affair which happened, at the Close of the Year 1773, but was not brought into Effect untill this Year 1774, mortified, chagrined, enraged & drove into right down Madness, *Adams* & all his Factious *Hydra*. It was a Grant from his Majesty, of a Salary to the Judges of the supreme Court.[18] Such a Grant was in Contemplation some Years before, when Mr. *Charles Townshend*, was prime Minister; but his Death delayed it untill this Time. The true Reason of the Grant was this: the Judges of that Court had the shortest Allowance, from the generall Assembly, of any publick Officer; even their Door Keeper had a larger Stipend. The Judges Travel on their Circuits was generally about 1100 Miles in a Year, & some Times it had been 1500 Miles. Their Circuit Business engrossed seven Months in the Year, & the Extremes of Heat & Cold in that Climate were submitted to. For all this Service, the highest Grant made to them was £120 Sterling p. Year, & it had been much less. The Chief Justice had £30. Sterling more. This Grant was annually made, tho' sometimes postponed, & it depended upon the Humors of the prevailing Partys. A late worthy chief Justice, who had a confirmed Character for Sense & Integrity, lived almost in Penury, & at last died insolvent; & one Year, there was an attempt, in the Assembly, to deprive him of his extra £30—because he had given an Opinion in Law, upon the Bench, contrary to the Mind of a Partizan in the lower House of Assembly: but the Affair was dropped, lest it should fix a Stigma upon the House, of gross Partiality. The Assembly endeavored to keep the Judges in absolute Dependance upon their Humor; & because they found them rather too firm to coincide with their Views in the Subversion of Government, they made them the Objects of their Re-

[17]A plea of Benefit of Clergy, in English criminal law, brought an exemption from the full penalties of the law.

[18] Oliver was the principal judge involved in this controversy.

sentment; & in Order to express it, they made two new Counties, of 100 Miles more Travel, & shortned their Allowance £37.10. Sterling in the Whole: in short, they seemed disinclined to do Justice theirselves, or to suffer others to do it.

Several of the Judges had repeatedly represented their Cases to the generall Assembly, praying a further Allowance: & in Case it should be denied to them, because they might be disagreeable to the Assembly, or to the Body of the People, they were ready to resign their Offices, to make Room for others who were in greater Esteem; but they were honored with no other Answer, but having their Memorials ordered to be laid on their Table.

His Majesty taking the Case of the Judges into his royal Consideration, from his known Justice & Benevolence, ordered them Salaries to be paid out of his Revenues in *America*; such Salaries as would keep them above Want & below Envy. This was striking at the Root of that Slavery which the Judges had always been held under; & to give up such an arbitrary, cruel & unjust Empire, did not comport with the Pride of the present ruling Powers; who now used every Art of suasion & cajoling by their Emissaries, & of Threatnings from theirselves, in Order to rivet the Chains which they had only locked before. In Order to effectuate their Purpose, they made a Grant to four of the Judges equal to his Majestys Grant; but they made it for one Year only. They knew that if this was accepted of, his Majesty's Grant would be forfeited of Course, & that the next Year they could return to their wonted Expedient, of attempting to bring them into a Compliance with their own Measures. To the chief Justice the Assembly granted an extra Sum, though very disproportionate to the Distinction his Majesty had made between him & the puisne Judges; but had their Grant to him been more than adequate to the King's Grant; he had too intimate a Knowledge of their past Conduct, to put any Confidence in the Justice, Honor or Generosity of a *Massachusetts* Assembly.

The Faction, who were the prevailing part of ye. Assembly, were anxious to know the Minds of the Judges, & appointed a Committee to ask their Determination; but as the Judges had no official Information of his Majestys Grant, they declined giving any Answer. This was towards the Close of the Year 1773, when the Term of the supreme Court was just finishing in *Boston*, where the general Court was then assembled. The Assembly were highly incensed at not receiving a categorical Answer from the Judges; they were just upon determining upon a Commitment of the whole Bench to Prison; but some of their *out-of-Door* Friends who had not breathed the pestilential Atmosphere of the Assembly Room, disswaded the *within-door* Leaders of the Faction from such an illegal Step; since, if it was taken, they could have no Remedy in Law in their litigious Suits, which were too common in this Province. Thus the Matter subsided for the present; the supreme Court finished the Term, & the Judges returned to their respective Homes; & had the Assembly finished their Sessions, & returned to their *long* Homes, it is probable that Rebellion herself would have returned to *her long* Home with them.

The Judges upon hearing, sometime before, of his Majesty's gracious Intention of such a Grant, had agreed to accept of it; but when the Dog Star raged with such a scorching Heat, four of them, who lived at and near that Focus of tarring & feathering, the town of *Boston,* flinched in the Day of Battle; they were so pelted with soothings one Day, & with Curses & Threatnings the Next, that they prudentially gave the Point up. One of the Judges, upon his Return home, sickened & died. The brutal Faction of the Assembly sent their Messenger to him, with Orders to deliver the Demand of an Answer to him personally, & receive his Answer; the Judge was within a few Hours of his Exit, when the Messenger arrived; he urged Admission to his dying Bed; it was granted, & he entered, & layed his Orders, in writing, upon the dying Man's Breast, who just declared his Non Acceptance of the Kings Grant, & soon after expired.

The Chief Justice was now left alone in the Combat: his case was peculiar; his Brethren had but lately been seated on the Bench. He had been 17 Years in the Service, & had sunk more than £2,000 Sterling in it.[19] He had conversed with many of the Members upon the Singularity of his Case, & had offered not to accept of the Grant (if his Majesty would permit him so to do) provided the Assembly would reimburse him one half of his Loss in their Service; & further, that he would resign his Seat on the Bench. Upon this Representation of his Case, they advised him to take the King's Grant. This they did out of Doors; but there was so great Virtue in the Boards & plaistering of the Assembly Room, that upon setting their Feet over its Threshold, they at once changed Opinions.

The chief Justice, very luckily lived above 30 Miles from *Boston,* or perhaps he would have followed the Suit of his Bretheren, in giving up the King's Grant; conformable to that only Truth which the

[19]Oliver told the General Court that he had spent £3,000 more than his salary during his tenure as Superior Court judge. Boston *Gazette,* March 7, 1774.

Devil ever uttered, *Skin for Skin & all that a man hath will he give for his Life*: but he considered, that Mobs, when they set out on their Expeditions, generally get a Spur in their Heads; & as he lived at 30 Miles Distance from their Head Quarters, in all Probability they would want a Spur in their Heels before they could reach him. He was not disappointed in his Conjecture, for he remained quiet in his Recess, untill the Assembly met again, 2 or 3 Months after; & then the whole Pack opened. A Message was sent to him, by the lower House, signed, *Samuel Adams*, Clerk, requiring him to make explicit Answer, whether he would accept of the Kings Grant, or of their Grant. He replied, that *he should accept the Kings Grant*—nothing less than Destruction now awaited him.[20] The Term of the supreme Court was now approaching—the Thunder Cloud gathered, black enough to crock Charcoal—instead of red, the Lightning flashed its white Streaks. There was a Gallery at a Corner of the Assembly Room where *Otis, Adams, Hawley,* & the rest of the Cabal used to crowd their Mohawks & Hawcubites, to echo the oppositional Vociferations, to the Rabble without doors. *Adams* now addressed his Gallery Men, to attack the Chief Justice when he came to Court; & they perfectly understood his Meaning. Even one of the Assembly Men, a Colo. *Gardiner,* who was afterward killed at the Battle of *Bunker's* Hill, declared in the general Assembly, that he himself would drag the chief Justice from the Bench if he should sit upon it. The Chief Justice's Friends wrote to him, that if he should go to Court his Life would be in Danger, but he not being conscious of such Danger; attempted to go, but a most severe Snow Storm happening the Night before his intended Journey, his Attempt ye. next Day, after a Mile or two of Struggle through Snow Drifts, was prevented by the Impassableness of the Roads.

The next Day, one of Mr. *Adams's* right hand Men arrived, with a Message from the general Assembly, signed again by Mr. *Adams* as *Clerk,* prohibiting the chief Justice his coming to Court—he obeyed. The Messenger was a Person who had been obliged, by him to whom he delivered the Message, & apologised for his being the Bearer of it. On conversing with him, he wept at the Situation of this Affair; & frankly acknowledged, that if the chief Justice had gone to Court, he believed that he might have walked the Streets in the Day, but that he would not be safe in the Night. It being Dinner Time, the Messenger was asked to dine & refresh himself, after his

[20]Oliver's reply and other papers are printed in the Boston *Weekly News-Letter,* March 3, 1774.

Fatigue; but he refused; & assigned for a Reason, that if they knew in *Boston*, (& they would ask him) that he ate in that House, it would give great Offence.[21] Thus these Christian *Liberty Men* resembled the inhabitants of *Judæa*, in that malicious Principle of not eating with a *Samaritan*, as well as in a Worse, that of thinking they did *God* good Service in persecuting & destroying all those who dared to be of different Opinions from them. Like to what *Ben Johnson* [sic] said of *King James* the first, *their Souls seemed to have been born in an Ally.*

The Assembly, finding that the chief Justice did not go to *Boston*, to have his Brains beat out by their Rabble, they attacked him in a new Quarter, where he happened to be Invulnerable. They ordered the Records of the supreme Court to be laid before them, hoping to find some Malfeazance in his Office; but they were disappointed; & every Disappointment put them upon scratching their Heads for new Matter. At last, finding that they were pushed to Extremity, they sprung a Mine which involved theirselves in the intended Ruin of him. They drew up an Impeachment of him, as Inimical to his Country in taking the Kings Grant, but at the same Time they did him the Honor of joining his Majesty with him in the Impeachment, as offering a Bribe to him, which he received. This was such an Insult to Majesty, that the Governor could not let it pass unnoticed, & accordingly closed the Matter against them. Thus ended all their legislative Attempts to ruin the chief Justice. The private Attempts of Assasination they reserved for future Opportunities; & several Plans were formed for his Destruction, which, by as many unaccountable Circumstances, he escaped from the Execution of. It was a little odd, that they should pursue him with such unremitting Vengeance when it is considered, that they had but just finished their Laugh at his bretheren, for being such Cowards as to quit their Hold of the King's Grants to them.

DEATH OF A BROTHER

In the Month of March 1774, the Chief Justice his Brother, who was Lieut. Govr. of the Province, died.[22] He had been Secretary of

[21] John Adams noted this danger to Oliver's life in his diary (*Works*, II, 328): "Some of these judges were men of resolution, and the Chief Justice, in particular, piqued himself so much upon it and had so often gloried in it on the bench, that I shuddered at the expectation that the mob might put on him a coat of tar and feathers, if not put him to death."

[22] Oliver's brother, Andrew, was the lieutenant governor. The harsh treatment accorded him was accurately described by Oliver. The funeral ceremonies were permit-

the Province many Years, to universal Acceptance; but he had been unhappily appointed, without any Application of his, to be one of the Stamp Officers, although he had wrote to his Correspondents in *England* against the Principles of the Act; before its being passed. He had been harrassed upon this Affair in the Year 1765, his House plundered, & himself Drove to their Tree of Liberty, & forced to a Resignation. He had also wrote, to a Friend in *England*, his private Sentiments on the Constitutions of the Colonies. Those Letters were also stole at the same Time when Govr. *Hutchinsons* Letters were pilfered. The Vengeance of the Faction was carried to, & beyond the Grave. Upon his Interrment a large Mob attended, & huzzaed at the intombing the Body; & at Night there was an Exhibition, at a publick Window, of a Coffin & several Insignia of Infamy—& at this Exhibition some Members of the general Assembly attended. *Could Infernals do worse?*

The chief Justice [felt] his risque of his Life was too great, for him to pay his final Visit to the Death Bed of an only Brother; & his Friends advised him not [to] pay his fraternal Respect to his Brother's Obsequies. The Advice was just; for it afterwards appeared, that had he so done, it was not probable that he ever would have returned to his own home. Never did Cannibals thirst stronger for human Blood than the Adherents to this Faction. Humanity seemed to be abhorrent to their Nature; & the whole Tenor of their Conduct to this Time will justifye the Observation.

I have been the longer on this Subject, as, perhaps, no one Transaction irritated the Faction more; it set them upon scratching where it did not itch, untill they felt sore all over. It was a Subject upon which the Dignity of the Laws much depended; but this Dignity they had been trampling under their Feet for many Years past. *Otis* had said, in the Year 1760, that there should be no Peace in his *Israel*, if his Father had not a Seat upon the Bench; & when he gave up his political Ghost, he bequeathed the Malignity of his Heart to *Saml. Adams* & his Faction Mongers, who received it with Avidity & have lived upon the Stock ever since.

---

ted, but the mourners were insulted by the mob, and Peter Oliver did not dare make a personal appearance. *Letters and Diary of John Rowe*, ed. Anne Rowe Cunningham (Boston, 1903), II, 265.

The Parliament, of this Year 1774, having taken into their Consideration the disordered State of the *Massachusetts*—that they refused to reimburse the *East India* Company for the destruction of their Tea; & that the Council of the Province was composed of Men who were inimical to british Legislation; for these, & otherwise Reasons, which were like to have a Tendency to establish Government, had they been as well pursued—passed several Acts: for *diminishing the Charter; for shutting up the Port of Boston; & for regulating Trials at Common Law.* Had the whole Charter been vacated, such an Abolition might have been justified, on the soundest Principles of Law & Equity; for they had forfeited it before now, & as justly as they had forfeited it, when it was vacated in *James 2d.* Reign. Upon this Alteration of the Charter, his Majesty had the Sole Appointment of his own Council, instead of leaving it to the Power of ye. People to chuse Men of their own Stamp to insult Parliaments, & abuse the regal Authority, *impuniter*; & in this Alteration it was put into the Governor's Power to appoint Judges, Justices, Sheriffs &c. in a course as conformable as possible to the british Constitution. This was founded on the soundest Principles of Government. The Port of *Boston* was shut up, on Account of the refusing to pay for the Tea which was destroyed; & it was to be opened when the Tea was paid for. *Salem* was the Port of Trade fixed upon, in Exchange. This employed many Carts in transporting Goods; & as the Act was called *Lord Norths* Act, it was diverting, to a Traveller, to hear the quaint Curses, which the simple Drivers of the Carriages would throw out at that great & good Statesman. If a Wheel run into a Rut, it always descended with a, *this is Lord North's Road*; if it Jolted hard over a Stone, the Rumble was accompanied with a *Damn Lord North!*[1] Even the pious Clergy propagated the Sound; & when they left their cart driving, & ascended the Desk, they had something to say in their Prayers about *Lord North*, either explicitly or by Implication: & one of them thinking it was best to be fair & above board with his Maker, uttered the following Expression, *O! Thou Lord of the East,*

---

[1] Frederick North, 2nd earl of Guilford (1732-92), was prime minister of Great Britain from 1770 until 1782. "Lord North was 'cursed from morn to noon, and from noon to morn by every denomination of people.'" Claude H. Van Tyne, *The Causes of the War of Independence* ... (Boston, 1922), p. 443.

& of the *West*, & of *ye. South! Defend us against Lord North!* Had Lord *North* been vulnerable by the Curses & the Prayers of those Carters & Parsons, he would not at this Day have stood at the Helm of Government, but both Pilot & Ship would have foundered long since.

As to the regulating Trials at Common Law, the Inconveniences of the late Practice of chusing Jurors hath been already mentioned, & publick Justice demanded a new Method; & that Method was appointed, which conformed to the Practice in *England*, which seems to be as impartial as the Policy of the Law could devise. But there was one part of the Act, which the Necessity of the Times, only could justifye, vizt. that in the Trial of certain capital Offences, if it appeared probable that the supposed Offender could not have a fair Trial in the Province where the supposed Offence was committed, a Trial might be had in a neighboring Province, or the Prisoner might be sent to *England* for Trial. It was probable that such an Offender would not stand a fairer Chance for his Life in one Government than in another; because it must be supposed that the same Influence would extend through the Whole; therefore, it would have been an heavy Charge, as well as great Inconvenience to Witnesses, to have crossed the Atlantick upon such Occasions—but the Trial of the Soldiers, already mentioned, as well as other Trials, would justifye any peculiar Hardships, upon such Refractoriness as had been exhibited by this Government.

Lieut. General *Gage* was appointed Governor of the *Massachusetts*, in the Room of Govr. *Hutchinson*, who sailed for *England*.[2] Soon after Mr. *Gage's* Arrival, on May 13th 1774, Mr. *Gage* acted both in the civil & military Department.[3] He was accompanied by 4 Regiments of Foot; & it was generally expected & hoped, that he had Orders to send to *England* several Persons, who had been declared by his Majesty's Law Servants to have been guilty of high Treason. Many of the guilty Persons dreaded what ought to have been their Fate; & many innocent Persons declared, that if they wanted Hangmen in *England* they would willingly undertake the Office: but unhappily for the Publick the People were disappointed & the Traitors felt theirselves out of Danger; by which means, many

---

[2] June 1, 1774 (Oliver's note).

[3] Oliver is accurate on the date of Gage's arrival. Gage arrived on May 13, 1774, and Hutchinson sailed for London on June 1, 1774. John R. Alden, *General Gage in America* . . . (Baton Rouge, La., 1948), pp. 203-204.

edged off to the Faction & they felt Security from an Increase of Adherents. This was the critical Moment to have given Stability to Government, & to have saved the enormous Sums which have been expended, & the Profusion of Blood which hath been shed in the Colonies. Timidity, in Suppression of Rebellion, will ever retard the Subdual of it.

Genl. *Gage* had both civil & military Government to conduct. The Task was arduous at this Juncture, & no Person could be more anxious than he was to support the former, tho' it was out of his Walk of Life. He was a Gentleman of an amiable Character, & of an open honest Mind; too honest to deal wth. Men, who, from their Cradles, had been educated in all the wily Arts of Chicane, & who never enjoyed greater Triumph than when they gain'd an Advantage by little low Arts of Cunning. Genl. *Gage* as a Soldier, preferred the engaging an Enemy in the *European* Mode, of an open Field. As Governor, he must engage an Enemy in the Mode of Bush fighting, which they had been bred in, but which he disdained. He called an Assembly to meet at *Salem*, & there he summoned those whom his Majesty had appointed for his Council, according to the new Act of Parliament; but when those Councellors met to be sworn into Office, several declined the Oath, as imagining that their Persons & Properties would be in imminent Danger, upon their taking it; but notwithstanding their Refusal, the People persecuted some of them, because they had been in Nomination, & were known to be well affected to Government. Their Refusal was of little Service to them, for some others, who had taken the Oaths, & were afterwards forced by the Mobs to resign, were in no worse Preedicament than their Selves. A great Number did undertake the Office, & hold it; but they were forced to repair to *Boston* for Safety, under the Protection of the Troops.

Mr. *Gage* had no great Trouble with his civil Government; for the lower House of Assembly locked their Selves into their Apartment, to pass some seditious Resolves; which, when he understood, he sent the Secretary to dissolve them. The Secretary could not gain Admission, & was obliged to discharge his Duty at their Door, instead of within their Room; but they had passed their Resolves before the Dissolution. Here ended the civil Government, both Form & Substance.

The People now went upon modelling a new Form of Government, by Committees & Associations. The County of *Suffolk* met &

passed a Number of high Seasoned Resolves, in the Month of *September*, sufficiently peppered to carry them through the approaching Winter. The wild Fire ran through all the Colonies; they all interested their Selves in the *Boston* Port Bill; & in a pretended Compassion to the Sufferers of that Town shipped Cargoes of Provision; but it was thought, that those who had the Distribution of them fared full as sumptously upon them as many of those did, for whom they were designed. The Lava from this Volcano at last settled into a Congress of 52 Men, from the different Provinces, who met in *September* 1774, & pass'd several notable Resolutions about Importation, non Importation & Exportation; all which, with their other after Resolves, have been so often printed, that the Pastry Cooks may furnish their selves with any Stock they may want, at every Book Stall in *London*, for their patriotick Pies; by which Means the Patriots may have the Advantage of eating their own Words again, without having them crammed down their Throats by Force of Law.

The People began now to arm with Powder & Ball, and to discipline their Militia. Genl. *Gage*, on his Part, finding that Affairs wore a serious Aspect, made Preparations for Defence. He began to fortifie the Town; he sent for Troops from *Quebec* & *New York*, & collected a respectable Force. The other Provinces dismantled the King's Garrisons; there being no Force to oppose them. The Rebel General *Sullivan* carried off some Cannon from the Fort at *New Ham[p]shire* together with some Shot wch. he designed to use with them; but he was so little acquainted with military Affairs, that he picked out Shot that were big enough for Cannon of double Bore to what he took away; he was so well versed in Iricism, that he could at any Time fire an eighteen Pound Cannon out of nine Pound Shot. The People were continually purchasing Muskets, Powder & Ball in the Town of *Boston*, & carrying them into the Country; under the Pretence that the Law of the Province obliged every Town & Person to be provided with each of those Articles. They urged another also, that there was Danger of a French War, which put them upon their Guard.

A Person who was more than stark Blind might have seen through such pitifull Evasions. Genl. *Gage* therefore took wise Precautions; he put a Stop to the carrying off any more; & as all warlike Stores, except private Property, are vested in the King, the Govr. therefore seized upon some of the Magazines, & secured the Powder under the Protection of his Troops. This provoked the People, & some of the Smuglers sent to the Dutch at *Eustatia*, & got a Recruit of Powder.

They also secured Cannon from Vessells, & some of the Kings Forts, & acted with great Vigor in all their Preparations; & thus passed the Remainder of the Year 1774, in Offence on one Side, & in Defence on the other.

There had lived in the Town of *Boston*, many Years, a *William Molineaux*, from *Wolverhampton* in ye. County of *Stafford* in *England*. He had been an hard Ware Merchant; but by minding the Rioting Business more than his own, he had reduced his Circumstances to a low Ebb, & maintained his Family upon the Effects of a Mr. *Apthorp*, a Merchant at *New York*, for whom he was Agent.[4] This Man was a most infamous Disturber of the Peace, & urged on the Mobs to commit their mad & desperate Schemes.[5] It was generally thought, that he had encouraged the french Boy to perjury, in the Trial of the Custom House Officers, already mentioned.[6] He had engaged the Mob to destroy the King's Troops, soon after General *Gage* came; but they being afraid to execute his Scheme, he grew mad with ye. Disappointment, & Mr. *Apthorp* at that Time, arriving in *Boston* to call him to an Account, he at once grew desperate; & instead of bringing on his designed Massacre of others, he retired to his House & finished his Life by Suicide. Thus was finished, a Man who had been a Pest to Society, for several Years before his Death.

The Term of the Supreme Court was, at the latter Part of this Summer, held at *Boston*. The Mob had threatned, in the highest Terms, to prevent its Session. Genl. *Gage* was but too apprehensive of the intended Mischief; & being always anxious to support the civil Power, he very politely offered his Troops to guard the Judges to the Bench. They determined to try the Force of the civil Power, & reserved the military to the last Extremity. The Mob assembled themselves, & the Judges assembled the civil Force. The former finding that the latter were determined, made an Opening Passage, & the Court was held without Opposition. Indeed, it was to little Purpose to hold the Court, except to make some Appearance of civil Author-

[4]Charles Ward Apthorp was the son of a great Boston merchant, Charles Apthorp. Wendell D. Garrett, *Apthorp House 1760-1960* (Cambridge, Mass., 1960), pp. 6-7.

[5]John Rowe, the diarist and merchant, had also a poor opinion of William Molineux. An entry for Oct. 24, 1774, reads: "This afternoon Willm Mollineux was buried—he has been famous among the Sons of Liberty. Many Things are attributed to him & tis believed he was the first Leader of Dirty Matters." *Letters and Diary of John Rowe*, II, 286.

[6]The commissioners of customs were miles away from King's Street on the evening of March 5, and the star witness for the patriots was a perjurer who was encouraged by William Molineux and others. Miller, *Sam Adams*, p. 188.

ity; for the *Suffolk* Resolves had forbid Jurors, & all others, to obey any Orders, but what they should issue themselves;[7] & the others Courts in the Province had been dissolved by Mobs; & some of them in a most brutal Manner, as may be seen in the *Appendix*, if You are not already too disgusted to throw your Eye upon it. Thus the *inter Arma silent Leges* was most strictly verified.[8]

LEXINGTON AND CONCORD

In the Spring of 1775, the War began to redden. Genl. *Gage* having Intelligence, that a Quantity of Warlike Stores were collected at *Concord*, about 20 Miles from *Boston*, judged it most prudent to seize them. Accordingly, just about Midnight of the 18th. of *April*, he privately dispatched about 800 Men for that Purpose: they executed Part of their Orders, but to no important Effect. This Party was attacked by a Number, who had previously Notice of their March. Much Stress hath been laid upon, who fired the first Gun. This was immaterial, for as the civil Government had been resolved by the *Suffolk* Resolves, the military Power had a right to suppress all hostile Appearances. But in the present Case, the commanding Officer ordered the armed Rabble to disperse, upon which some of the armed Rabble returned an Answer from their loaded Muskets. The King's Troops then returned the fire—the Alarm spread, & 10 or 12000 Men, some say more, flanked them & kept in the rear, at turns. The Battle continued for the whole Day. After this first Corps had fought, on their Return, for many Miles, they had expended most of their Ammunition, & must have submitted as Prisoners, had not Ld. *Percy* met them with a fresh Brigade, with two Pieces of Artillery.[9] This fortunate Circumstance saved them from a total Ruin. When united, they still fought, but the Cannon checked the Progress of the Rebels; who kept at a greater Distance, & chiefly fired from Houses, & from behind Hedges, Trees, and Stone Walls. As the King's Troops approached their Head Quarters, ye. Battle thickened upon them; for every Town, which they passed through, increased the numbers of their Enemys; so that they had not less than 10 or 12000 to combat with in the Course of the Day.

[7] The Suffolk Resolves of Sept. 9, 1774, declared (in Resolution 5) that all officials of the courts who held their tenure under any authority other than the Massachusetts charter were acting unconstitutionally.

[8] "Amidst the clash of arms the laws are mute."

[9] Hugh, Earl Percy, the son of the first duke of Northumberland, was in charge of the British forces marching to Lexington and Concord.

At last they arrived at a Hill, on the same Range with that of *Bunker's* Hill: here Lord *Percy* took Post, in so defensible a Place, that there was no danger of being annoyed by the Enemy; but unhappily this Post was quitted in a few Days; for the principal Men of *Charlestown*, in which this Hill was situated, interceeded with Genl. *Gage* not to fix any Troops there, lest it should injure the Town; & they gave their Words & Honor, and some of them were men of Honor, & Friends to Government, that if there should be any Attempts to throw up Works to annoy the town of *Boston*, they would give timely Intelligence of them. But neither Genl. *Gage* or they calculated the Probability of the Rebels guarding the River in such a Manner as to prevent any Intelligence across it to the Town of *Boston*—and this Mistake was the Occasion of the Battle of *Bunkers Hill*, two months after. This was a Battle of *Chevy Chase*, & many have had, & others will have Reason *to rue the hunting of that Day*.[10] This was called the Battle of *Lexington*, because it was at that Town, abt. 15 Miles from *Boston*, where it first began.

Many were the Exploits of that Day, variegated wth. Courage, Generosity, & Barbarity. Lord *Percy* was distinguished by Conduct & Gallantry; & the other Officers & Soldiers by great Bravery. Some of each Rank travelled 50 Miles that Day, wthout. a Morsel of Food.

Many were the Instances of the british Soldiers great Humanity, in protecting the aged, the Women & the Children from Injury; notwithstanding the great Provocation they had to a general Slaughter. One among the many was this, vizt. A Soldier seeing an old Man, with a Musket, who had been in the Battle, much wounded & leaning against a Wall; he went up to him, tore off the Lining of his own Coat & bound up his Wounds, with it, desiring him to go out of Harm's Way. The Soldier had scarcely turned from him, when the old Man fired at his deliverer: human Passion could not bear such Ingratitude, & the Man lost his Life by it. Another Instance was this: from one particular House the Troops were much annoyed; a Capt. *Evelyn* rush'd in; but finding no Body below, he ran up Stairs, &

---

[10]"The Hunting of the Cheviot," in *The English and Scottish Popular Ballads*, ed. Francis James Child (Boston, 1886-98), III, 311 (Verse 2):

> To drive the deere with hound and horne
> Erle Pearcy took the way:
> The child may rue *that* is unborne
> the hunting of *that* day!

Apparently Oliver is referring to a local story told of Lord Percy's march. A Roxbury schoolboy laughed at the tune of the fifers and observed: "To think how you will dance by and by to Chivy Chase."

a Woman in Bed begged her Life: he told her she was safe, & asked where her Husband was? She said that he was just gone out of the Room; upon which Capt. *Evelyn* returning to the Door, the Man, who was under the Bed, fired at him: Capt. *Evelyn* then put the Man to death.

There was a remarkable Heroine, who stood at an House Door firing at the Kings Troops; there being Men within who loaded Guns for her to fire. She was desired to withdraw, but she answered, only by Insults from her own Mouth, & by Balls from the Mouths of her Muskets. This brought on her own Death, & the Deaths of those who were within Doors.

Many Lives were lost this Day; the King lost about 90 Men, & the Rebels at least as many. Many were wounded on each side. Two of the British Troops, at fewest, were scalped, & one of them before he was dead. Let Patriots roar as loud as they please, about the Barbarity of an Indian scalping Knife; but let them know, that an Indian Savage strikes the deadly Blow before he takes off the Scalp. It was reserved for a *New England* Savage, only, to take it off while his Brother was alive.

Messrs. *Hancock* & *Saml. Adams* happened to be at *Lexington*, on the Night before the Battle. They heared, the Kings Troops were coming out; & their Guilt whispering in their Ears, that the Design was to take them into Custody, they fled. Their Flight confirmed that observation made by *Solomon*, viz. *the wicked fleeth when no Man pursueth.*[11] There was also a Colo. *Lee* of *Marblehead*, a weak but violent Partizan of Rebellion, who was there; & he imagining the same Design of seizing him, fled also, ran into Distraction & died miserably; this Man had great Influence, as he was supposed to be a Man of a large Estate. Several Men of Estates, from Ambition & a mistaken private Interest, as well as from Resentment, engaged in this Rebellion; but upon settling their Books found the Ballances against them. Others who were firmly Attached to Government fared no better; for what with Sequestrations & enormous Taxes & an illegal Prevention of recieving the Debts due to them, they were mowed down to a Level with the others. Never did the World exhibit a greater Raree Show, of Beggars riding on Horse back & in Coaches, & Princes walking on Foot. One Instance is Striking, of a Sand Man who carried Sand to the Doors of the Inhabitants in *Boston*, & is now riding in a Coach. This material World is turned

[11] Proverbs xxviii.1.

topsey turvey every Day; & doubtless, it is necessary that the System of the political World should under & overgo too, a similar Rotation—

Variety alone doth Joy,
The sweetest Meats do soonest cloy.[12]

After the Battle of *Lexington*, there was a general Uproar through the Neighbouring Colonies; the Echo of which soon extended throughout the Continent. *Adams*, with his Rabble Rout, & his Clergy sounding the Trumpet of Rebellion to inspire them, had blown the Bellows so long, that the Iron was quite hot enough to be hammered. The News of the Battle flew with Rapidity; one Post met another to tell the dolefull Tale, of the Kings Troops burning Houses & putting to Death the Inhabitants of Towns. Industry never labored harder, than the Faction did, in propagating the most atrocious Falshoods, to inspirit the People to the grossest Acts of Violence; & they had a great Advantage in doing it, by engrossing the tale almost to theirselves, & by suppressing the true State of Facts. At last, indeed, Genl. *Gage*, by great Assiduity, found Means to undeceive those who had preserved any Coolness of Temper. As for the *qui vult decipi decipiatur*,[13] he there could make no Impression—thus the Rupture could not be closed.

MR. PUTNAM

Amidst this general Confusion, the famous Mr. *Putnam*, now a Brigadier General in the Rebel Service, went to *Boston*, & offered his Service to Genl. *Gage*, & proposed for himself a Birth in the royal Artillery; but Mr. *Gage* having no Vacancy above 3/6 p. Day, he did not incline to accept, saying at the same Time, that 10/p. Day was the utmost of his Ambition. It hath been wished by many, that Genl. *Gage* had secured him to the royal Interest. It possibly might have turned out *well*, had he have done so, but I imagine it hath turned out *better*, by not engaging him; for Mr. *Putnam* hath not only been the least obnoxious Man in their Service, but he hath really exercised great Humanity to Prisoners taken by the Rebels; & had there been no worse Men to conduct their Opposition than

---

[12]Matthew Prior, "The Turtle and the Sparrow," *The Literary Works of Matthew Prior*, ed. H. Bunker Wright and Monroe K. Spears (Oxford, 1959), I, 536, ll. 232-233:

Variety alone gives joy,
The sweetest Meats the soonest cloy.

[13]"Who wishes to be deceived will be deceived."

he is, I have no Doubt that the Rebellion would have ceased long since.[14]

As Mr. *Putnam* hath been a Subject for News Paper Paragraphs, & as his Picture hath been exposed in the Windows of Print Shops, both of Town & Country, although very unlike him, it may not be amiss to give you some Traits of a Semblance. I am pretty sure, that they will be less disgustfull than some others I feel myself obliged to give you very soon. Know then, that he was a Person who commanded a ranging Party when General *Amherst* reduced *Canada* to British Subjection. In that Service he distinguished his self with Fidelity, Intrepidity & Success. After the Campaign was over, he returned to his small Farm in *Connecticut*, & to his old Business, as a Retailer of Cider & Spirits, in which he gained something to the Support of his Family.[15] He was well esteemed by those who knew him, according to the provincial Phrase, as an *honest, good Sort of Man*—his Parts are not brilliant, but he is hardy, bold, & daring in Execution. His Courage is of that Sort which hath sometimes been deemed, fool hardiness. An Anecdote or two, which have been currently believed in *New England*, may be explanatory of the latter. It is said, that some Years ago he had a few Sheep upon his Farm, which a Wolf had destroyed; he was determined to avenge his loss by the Death of ye. Robber. He accordingly took a Companion, & repaired to his Den, then tied a Rope around his Waist, & with his Gun crawled on his Hands & Knees into the Den; when he soon

[14]The following passage was crossed out in the manuscript, and this explanation was given: "This Article is a Mistake: it was not Mr. Putnam, but Genl. Green who conveyed the Lady to her Father." The passage reads: "I will give one Instance, from the best Authority, of the humane & generous Feelings of his Mind; vizt. a Lady, who was known to Mr. *Putnam*, but whose Husband, as well as herself, had been long obnoxious to the Faction, embarqued for *London*, about the Time the King's Troops evacuated *Boston*. The Pacquet, in which she embark'd, was detained in the Harbor, untill the Rebels had taken full Possession of the Town of *Boston*; but she being in such a Situation, as discouraged her from the Voyage, returned to a Friend's House, where she was secreted in a Chamber. It so happened, that Mr. *Putnam* dined at this House, where he observed, that Plates of Food were sent from the Table to an Invalid above Stairs; he desired to know who was above, & after some hesitancy he was told. He then desired to see the Lady, who was alarmed at such a Visitant & when he was admitted, he desired her not to be uneasy; & very humanely, as well as politely, asked her, whether he could be of any Service to her? She replied, she only wished to go to her Father at *Rhode Island*, about 70 miles off. Mr. *Putnam* immediately procured a Coach for her, conveyed her there in Safety, & relieved her of her Anxiety. Let this Instance of Charity cover a Multitude of his Errors."

[15]Israel Putnam (1718-90) served in many campaigns during the Seven Years' War, with bravery and distinction. After the death of his first wife he settled at Pomfret, Conn., where he married again and became active in local and colony politics.

percieved the Wolf with his Eyes glaring, at the further End of it; he fired his Gun & killed him; & seizing him by the Ears, gave the Signal to his Comrade, who pulled them both out. This rash Action was bruited about, & his Minister under took to expostulate with him upon it; but he closed the Dispute by saying, "that if the Devil himself had stolen as many of his Sheep as the Wolf had, he would have gone into his Dominions & pulled *him* out by the Ears." Another Story they tell of him, is; that he was taken by the Indians in the last War & having destroyed many of their Tribe, they were determined to destroy him; & accordingly bound him to a Tree, & retreated to a Distance, to fling their Hatchets into him; when he, just as the fatal Stroke was to be given, laughed in their full View. The Indians, being always pleased with a brave Action, immediately released him. These Instances are Characteris[tic]k of some Sort of bravery, which though it may not be justified upon the Principles of true Courage, yet often meets with Success: & as far as it coincides with true Courage, it will confirm that part of Mr. *Putnams* Character which I at first mentioned, agreeable to that Maxim, vizt. "a Man of true Courage is always a Man of Humanity": & I make not the least Doubt, that when a List of the Barbarities which have been committed by *Washington* & his Savages may be published, *Putnam's* Name will be in vain searched for as one of the Perpetrators.[16]

BUNKER HILL

I now return to the disagreeable Situation, after the Battle of *Lexington.* The old Bickerings continued, & new ones increased. Genl. *Gage* was obliged to fortifie the Town, to secure his Troops & those who had resorted to them for Protection. The People, on their Parts, complained of his so doing; pretending that the Inhabitants could not be supplied with Provisions from the Country. This they knew to be false, but used it as a Pretence to keep the Town exposed to the inroads of the Numbers they designed to bring in, to take Possession: & had not the General taken those Precautions, it is probable that the Loyalists, who had fled to the Town, would many of them have been massacred; & others of them have fared but little better. The Faction, who were out of the Town [were] constantly urging the Inhabitants to quit the Town, & threatning to

[16]Similar tales of Putnam's heroic deeds are retold in George Canning Hill, *Gen. Israel Putnam* (Boston, 1858), pp. 16-27 (wolf tale), 39-48. See also [David Humphreys], *Memoirs of the Life . . . of Israel Putnam* (Ithaca, N.Y., 1834).

destroy it. Many went out, & it was with great Hardships & Difficulties that they could find where to lay their Heads; insomuch, that of 10 or 12,000, who left it after that Battle, 1200 died by *November* following. The Operation of that Battle occasioned so great an Evacuation, that the Town was reduced to a perfect Skeleton.

In May Generals Howe, Clinton, & Burgoyne, arrived from *England*; but, little else was done but fortifying, untill the Battle of *Bunker's Hill*, on the 17th. June, cut out Work enough for the Troops, not only for that Day but for nine Months after. That memorable Day exhibited a Scene, which crowned british Valor with Laurels of unfading Honor; but it was much to be lamented, that the Laurels were not to be obtained without the Sacrifice of a greater Disproportion of heroick Officers than perhaps ever fell in one Battle; owing to that savage Way of fighting, not in open Field, but by aiming at their Objects from Houses & behind Walls & Hedges. The Battle came on thus. It hath been already said, that the principal Inhabitants of *Charlestown* had told Genl. *Gage*, that he should have Intelligence of any Designs against him from that Town; but they were either disinclined, or not able to give the Information; so that, on the Night of the 16th. June, about 3 or 4000 Men were busied in throwing up a Redoubt, to contain 500 fighting Men; in fixing down 13 Rail Fences in the Front of it; & in making an impenetrable Hedge, which ran from the Redoubt to the Water's Edge, several hundred Feet. The other Part of the Redoubt was flanked by Dwelling Houses, from whence they fired with great Security; by which Means they could take Aim at the Officers of the british Troops, whom they made the particular Objects to be fired at. Thus prepared, & never was a more advantageous Defence prepared, they began early in the Morning of *17th. June* to fire upon the Town of *Boston*, from their Redoubt of 3 peices of Artillery, of 3 Pounds Shot; & they might have fired untill this Time, without doing little other Damage than by keeping the Town in constant Alarm, & keeping up their own Spirits.

Charlestown is a Peninsula made by an artificial Ishtmus [sic] about 2 Rods wide. On one Side a Gondalo with Cannon could pass almost to the Neck of Land, at high Water, & on the other Side, a Vessell of considerable Force could approach very near, to meet the opposite Gondalo. *Charles River* is the Boundary between *Boston* & *Charlestown*. At the Ferry it is not ½ a Mile in Width—at the North Part of *Boston* is an Hill, called *Copp's* Hill, which was well fortified with heavy Cannon. This Hill is opposite to *Bunker's*

Hill, about ¾ of a mile Distant. From this Hill the Redoubt of the Rebels was battered; & it did some Execution, by damaging the Redoubt, & by killing about 40 Men in it; & this Battery plaid untill the Kings Troops were in Action, about 2 or 3 o'clock in the Afternoon. The Fatalities of War, attending this Days Action were singular in their Quality, but not so in their Number; as may be observed in the following Relation, & the Day was remarkably hot, as well as the Action.

Genl. *Gage* found it necessary to dislodge the Rebels; a further Indulgence to them would have been irremediable. He accordingly proposed to the Admiral, to send an armed Vessell on that side of the Enemy's Encampment, where they could have been effectually annoyed. The aforesaid Hedge which concealed great Numbers, who afterwards galled the King's Troops, would have been so flanked, that not a Rebel could have stood his Ground. Besides which, there could have been no Retreat for them, as such a Vessell would have lain near to the Isthmus & prevented it. This Manæuvre would have made Prisoners of near 4000 Rebels, & perhaps put an End to the Rebellion. But it seems, that, at this Time, & during a great Part of this american Contest, the King's Ships were looked upon in too sacred a Light to be destroyed by any Thing, except by Storms, Rocks & Worms. In this Case, a Vessell of £200 Value, would have been as effectual as one of £20,000. This I term the Fatality of Fatalities of this memorable Day.[17]

It was high Water about one o'clock after noon. About 1700 of the Kings Troops then embarked, & landed without any Opposition. They formed, & marched towards the Redoubt on their March. They were fired upon, through the aforementioned Hedge by two pieces of Cannon peeping through it: upon which Genl. *Howe,* who commanded, called for his 6 Pound Artillery; but when they began to load them, they had only 12 Pound Shot for 6 Pound Cannon. Here was a second Fatality. Genl. *Howe* then, with true british Courage, said that "they must do as well as they could with their Muskets," & marched on. When the Soldiery came to the Fences, they attempted to break them down; but they were so well fixed, that the Ardor of the Troops could not wait to level them, but climbed them. This Sort of Attack was fatal to them; for they were now Objects of Aim, from the Houses as well as the Redoubt.

[17]Charles Stedman, *The History of the . . . American War* (London, 1794), I, 125-129, agrees that a better use of naval power would have changed the character of the battle.

At this Time, the Encampment, upon *Copp's* Hill, seeing the Troops so much distressed from the Houses, flung a Shell, which fell upon a very large Meeting House built with Wood, which instantaneously kindled; & the wind blowing in the Course of the Buildings, the whole Town became one general Conflagration.[18] The british Troops by repeated Efforts had made a Passage through the Fences, & were marching to the Redoubt; but in great Disorder. Mr. *Howe*, observing it, ordered a Retreat, he was obeyed. He soon formed them, & they marched on again in good Order; & immediately, upon one or two having mounted the Parapet, the Rebels fled from the Redoubt. Major General *Warren*, who commanded in the Redoubt, exerted himself to prevent their rushing out at the Passage, but all in vain. He was the last Man who quitted it; & while his Men were running off, he very slowly walked away; & at about 20 or 30 Yards distant from the Redoubt he dropped; a Bullet having entered the back Part of his Head, & gone through it so far as to occasion a Prominence on his Forehead.[19]

Thus the Battle ended. And why there was no Pursuit is an Arcanum that must reside in those Breasts where many other Mysteries have been locked; but, of which, a Key hath been found to open many of them to publick View. The Gondalo, which came at no great Distance from the Isthmus, did some Damage, & served *in terrorem* to those who were going to assist at the Redoubt. Had it gone nigher, as it might have done, there would have been great Slaughter of the Rebels—a Remarkable Circumstance attended the firing from the Gondalo. A Colo. *Mc. Clary* was leading on a strong Party of Succours, across the Isthmus. Some of his Men flinched, through fear of the Canonade from this armed Boat; the Colo. seeing it, cryed out, "Come on brave Boys! that Shot is not yet cast that is to kill me." The Words were scarcely spoke, before a Cannon Ball cut him almost to Peices.

Colo. *Putnam* was at the Redoubt, when the british Troops were marching up to it. He knew their Bravery, & the Rawness of the Rebel Army. He said to the commanding Officer of the rebel Army;

[18]The burning of Charlestown apparently was started by shells from Copp's Hill. Willard M. Wallace, *Appeal to Arms: A Military History of the American Revolution* (New York, 1951), p. 41.

[19]Joseph Warren (1741-75) "mingled in the fight, behaved with great bravery, and was among the last to leave the redoubt. He was lingering, even to rashness, in his retreat. He had proceeded but a few rods, when a ball struck him in the forehead, and he fell to the ground." Richard Frothingham, Jr., *History of the Siege of Boston . . .* (Boston, 1849), pp. 170-171.

"I know the british Troops, I have acted with them; We must retreat, for they will defeat us;" upon which he was sent off to *Cambridge*, about 3 Miles Distance, for more Men; but the Battle was over before his return.

The Kings Troops had about 1000 killed & wounded, & of the latter many died of their Wounds, through the excessive Heat of the Season. The Rebels did not lose one half that Number: about thirty of them, who were wounded; were lodged in Prison, at *Boston*, & were as well tended as the Kings wounded Troops. Among the rest was a Colo. *Parker*, who died with his Wounds not long after the Battle. This unhappy Man lamented the Ambition that led him into this Mistake, & sent Word, to some of his active Friends, to quit the Cause, as he now too late found himself in the wrong.

HEROES AND REBELS

This Day was distinguished by as many Acts of Heroism as so short a Time could be well be crowded with. One of which was relative to the above Colo. *Parker*; who being wounded, sat upon a Stone in great Anguish begging for a little Water.[20] A Soldier seeing him was going to run him through with his Bayonet, to ease him of his Pain. A Grenadier, at that instant, interposed & prevented the fatal Stab, saying to the Soldier, "Go fetch him some Water; let him live to know that a British Soldier is humane as well as brave." After the Battle, the Kings wounded Troops were carried to *Boston*; & it was truly a Shocking Sight and Sound, to see the Carts loaded with those unfortunate Men, & to hear the piercing Groans of the dying & of those whose painfull Wounds extorted the Sigh from the firmest Mind. As I was a Witness to one Instance, in particular, of Stoicism, I will relate it. I was walking in one of the Streets of *Boston*, & saw a Man advancing towards me, his white Waistcoat, Breeches & Stockings being very much dyed of a Scarlet Hue. I thus spake to him; "My friend, are you wounded?" He replied, "Yes Sir! I have 3 Bullets through me." He then told me the Places where; one of them being a mortal Wound; he then with a philosophick Calmness began to relate the History of the Battle; & in all Probability would have talked 'till he died, had I not begged him to walk off to the Hospital; which he did, in as sedate a Manner as if he

[20] John Parker (1729-75), born at Lexington, Mass., was a farmer and mechanic before the revolution and was leader of the guard that protected Samuel Adams and John Hancock at Lexington.

had been walking for his Pleasure. I forbear to mention others lest you should complain of Tediousness.

As I have mentioned Major Genl. *Warren*, it may not be amiss to give you a short Sketch of his Character. He was born near to *Boston*; & when young, was a bare legged milk Boy to furnish the *Boston* Market. He was a proper Successor to the bare legged Fisher Boy *Massianello*, & his Fate was almost as rapid.[21] Being possessed of a Genius which promised Distinction, either in Virtue or Vice, his Friends educated him at the College in *Cambridge*, to take his Chance of being a Curse or a Blessing to his Country. After he had been graduated, he studied Physick under a Capital Physician in *Boston*. But in that Town, a Man must look one Way & row another to get any Way a head; & that will not always do; if it would, Mr. *Warren* had a Mind susceptible of all Duplicity—and in his Profession, his Practice was not very rapid. He therefore look'd out for other Means of Subsistance. He married a tolerable Sum of Mony:[22] he also took Administration on Part of a Gentlemans Estate which he appropriated to his own Use. Being of a very ambitious Cast, he listed under the Banner of the Faction, & urged on the boldest of their Schemes; untill his close Attendance, at the Altar of Sedition, had reduced his Finances to a very low Ebb. He was now forced to strike any bold Stroke that offered. Conquer or die were the only alternatives with him, & he publickly declared, that "he would mount the last Round of the Ladder or die in the Attempt."[23] The Prophecy was ambiguous, he met his Fate in the latter. Had he conquered, *Washington* had remained in Obscurity; at least, he would not have been honored with the Eclat of a Coffee house, or of any other Assembly of Politicians, as the american *Fabius*. That Honor would have been reserved for those celebrated Heroes, who retard every Operation that tends to the Salvation of their Country.

An Engineer, who served at this Battle, & was wounded in it, was a Mr. *Richard Gridley*. At the taking of *Cape Breton*, in 1745, he acted in the same Capacity, & executed his Office with great Applause. Being a Man of Ingenuity, he, since that Time, had turned Projector, & met with the common Fate of Projectors, who, by attempting a Transmutation of other Substances into Gold, gener-

[21]Masaniello was a Neapolitan fisherman who led a revolt of the inhabitants of Naples against their Spanish rulers.

[22]Warren married Elizabeth Hooton, daughter of a Boston merchant.

[23]See "An Address to the Soldiers," p. 159.

ally find a *Caput Mortuum* at the Bottom of their Crucibles.[24] Thus being reduced, & swelled with great Self Importance, he deviated into the Road of Rebellion, in order to acquire Fame & a Subsistance. His Wound hath immortalized his Fame, as a Rebel. But as to increasing his Hoards, it is not probable that Congress Paper Dollars will increase them, except in Bulk; for they are too like the *New-England* Parson's Description of Self righteousness, vizt. "that the more a Man hath of it, the poorer he is."[25]

A Mr. *Henry Knox*, who now fills the chief Departments in *Washington's* Artillery, is another high Partizan in the Rebellion. He was a Bookseller in the Town of *Boston*, but he was too Deep in Debt, for his Stock, to hesitate a Moment at any Scheme to extricate himself.[26] Rebellion first offered her Services, & he accepted them. Some of the late intercepted Letters are descriptive of his present Situation, & it appears by them that he can not expect to make a Fortune by the Congress Paper Dollars. It takes so great a Quantity of them to crowd into a Man's Stomach for one Dinner, that an hard Mexican Dollar is much easier of Digestion. In Short, if we review the List of those Heroes who compose Congresses, Committees, mock Government, & the chief army Departments, we shall find it filled up with Men, desperate in Ambition or in Fortune. As for those who follow their Leaders, they stand upon ye. compassionate List, for they know not what they do. The Foundation & Progress of this Rebellion may be epitomized in the Moral of the following Story.

Among the Prisoners who were wounded, & confined in the Jail at *Boston*, was a Lieutenant, by the Name of *Scott*, a Person of a good natural Understanding.[27] A Gentleman of Humanity went to the Jail to visit & converse with the wounded, & to offer the *Samaritan* Service, of pouring Oil & Wine into their Wounds. Among the rest, he found this *Scott* to be a sensible, conversible Man; he offered to send him some Refreshment, to alleviate his Distress. *Scott* seemed surprized at the humane Offer, & said to him, "are you

[24]Probably taken from the Boston *Weekly News-Letter*, April 16, 1773.

[25]Richard Gridley (1711-96) served as an engineer in the battle of Louisburg in 1745 and was a commander of the artillery in the Crown Point expedition of 1755. He constructed breastworks for Breed Hill in 1775.

[26]Henry Knox (1750-1806) owned the London Book Store in Boston. Worthington C. Ford, "Henry Knox and the London Book-Store in Boston, 1771-1774," *Proceedings of the Mass. Hist. Soc.*, LXI (1928), 227-303.

[27]Ezekiel Scott?

in earnest Sir?" The Gentleman replied, "that he was; & if a Bottle or two of Wine, or any other Thing would be acceptable, that he'd send it to him." Such a kind Offer did *Scott's* Heart good equal to the Medicine itself; & he accepted the Offer. The Gentleman then addressed him in this Manner: "*Scott!* I see you are a sensible Man; pray tell me how you came into this Rebellion?"

He returned this Answer: "the case was this Sir! I lived in a Country Town; I was a Shoemaker, & got my Living by my Labor. When this Rebellion came on, I saw some of my Neighbors get into Commission, who were no better than my self. I was very ambitious, & did not like to see those Men above me. I was asked to enlist, as a private Soldier. My Ambition was too great for so low a Rank; I offered to enlist upon having a Lieutenants Commission; which was granted. I imagined my self now in a Way of Promotion: if I was killed in Battle, there would be an end of me, but if my Captain was killed, I should rise in Rank, & should still have a Chance to rise higher. These Sir! were the only Motives of my entering into the Service; for as to the Dispute between *great Britain* & the *Colonies,* I know nothing of it; neither am I capable of judging whether it is right or wrong." This Instance will solve many Conjectures, relative to the Unanimity of the Colonists in this Rebellion; & seperate such Instances from the Numbers collected in carrying it on, the Justice of their Cause, when weighed in the Ballance, will be found wanting.

After the Battle of *Bunker's Hill,* Genl. *Howe,* took Post on an Hill, of the same Range of Hills, near to the Isthmus, where there could be no Approaches to discommode him. Had this Post been maintained after the Battle of *Lexington,* it is now evident, that all the Carnage of the 17th. June would have been prevented—all that was to be done, now, was to endeavor to do better next Time—*felix quem faciunt,*[28] was a Lesson to be well learned, but there are some Persons, who grow so callous upon a severe Flogging, that they seem unsusceptible of future Instruction; similar to the Discipline of the celebrated *Dr. Busby,* who, it was said, had whipped more Understanding *out* of his Pupils, than he had ever whipped *into* them.[29]

The Rebels took Possession of some very strong Posts, opposite

[28]"Happy the man whom the horns of others make wary." Happy the man who is warned by others' bad luck.

[29]Richard Busby (1606-95) was notorious for his methods of enforcing discipline as a schoolmaster.

to those of Mr. *Howe*, at about a Mile's Distance; & they very rapidly extended them for 13 Miles, untill they had surrounded the Town of *Boston*, except where the Tide flowed to intercept them; & thus was the Town changed into a Prison. Mr. *Washington* was now fixed upon, by the Congress, to take upon him the Command of the continental Army. He had the greatest Reputation, as a Soldier, among the Southern Colonies. He was polite, humane, & popular. He soon came to the *Massachusetts*, & encamped in & about *Cambridge*, in View of the King's Troops. He had been promised, by the *Massachusetts*, a Body of 20,000 Men, well cloathed & armed; but when he came, he was much disappointed. However, as he had engaged in the Service, he was resolved to make the best of it, & discipline his Men to the most Advantage. Ammunition & Artillery he much wanted; otherwise he might have done more than was done; for it seemed to be the principal Employment, of both Armies, to look at each other with Spy Glasses. The Rebel Army was so destitute of Artillery, that they sent to *Ticonderoga*, 200 Miles distant, to bring down a single Mortar, by Land; but luckily for them, tho' unfortunately for the british Troops, they had a Supply of War Stores, by taking an Ordnance Ship loaded for *Boston*. This gave them another Mortar. Powder also had been much wanted untill the Winter, when they were supplied with that also.

In the mean Time, both Armies kept squibbing at each other, but to little Purpose; at one Time a Horse would be knocked in the Head, & at another Time a Man would be killed, or lose a Leg or an Arm; it seemed to be rather in Jest than in Earnest. At some Times, a Shell would play in the Air like a Sky Rocket, rather in Diversion, & there burst without Damage; & now & then, another would fall in the Town, & there burst, to the Terror or breaking of a few Panes of Glass; and during the whole Blockade, little else was done but keeping both Armies out of the Way of Idleness, or rather the whole Scene was an idle Business. But as little as the red Regiments performed, the black Regiment played its Artillery to some purpose, and

> The Pulpit, Drum ecclesiastick
> Was beat with Fist, instead of a Stick[30]

to such Purpose, that their Cushions contained scarce Feathers, sufficient for the Operation of tarring & feathering one poor Tory.

[30]Samuel Butler, *Hudibras. In Three Parts* ... (London, 1726), Part I, canto i, p. 16, ll. 11-12.

The Name of the Lord was invoked to sanctifie any Villainy that was committed for the good old Cause. If a Man was buried alive, in Order to make him say their Creed, it was done in the Name of the Lord. Or if a Loyalist was tyed to an Horses Heels, & dragged through the Mire, it was only to convert him to the Faith of these Saints. It was now, that Hypocrisy, Falsehood & Prevarication with Heaven, had their full Swing, & mouthed it uncontrold. Mr. *Washington* was provided with a Chaplain, who, with a Stentorian Voice & an Enthusiastick Mania, could incite his Army to greater Ardor than all the Drums of his Regiments; but he, unhappy Man! not long after, retired to his Home & *made himself away*, from future Service.[31]

INDIAN WARRIORS

Much hath been said, & many Exclamations thrown out, even in Parliament, by some popular Orators in the Opposition, against employing the Indians, to whom they gave the Appellation of, *Savages.* Savage is a convertible Term. It properly designated a Person who acts contrary to the Principles of Humanity: An Englishman who hath been educated in Rules of civil Society, may, by a certain Tenor of Conduct, contract a Savageness of Manners which may exceed any Action which an Indian hath been guilty of; as you may, by & by, see, if you please, in the Appendix. Every Nation hath something Peculiar in its Mode of War. An Indian prefers the Mode of fighting behind a Tree, or of skulking in Bushes. He prefers the Hatchet, the scalping Knife & the Tomahawk, to the Bayonet, the Sword & the Cutlass. His Weapons give, at least, as sudden, if not a less painfull Death, than the Englishman's Weapons. It is true, he doth not discover what is called english Courage, of standing undaunted in open Field to be shot at; he rather chuses to be safe in his own Person, whilst he destroys the Person of his Enemy; but this is all, the Custom of Particular Nations. If you incline to put him to Death in a painfull Manner, he will convince You, that he can undergo the most excruciating Torture, without a Groan. This perhaps would be called, by a civilized European, a *Savage Temper.* The Definition of Courage is arbitrary. As to taking the Scalp off a dead Man, it will not give any great Pain; & this is the Trophy of their Victory, which they return Home with as their Voucher; & as to any Damage it may do to a dead Person, it is of no more Consequence than taking off the Shirt of his Garment.

[31]By cutting his throat (Oliver's note).

This Scalping Business hath been encouraged, in the Colonies, for more than a Century past. Præmiums have been given, frequently, by the *Massachusetts* Assemblies, for the Scalps of Indians, even when they boasted loudest of their Sanctity; & I have seen a Vessell enter the Harbor of *Boston*, with a long String of hairy Indian Scalps strung to the rigging, & waving in the wind; but I never heared of an Englishmans scalping an Englishman, untill the Battle of *Lexington* told the savage Tale. And in the last Century, a War was waged with the Indian King *Philip*, who would have been equal to *Julius Cæsar* had their Education been equal. A certain Warrior had acquired a great & a just Fame in his Victories over the French & the Indians, & had hunted King *Philip* down at last; but his Enmity subsisted, after he had killed him; for he most shamefully cut off his Hand, to preserve it as a Trophy; & not contented with so mean a Revenge, he condescended, in a spitefull Manner to chop his backside with a Hatchet; insulting the dead, whilst in the Operation, with ignominious Language. This seemed to be done with the Air of savage Cowardice; as it doth not look fair to attack a Man behind; unless an Attack upon a dead Body will exculpate a Man from Cowardice. Whether King *Philip*, or the Province who employed this Warrior, found any Fault with this mean & base Transaction, the History is silent.

But let Opposition roar, as loud as they please, against the employing Indians in the present Contest with Rebellion; they cannot but remember, that Gen. *Amherst* employed them, under the Sanction of their late Patron, against the French of *Canada*; & surely, there cannot be a worse & baser Enemy than a Rebel, to whom the English Law has assigned the most ignominious Punishment. Besides, those very Men, whom the Opposition have encouraged in this Revolt, appointed a Committee to meet the *Iroquois*, or *Five Nations*, at *Albany*, in Order to engage them against their old Ally, *Great Britain*. Each Party met; &, agreeable to the ancient Custom of such Treaties, the Indians had the usual Frolick of the roasted Ox. The Parties then met upon their Business. The Commissioners proposed to the Indians, that they should join them against their Mother Country; but no Bribe was offered. The Indians were silent; the Convention was adjourned. The Blankets and other Presents were prepared against the next Meeting, to the Value of above £2000 Sterlg. The next Meeting came, according to appointment. The presents were made, & when the Indians had full possession of them, they made this Reply, vizt. "This is a Quarrell between Father &

Children; we shall not meddle with it." Thus were these notable Commissioners outwitted in Indian Cunning. But they profited of their Disappointment, for the *Saratoga* Convention will be a standing Witness of the Infidelity of an american rebel Treaty.

Another Example was set, for the Use of the scalping Knife, by these very Men; who never complained of the Use of it untill they were disappointed in their Aims to bring it into Fashion. There was a Tribe of Indians who lived about 150 Miles from *Boston*, at a Place called *Stockbridge*, who were incorporated with the English Settlers. These Indians were brought down into the Rebel Incampments near *Boston*. They would approach nigh to the british Lines, & there flourish their scalping Knives, & yell, by Way of Insult. But these new Allies did not continue, for any Length of Time, among them; they were too fond of Liquor; they grew troublesome to them; there was no Bush fighting to employ them in; & they were dismissed. Hence forward, let Patriotick Oratory & american Complaints, about the scalping Knife & Indian Savages, be controled by everlasting Silence.

VIII. COURSE OF THE REVOLUTION

In this Year *1775*, two Transactions of the Congress will render this Æra memorable in future History. One was, a Bead-roll of Addresses, to the King; to the People of *England*; to the People of *Ireland*; & to the Inhabitants of *Canada*. And not long after, they added a List of colonial Greivances, like ye. Rattles in the Tail of the Rattle Snake, in order to make the other Parts more formidable. The other Transaction was their Expedition to conquer Canada.

As to the first, they addressed his Majesty as an absolute Monarch, who had the Regulation of the State solely in his self. They fawned, they flattered, they were guilty of the most palpable Falshoods, they complained of his Ministers & his Parliament. What was something remarkable; this high & mighty Congress consisted of 52 Persons, & one fourth Part of them were Lawyers; yet this fourth Part, who ought to have known something of the English Constitution, contributed their Interest to address a King, who, in his political Capacity, was but one third Part of that Body politick which could redress their pretended Greivances; & these very Men sacrificed their Understandings, in Order to make themselves of Consequence in a Republick. His Majesty had too much good Sense, not to see into the natural Consequences of their Schemes, & was too much of a Patriot King to listen to them.

In their Addresses to the People of *England* & *Ireland*, they soothed them with dolefull, false Tales, of their Distresses from an arbitrary Government, & made such Representations of their Case, as that though they theirselves were the first Morsel that was to be devoured by the Tyrant *Polypheme*, yet it would soon come to the Turn of *England* & *Ireland* to be devoured also. They also interlarded their Addresses, as artfull Cooks do some Species of Fowls, with Dissertations upon Popery; representing the Views of Parliament to make the Realm & its Dominions to be a *Smithfield* of Fire & Faggots;[1] & warning *England* of its approaching Martyrdom. Every base & false Art was used to incite a Rebellion throughout the Realm, to keep Pace with that which they had raised in *America*; & they were well supported, by no ignoble Coadjutors, in *England*. But

[1]Smithfield was a place where executions were held outside the city boundaries of London.

there was something defective in the Automaton. Some of the Cogs of its Wheels did not play well into the others, so that it did not keep regular Time to the Satisfaction of the Congress. To make their Scheme more perfect, & to raise the Spirits of the Colonists, it was bruited throughout *America*, that the People in *England* were in Alarm on their behalf; that the Nation was bankrupt, & that Mr. *Wilkes*, with 100,000 Men at his Heels, was going to storm the Parliament House, & beseige *Windsor Castle*, to take the King as a Prisoner, & to do something else with him. All this was swallowed by wholesale, by their credulous Followers; & thus the Ball was kept up.

Let us now cast an Eye upon their Address to the popish Inhabitants of *Canada*. We do not find, in that, a Word about the Rags of Popery, about a *Smithfield* Fire, or an Inquisition Coach. No! God & Nature had made them free; they had a Right to exercise their own Religion, & to worship God according to their Consciences. But the English Nation were attempting to make Slaves of them all. Will Posterity beleive, that such a Compound of Absurdity, Weakness of Head, & infernal Wickedness of Heart, could be mixt by 52 Men, in whom was consolidated the Sense of thirteen united Colonies? They surely imagined, that no others would read their different Addresses, but those to whom they were addressed; but could an Hottentot have read them all, even *his* Stupidity would have classed them, on the List of errant Folly or knight Errant Villainy.

As to their after List of above 20 Articles of colonial Greivances, which they published to all *Europe*, it would be too tedious to enter into the Minutiae of them. Besides, they have been so compleatly answered, in two Treatises already published, & both in the Year 1776, vizt. one entitled, *Strictures upon the Declaration of the Congress*, by Govr. *Hutchinson*—the other entitled, *an Answer to the Declaration of the american Congress*, by *John Lind* Esqr., of the Temple;[2] that whoever would wish to know the true State of the Case, by adverting to these, will find such masterly Reasoning on the Subject, such a Developement of the Facts, such a Detection of Weakness & Malevolence, that if the Congress had consisted of ten Times the Number which composed it, their united Force could

---

[2] [Hutchinson], *Strictures upon the Declaration of the Congress at Philadelphia: In a Letter to a Noble Lord, &c* (London, 1776); [John Lind], *An Answer to the Declaration of the American Congress* (London, 1776).

not have supported their Cause against such Opponents; but they would have felt the force of that Maxim, *magna est Veritas, et prævalebit.*[3]

THE CONQUEST OF CANADA

The Expedition to *Canada* was as follows: & know all Men by those who were present at the Congress, that whilst the Clergy, by Prayers, fasting & preaching, were trying to move Heaven; & the Congress, by Addresses, were moving Earth, to bring an Accomodation with *Great Britain*; that this very Congress, with all the base Duplicity that the human Mind can be guilty of, at the same Moment formed this Expedition, to wrench *Canada* out of the Hands of the Mother Country. In Order to make sure of its Conquest, they formed two Armies; one to march by the Way of Lake *Champlain*, under the Command of General *Schuyler*, tho' General *Montgomery* was the Man who executed it: Colo. Benedict *Arnold* & Colo. *Ethan Allen* having previously scoured the Lake of what little british Force was upon it.

The other Army was to go up *Kennebeck River*, in the eastern Parts of the *Massachusetts* Province; & to be commanded by Colo. *Arnold*, who was to meet *Montgomery* at *Quebec*; the latter's Rout being by *Mon[t]real*, about 170 Miles above *Quebec*.

That the Conquest might be easier, Emissaries of popish Priests from *Maryland*, where they abounded, were sent forward to *Canada* amongst the french Settlers, to seduce them; this was no difficult Task, & it was effectuated. The Congress, who pretended to be such warm Sticklers against Popery, now made it evident, that they thought Evil might be committed, if they could squeeze any Advantage from it to answer their own Purposes.

Perhaps you would be willing to know the Characters of those who have been mentioned as the Conductors of this Expedition.

Schuyler was of Dutch Extract, of Albany.[4] He had served in the last War, in the Conquest of *Canada*, & had picked up in the Service, enough to make him a Man of Consequence.

Arnold had been a *Connecticut* Horse Jockey.[5] He had been in

[3]"Truth is mighty and will prevail."

[4]Philip John Schuyler (1733-1804) was a delegate to the Continental Congress in 1775 and served in the revolutionary army.

[5]Benedict Arnold (1741-1801) was born at Norwich, Conn., and saw service as a volunteer in the French and Indian War. For a time he was a druggist and bookseller at New Haven and invested his money in the business of selling horses and mules to West Indian plantation owners.

Canada, as well as other Places, purchasing Horses for shipping to the *West Indies*, & for other Purposes. He was a bold, daring Man, & calculated for any arduous Enterprize: & for such Purposes, only, he was held in any Estimation.

Ethan Allen was of *Connecticut* also; of a bad Character, & had been guilty of Actions bad enough to forfeit even a good one.[6] He was brave, but unprincipled; & after he had been a Prisoner in *Canada*, sent to *England* in Irons, as a Rebel, & afterwards dismissed, he openly acknowledged, when he was at *Falmouth*, that it was indifferent to him for whom he fought; whether the King of *Great Britain*, the King of *Spain* or for *America*; they who would give him the best Pay should have his Service. He went to *New York*, & was on his Parole of Honor; but soon broke it, & left the Peices of it with the british General, who might have known, that a Man who possesses no Honor can neither give or lose any. This Man afterwards collected a Number of Adherents, & settled a District to the northward of *New York*, called *Vermont*; which he maintained against the Power of the Congress, whom he brought into a great Dilemma, as that Tract of Land was in Dispute between two of the 13 Stripes; & they were loth to disoblige either of the contending Parties. However, the matter now is *sub silentio*, since *Ethan Allen* has lately broke his Parole of Honor with *them*, & gone over to the King's Garrison at *Ticonderoga*; carrying with him a large Number of Men. This Man seems to be so overstocked with Honor, that there will never be an End of its Dissipation.

General *Montgomery* seems to have possessed an amiable Character.[7] He certainly exhibited one, of great bravery. He had formerly served in the british Army, wth. great Reputation, but having sold his Commission, he married into a Dutch republican Family, in *New York* Government, & imbibed a large portion of that Spirit so inimical to the British Constitution, that whoever is under the Influence of it, as rapidly runs into Rebellion as the *Gadarene* Swine did into the Lake; & very often, too, meet with the same or a similar Fate; for what the Sea refuses the Gallows accepts of.

[6]Ethan Allen (1738-89), born in Litchfield, Conn., was captured in the Canadian expedition of 1775. He was exchanged as a prisoner in 1778 and was recommissioned by George Washington. His negotiations with the British during 1780 compromised his reputation as a patriot.

[7]Richard Montgomery (1738-75) was Irish born and educated. A British army officer until 1772, he saw service in the battles of the Seven Years' War and was a member of the House of Commons. He came to America in 1772 and soon married Janet, the daughter of Robert R. Livingston.

Montgomery set out from *Albany* in August 1775, with 1100 Men. *Schuyler* afterwards followed with another large Body, but he himself soon left the Army to the Care of *Montgomery*. On the 13th. of November, *Mon[t]real* surrendered. On the 30th. of November, *Montgomery* sailed from *Mon[t]real*, with about 1500 Men, & arrived before *Quebec* on the 5th. December, where he met *Arnold*.

Arnold left the rebel Camp at *Cambridge* on the 13th. September, with about 11 or 1200 Men; he embarqued at *Newbury Port* for *Quenebeck* River, & went up the River as far as the Batteaux could go; having, with great Labor, transported his Provisions & Batteaux, by Portages occasioned by many Falls; & arrived at *Point Levy*, opposite to *Quebec*, on the 11th. Novr. About 200 of his Men left him soon after he had entred the River *Quenebeck*; some by Reason of Sickness, & others through Dread of approaching Hardships: so that what by Deaths & Desertions he had not conducted to *Point Levy* above two thirds of the Army he set out with. This Expedition was a most extraordinary Instance of Rapidity, Resolution & Perseverance. And this very Man hath, in *January* last, given another Instance of Courage & Conduct, in the Kings Service, by burning, destroying & capturing, the Rebel Magazines of Provisions, war Stores and Vessells up the Bay of *Chesepeak* in *Virginia*; tho' not with so great Risque & Fatigues as what he met with in reaching *Quebec*; for here were Mountains to be climbed; Rivers to be forded; Hunger to be grappled with, to such Degree that they were obliged to eat their Dogs & the Leather of their Shoes. Almost impenetrable Forests were to be forced; & every Obstacle, that the Wildness of Nature could throw in their Way, was to be surmounted; insomuch, that it was scarcely to be parallelled in the Records of History, but by *Xenophons* Retreat out of *Persia*.

On 31st. December *Quebec* was attacked by *Montgomery* & *Arnold*. The Matter was soon determined. *Montgomery* lost his Life, & *Arnold* was wounded in his Ankle; & thus ended the Congress Expedition, on which they founded the warmest Expectations. The whole of this Expedition is minutely & faithfully related, in a Publication, entitled, *The History of the civil War in America*, wrote *by an Officer of the Army*,[8] who was in *America* about that Time; in which is given a Detail of Facts from the Year 1765 to the quitting

[8]*The History of the Civil War in America … 1775, 1776, and 1777. By an Officer of the Army* (London, 1780).

of *Philadelphia* by the british Army in 1778. It is sensibly wrote, & the Facts are faithfully related; & it is well worth adverting to for Information.

THE SIEGE OF BOSTON

I shall now leave the Congress at *Philadelphia*, & return to *Boston*, if I can get a Passport through the Rebel Army, which every day blockades the Town closer than the preceeding. I must leave all the Delicacies that so important a Body of men are epicurizing upon, & return to my former Fare of coarse Salt Beef on one day, & upon nothing the next; but which to give the Preference to, I am at a loss. If I can be excused from Shells & Shot, I shall be content with the latter, for they are much harder of Digestion, than nothing at all.

In the Autumn of *1775*, difficulties increased upon the British Troops & the Inhabitants, in *Boston*, whilst the rebel Army increased in Resources of Men & Stores, of which they had a full supply. Many Vessells, which were coming from *England* & *Ireland*, with Provisions & Stores for the Army & for the Inhabitants, were captured within a few Leagues of *Boston*; and the Rebels Vessells arrived safe with Supplies for *them*. Genl. *Gage* embarqued for *England* in October, & left the Command of the Civil, or rather no Government, to the Care of Lieut. Governor *Oliver*;[9] & of the Army to General *Howe*.

It was rather Astonishing, that so many Vessells should be captured, & so near to so many King's Ships; when a great Part of them might have been saved. For, at a Place called *Salem*, within 3 or 4 hours Sail from *Boston*, & another Place, vizt. *Newbury*, at abt 7 or 8 Hours Sail from *Boston*, were hauled up 7 or 800 Vessells of various Sorts, which might have been easily taken or destroyed. Had this been done, their privateering Resources of rigging & Sails would have been ‘destroyed, for some Time at least. Besides, those two Towns of *Salem* & *Newbury* were deep in Rebellion, & if they too had been destroyed, such Destruction might have been justified on the common Principles of War, & of Humanity also; for had such Measures been taken at first, there is the highest Probability that thousands of Lives would have been saved, as well as enormous Expences of Treasure, to both *England* & *America*. But the Plea then was; that if such Measures were pursued, it would irritate the

---

[9]Thomas Oliver (1734-1815) was no relation of Peter and Andrew Oliver. Thomas became lieutenant governor in 1774. Kenneth B. Murdock, "Lieutenant Governor Thomas Oliver, 1734-1815," *Pubs. of the Colonial Soc. of Mass.*, XXVIII (1935), 37-66.

Americans & make them desperate. Those who have made this Plea have lived to see the Erroneousness of their Calculations; & that ill-judged Lenity & a Forbearance to irritate have thrown Rebellion into the utmost Desperation. In short, it seemed to be the Business, of Navy & Army, to help each other in doing nothing, except parrying of the Knife which was held to their Throats; without disabling the Hand, which held it, from Execution.

In the Winter of *1775*, the severe cold Northwest Winds blew off the Coasts several Vessells with Troops & Provisions, that were transporting Relief for the Garrison at *Boston*; and the Rebels had received such Supplies of Ammunition, so as to be ready for an Attack on the Opening of the Spring. It was expected that they would have made an Attack, upon the Ice, which surrounded the Town in the Depth of Winter. The Soldiers of their Army expected it, & the chief Men of their civil Government expressed their Uneasiness to Mr. *Washington* that he did not suffer it; when he told them that he had scarce a Round of Powder to a Man; but they soon had a Supply after the Severity of Winter was over, & then they began upon Exertions to drive off the Kings Troops from their strong Holds.

There was an Hill, called *Foster's Hill* on *Dorchester's* Neck, to the South East of *Boston*, across an Arm of the Sea, & within point blank Shot of the Town; from whence only, it seemed that the Town could be greatly annoyed. It had often been wished that this Hill had had proper Attention paid to it; & it had been repeatedly mentioned, that it was of the last Necessity to secure such a Position; but the general Answers were, that there was no Danger from it, & that it was to be wished that the Rebels would attempt to take Possession of it, as they could soon be dislodged—We shall presently see how wise those military Calculations were.

There was another Hill, a little to the Southward of *Foster's Hill*, still higher; a Redoubt upon which, with a small Force, would have been tenable against a very large Army of so undisciplined Troops as surrounded the Town: but perhaps it was against the Rules of War to have fortified either of those Hills. We are now to see the Consequences of such Conduct.

The Weather now opening, to begin military Operations, the Rebels mustered between 20 & 30,000 Men: about 10 or 11,000 of whom began to throw up Works on the last mentioned Hill. This being observed from *Boston*, Genl. *Howe* determined to attack them. Accordingly he ordered a Corps of about 1700 Men to embark in large Vessells & Boats, to cross the Water, to attack them; he himself designing to march by Land to flank them, with another Corps. The first Corps were embarqued & sailed; but a most severe Storm arising at South, some of these Vessells grounded, & a Retreat was ordered. It was an happy Disappointment, for had the Attack been made, this steep Hill must have been climbed with Musquetry only; & the Rebels had placed Rocks & large Stones on the Top of it, to roll down & break the Ranks of the Kings Troops, whilst they theirselves were discharging their Balls at them. I have no doubt but the Kings Troops would have defeated the Rebels; but it would have been another *Bunker's Hill* affair; the Carnage would have been great, & Men could not have been so well spared as then; & after so many of them had been used up, there were no Resources for a Recruit. Thus this Expedition failed.

The Month of March 1776 opened with a new Scene. The Rebels had waited long enough for the King's Troops to fortifie *Foster's Hill*; & since they would not do it, the Rebels thought it a Pity so fine a Situation should not be occupied, and so fortified it theirselves. It was done thus! They had prepared a large Timber Battery, in seperate Pieces, as also a large Quantity of screwed Hay to fill between the Timbers when they were put together. There was no Suspicion of such a Battery being in Preparation, untill after a long dark Night it arose in full View, & began to play upon the Town. It was now Time for the Troops in Town to make the best Terms for theirselves, & to get off as fast as they could; for in vain would they have fired to destroy this Battery, made of Wood & Hay; they might have fired at it 'till this Day & would have made but little Impression. Although the Weather was cool, yet the Town was hot enough; for the Rebels kept up an incessant Fire with Shells & Shot into it, for 6 successive Nights; but, to the astonishment of all, with scarcely any Damage.

Affairs being in this Situation, & Genl. *Howe* having had Orders from Home to evacuate *Boston*, he gave Notice to Genl. *Washington* of such his Purpose; informing him, that if he would suffer him to embark unmolested that he would not injure the Town; otherwise, that he would lay it in Ashes. Some of the Rebels were for suffering the Town to be demolished; but there being so many good Buildings & so much Treasure in it, the major Part prevailed, & his Proposal was complied with. Immediately all Hands were at Work for evacuation; & the Cathartick was of so drastick a Nature, that by the 17th. of the Month, *Boston* was emptied of it's late Inhabitants, & a new Generation supplied their Places. Notwithstanding of the great Assiduity in embarking, Genl. *Howe* was obliged to leave many valuable Stores behind him.

The Destruction of that fine Fortress, *Castle William,* took up about a Week; & on the 20th. of March it was finished.[10] On the 27th. the last Division of the Fleet of Troops & Inhabitants sailed from *Nantasket* road, about 9 Miles from *Boston,* & on the 2nd. of April arrived at *Hallifax.*

[There were] Vast Numbers of the Inhabitants of *Boston* & of those who had fled thither, as to an Asylum, from the Cruelties of Rebellion. Many Loyalists were left behind, who had nothing to support them from their Homes; & many, who had Families which they were loth should be separated, as there was not Transports for all who would have been willing to have embarked. These were obliged to take their Chances of ill Usage, & some of them felt it severely; particularly six Gentlemen of good Reputation. One of these six, in particular, was used in a strictly diabolical Manner; he was a Loyalist, but an inoffensive one in his Behavior; he had an amiable Wife & several amiable Children; the Rebel Cart, in Imitation of the Inquisition Coach, called at his Door in the Morning, & they ordered him into the Cart, not suffering him to take his Hat with him; his Wife, at the same Time, begging on her Knees, to spare her Husband; & his Daughters crying, with Intreaties. This infernal Crew were deaf to the Cries of Distress, & drove on, untill they had got the six into the Cart; whom they carried to the Kings Lines, at the extreme Part of the Town, & there tipped up the Cart, & tumbled them into a Ditch; & not content with this diabolical Barbarity, they forbad their entring the Town again; & at the same Time, also, forbad the People in the Country to give them Food or to shelter them. Step forward thou *Iroquois* Savage! & drop *your* Tear of Humanity over this horrid Scene of Barbarity, perpetrated in a Town which for many, very many Years past, hath boasted of the Sanctity of Christianity!

It is in vain to plead Excuse, that this & many other like Diabolical Cruelties were acted by Mohawks, or the Rabble: they, & this also,

[10]Oliver went aboard the *Pacific* on March 10, 1776, but the ship did not leave the harbor until March 21, giving Oliver the opportunity of seeing Castle William blown up by the retreating British: "The blowing up of the Castle Walls continued: and at night all the combustible part of the Castle was fired. The conflagration was the most pleasingly dreadful that I ever beheld: sometimes it appeared like the eruption of Mount Etna. . . ." *The Diary and Letters of . . . Thomas Hutchinson . . . ,* ed. Peter Orlando Hutchinson (London, 1884-86), II, 47.

were transacted in open Day, that the Sun & the civil Government might be Witnesses to the horrid Deeds, but Heaven, in this Instance, interposed, & inspired into the Hearts of some People in the Country so much Humanity, as to save these unhappy Sufferers from meeting the cruel Deaths assigned to them by their Persecutors, and even a Colo. of a rebel Regiment, who was quartered near the Town, was so roused wth. a compassionate Resentment, that he succoured them; & declared to his Employers, that if such Inhumanity was suffered, he would resign his Commission & quit their cause.

A FINAL REVIEW OF THE REBELLION

I have now Sir! finished my Narrative of the *american Rebellion*. I have brought it down to the Æra I first proposed to myself. I have confined it chiefly to the Province of the *Massachusetts Bay*; although I have now & then made an Excursion to some of the other british Colonies. What relates to this Rebellion, after the evacuation of *Boston*, I must refer you to authentick Documents, which have been published, according to the Series of Transactions wch. have occurred since that Time. My intent was to elucidate the original, as well as the occasional Causes, which tended to stimulate the Seeds of this Rebellion to a progressive Vegetation. If I have thrown any Light upon the Subject, I shall be pleased in having executed my Intention. The Narrative hath been Lengthy. I wish it may not have been tedious to You. Many of the Shades of the Portraits, both of Persons & Times, I confess are very dark: that is not my Fault. My Business was to draw true Portraits. If Nature hath been distorted by the wild Freaks of the various human Passions, neither she or I ought to be blamed. If she had been suffered to proceed in her own Operations, I should have been saved the Trouble of relating such disagreeable Facts; & you Sir! would have escaped the Chagrin of reading them. Upon a Review of this Narrative, I am not conscious of the least Exaggeration—to a Man at Ease, & unacquainted with the Deformity of the human Mind; it might appear all Exaggeration where Deformity is depictured; but I have adhered strictly to what I esteemed to be Truth. Many of the Facts I was personally acquainted with, & others I have the best Authorities for; such Authorities, which I would give almost equal Credence to Facts, as to my own Knowledge of them. Such Facts of Consequence, as have occurred to my Memory, of Importance to be related, I have thrown out to you. Many disagreeable *Minutiæ* I have omitted, &

should have been better pleased to have thrown a Veil over the whole, had not the *fiat Justitia, ruat Cælum* stimulated me to give the Truth, & nothing but the Truth.[11] I hope the Distortions of Nature will not put either of us out of Conceit with Nature herself, but put both of us upon following one of her most usefull Dictates, that of pitying those whom we are obliged, in justice to Mankind, to blame.

Let me detain You a few Minutes longer, in reviewing the Subject. We have seen Englishmen quitting their *Natale Solum,*[12] to migrate into a new & distant Country, under the Pretence of enjoying, that unalienable Right of all Mankind, the Liberty of worshipping *God* according to the Dictates of their own Consciences. We have seen their Solemn Declarations, of their most sincere Affection to the *Church of England*, in the Pale of which they were born & nurtured, and we have seen, too, their sudden Defection from, & discontinuance of, that very Church, as well as the Persecution of their Bretheren who differed from them in religious Sentiment.

We have seen a Set of Men favored with the Liberty & Charter Grant of an extended Country, under ye. Auspices of the english Government; & protected by it; but under an Obligation to conform to such Regulations as should be made by its Authority. We have seen these new Settlers, for a long Series of Years, paying all due Deference to those Regulations, as stipulated in their Charter. We have seen them also rising, by easy Gradations, to such a State of Prosperity & Happiness as was almost enviable, but we have seen them also run mad with too much Happiness, & burst into an open Rebellion against that Parent, who protected them (upon their most earnest Entreaties & humble Solicitations) against the Ravages of their Enemies. This, in private Life would be termed, base Ingratitude; but Rebellion hath sanctified it by the Name of, Self Defence— and why is the sudden Transition made, from Obedience to Rebellion, but to gratifye the Pride, Ambition & Resentment, of a few abandoned Demagogues, who were lost to all Sense of Shame & of Humanity? The generality of the People were not of this Stamp; but they were weak, & unversed in the Arts of Deception. The Leaders of the Faction deceived the Priests, very few of whom but were as ignorant as the People; & the Wheel of Enthusiasm was set on going, & its constant Rotation set the Peoples Brains on Whirling; & by a certain centrifugal Force, all the Understanding which the

[11]"Let justice be done, though Heaven should fall."

[12]"Native soil, native country."

People had was whirled away, as well as that of the Clergy; & a Vacuum was left for *Adams*, & his *Posse* to crowd in what Rubbish would best serve their Turn.

The Ingratitude of this Rebellion must appear in a most striking Point of View, when it is considered, that *Great Britain*, (the Parent State) had given her Millions, in Bounties, to encourage the Growth & Produce of her Plantations. Nay she had discouraged the raising some Articles within the Realm, particularly *Tobacco*, in order that her Dominions might monopolize the Growth of it. She gave Bounties also upon Pitch, Tar, Deals, &ca. And she had expended many more Millions, in defending the Colonies against the Incursions & Conquests of their as well as of her Enemies; & the *Massachusetts Province*, in particular, where this Rebellion began, had often felt the strongest Instances of a Parent's Regard & Tenderness. This Province had for many Years groaned under the Incursions of various Tribes of Indians, who were instigated by the french Government of *Canada* to break up the english Settlements, & murder the Inhabitants of them; insomuch, that the french Governor of *Canada*, *Monsieur Vaudreil*, had a large Room hung round with English Scalps, with which he frequently insulted the English; agreeable to the Politeness of a french Barbarian. Those Incursions of the Indians, who were headed by french Partizans, grew intolerable. The *Massachusetts*, in the Year 1745, undertook the Risque & the greatest Part of the Expence of conquering *Cape Breton*.[13] The Charges were so great, that they theirselves thought, that if the Expedition failed it would compleat their Ruin—by a *numine favente*[14] it succeeded, & *great Britain* reimbursed their Charges, by remitting them in Mexico Dollars; with which they redeemed their most infamous fallacious Paper Currency, similar to the present Congress Paper Dollars; & instated them in Peace & Plenty.[15]

In about 10 Years after, a new War, between *Great Britain* & *France* broke out—the french Government were determined to avenge themselves on the *New England* Governments, for the af-

[13]Richard W. Van Alstyne, *The Rising American Empire* (Oxford, 1960), pp. 1-27; Schutz, "Imperialism in Massachusetts during the Governorship of William Shirley, 1741-1756," *Huntington Library Quarterly*, XXIII (1960), 221-225.

[14]"Fortune favoring."

[15]Hutchinson used his vast political power, in association with that of Governor William Shirley, to force a sound currency through the legislature. Some politicians never forgave Hutchinson for this action. Malcolm Freiberg, "Thomas Hutchinson and the Province Currency," *New England Quarterly*, XXX (1957), 195-208.

front offered by them in the Capture of *Cape Breton* in the last War. These Governments were in the greatest Anxiety & Alarm; they Petitioned the Parent State, in the most suppliant Terms, for Aid against their Enemies; they represented their Danger in the most piteous Accents. Their Prayers & Supplications were heard. They acknowledged their Dependance upon the best Government existing upon Earth. In Consequence of their Intreaties & from a Sense of the Importance of the Cause, *Great Britain*, if I may so term it, threw away 50 Millions more, & conquered *Canada*, with all its Dependencies; & *America*, was liberated from her fears of her old perfidious Enemies.

Such a Liberation, it might have been reasonably thought, would have inspired the Colonists with the warmest Sense of Gratitude & Respect to their Benefactor. It was rather the Reverse. The Faction (for there was always a Faction in the *Massachusetts* Province, particularly in *Boston*) seemed to exult in the general Joy; but they exulted also that they had got rid of a formidable Enemy, who stood in their Way of entering the List with *Great Britain*. They rendered it an Affair of little Consequence to them, & boasted of their great Efforts in furnishing so many Men for the Conquest, as they had sent to join the british Troops. It is true, that this Province did send great Numbers of Men, but they served little other Purposes, but to assist the british Army in Camp Labours & scouting Parties; for as to the fighting Part of the Business, *Canada* might have rested in Peace from any Fear of them: and it was but two Years before the Conquest of it, that the French General *Montcalm* was making his Inroads on these *New England* Governments, with but 4000 Men; when this very Province, consisting of above 40,000 fighting Men, were in so great Consternation, when the french General was above 150 Miles from *Boston*, that publick Orders were just upon being issued, to drive all the Cattle in, & bring off or destroy the Carriages. This boasted Supply of Men was of great Service to the Province; for the Pay of them & the Supply of Provisions & other Necessaries for the Army, added to the general Stock of Wealth: & Silver & Gold were so plenty among the lower Degrees, that I have known Men, who, before these Campaigns, might have searched their Pockets in vain all Day for an half Penny, & could now shew & brag of their *Dollars* & their *Johannes*. Now the Faction said, that they did not care if the French had it again; & this they said, because they knew that they could not have it again—and there were many Loyalists, who wished the same Thing, but from a different Principle.

They saw the Buds of the present Rebellion began to swell. They had exerted theirselves in the Subdual of *Canada*, not weighing the Consequences of it; 'till it was too late. They now saw, that had *Canada* remained in the Hands of its former Possessors, it would have been attended with less ill Consequence than what was likely to ensue upon the Conquest of it: & it is now apparent, that had that been the Case, the present Rebellion might have remained in Embrio, untill some future Age had brought it into publick Existence.

The Congress, in *1776*, published their Declaration of Independence. The Minority, or Opposition in Parliament said, that the Ministry had drove them into it by Oppression, & that Oppression would make a wise Man mad. The Faction in *America* seem to have made Dupes of all they had to do with. They duped the Clergy, they duped the People & they duped the wise Men of *Gotham* in *England*. If these wise Men disown ye. Shame of being duped by an American, they must take the Shame of being the Betrayers of their Country, by encouraging them to the bold Stroke which they have struck for Independence. The Alternative is in their Choice. But they are mistaken in their Fact. Independence, it is true, was declared in Congress in 1776, but it was settled in *Boston*, in 1768, by *Adams* & his Junto. I have Authority for this Assertion; the Authority of a Gentleman who was tampered with by the aforementioned Major Genl. *Warren*, who was a most active Man among the Faction. *Warren* was in Hopes to take this Gentleman into their Number, & laid open their whole Scheme. He told him that "Independence was their Object; that it was supposed that *great Britain* would resent it & would lay the Town of *Boston* in Ashes, from their Ships; that an Estimate had accordingly been made of the Value of the Estates in Town; & that they had determined to pay the Losses of their Friends from the Estates of the Loyalists in the Country." The Gentleman refused to join with them, but *Warren* replied, that they would pursue their Scheme. This Scheme was not divulged to the People, for had it been generally communicated to the People, I beleive, they would, *then*, have been shocked at the Proposal; although they have, since that, had the Changes of Popery & Slavery so often rung in their Ears, that they are now reconciled to it.

As to the Effrontery of the Congress, in publishing so many false Facts to the World, it is evidential of Foreheads capped with Brass & Hearts lined with Steel. Their Arguments of Defence have been often confuted by able Pens, upon the Principles of Government in general, & the english Constitution in particular; & their Falsity of Facts, as frequently detected. The Issue hath been, that a fine Country, like the Land of *Canaan*, flowing with Milk & Hony, is turned into a dreary Wilderness, enstamped with Vestiges of War, Famine & Pestilence.[16] The Inhabitants of this Country bewailing the Loss of *70 or 80,000* Thousands of their Friends and Neighbors by Sword & Pestilence. And instead of their usual Happiness, of sitting under their own Vines & Figtrees in Peace, [they are] now constantly terrified by the Din of Arms, & [are] groaning under the Weight of *60 or 70* Millions Sterg. Taxes, which scarce any thing can redeem them from but the kind Hand of Death. And all these Distresses they have been plunged into, by an *Otis*, an *Adams*, a *Franklin*, & a few others of the most abandoned Characters, aided by a Set of Priests, who are a Disgrace to Christianity, & would have been the Opprobrium of even Mahometism. And let me add that this Rebellion would never have come to its present Maturity, by all the Efforts that could have been made by any or all of the factious Colonists, as there were Loyalists among them, sufficient in Numbers, Sense & Virtue who could have banked out the Inundation, but a most detestable Opposition offered & lent their Aid to encourage it. An Opposition in *England*, compounded of all Orders & Degrees: the Merchants from a View to gain; the Clergy from a View to introduce Republicanism; the Orators from a View to Popularity & to distress Administration; & as they had behaved with Infamy when they were *in*, so they were determined to retain their Characters now they were *out*. Majesty hath been insulted. The most amiable, benevolent & Patriot Sovereign hath been treated with that Contempt which a private Subject would not have past unnoticed. Every Species of Chicane hath been practised, to distress, & to subvert the Foundations of a Government, which hath long been the Admiration and Envy of Foreigners; & have brought it so near the Verge of Ruin, as to set Fire to the Metropolis of *Europe, London*, which had almost involved it in a general Conflagration, that would have plunged the Nation into Bankruptcy: & after all, some of those very Men complaining of the Exercise of that military Force which, alone, suppressed the Fury of the Flames. Besides these Efforts, they have drove two Millions of happy Colonists to the Precipice of almost irremediable Ruin; & have so changed the Temper of their

[16]These words are omitted from the Huntington Library copy of the manuscript.

Minds, as exactly conforms to the Character of the *Jews*; of which the following Lines of *Dryden*; in his *Absalom & Achitophel*, are so descriptive, vizt.

The *Jews*, a head strong, moody, murmuring Race,
As ever tried th' extent & stretch of Grace:
God's pamper'd People, whom, debauch'd with Ease,
No King could govern, nor no *God* could please.
These *Adam*—Wits, too fortunately free,
Began to dream they wanted Liberty,
And when no Rule, no Precedent was found,
Of Men, by Laws less circumscrib'd & bound;
They led their wild Desires to Woods & Caves,
And thought that all but Savages were Slaves.
Those very *Jews*, who at their very best,
Their Humour, more than Loyalty exprest,
Now wonder'd, why so long they had obey'd
An Idol Monarch, which their Hands had made;
Thought they might ruin him they could create,
Or melt him to that golden *Calf*, a State.
The sober Part of *Israel*, free from Stain,
Well knew the Value of a peacefull Reign;
And looking backward with a wise Affright,
Saw Seams of Wounds, dishonest to the Sight;
In Contemplation of whose ugly Scars,
They curst the Memory of civil Wars.
For *David's* Mildness manag'd it so well,
The bad had no Occasion to rebel.
But when to Sin our byass'd Nature leans,
The carefull Devil is still at Hand with Means;
And providently pimps for ill Desires;
The good old Cause reviv'd, a Plot requires.[17]

[17]The "good old Cause" was a Whig euphemism that justified the cause of liberty against tyranny and implied the legality of armed resistance against tyrants. The phrase was used by the Whig martyr Algernon Sidney on Dec. 7, 1683, as a climax of his speech from the scaffold: "Grant [O Lord!] that I may die Glorifying Thee for all Thy mercies; and that at the last Thou hast permitted me to be singled out as a Witness of thy Truth; and even by the Confession of my Opposers, for that OLD CAUSE in which I was from my Youth engaged; and for which thou hast Often and Wonderfully declared thyself." An account of the popularity of Sidney in revolutionary America can be found in Caroline Robbins, *The Eighteenth-Century Commonwealthman* (Cambridge, Mass., 1959), pp. 45 ff. For John Dryden the old cause was the original sin of disobedience instigated by the Devil, and so with William Baron, *Regicides: No Saints nor Martyrs* (London, 1700), pp. 8, 16, 27.

> Plots, true or false, are necessary Things,
> To raise up Commonwealth & ruin Kings.[18]

I have now finished, & as I have wrote with a *currente Calamo*,[19] I can see many Faults in the Mode, which I have not Leisure to correct but none in the Substance. Perhaps you will see more in the former than I do. These I submit to your Candor for Excuse. As to the Substance, I neither ask Pardon of You or myself, as I am not conscious of any Disguise of Truth in the Relation of Facts.

If I have given You Information, my End is answered. It is what you desired, & what I have aimed at. If you are pleased, it will give a particular Satisfaction to him who assures You, that he is

Sir!

Your faithfull Friend
& humble Servant.

T–W–Esqr.

---

[18]*The Works of John Dryden*, ed. Saintsbury, IX, 232-233, ll. 45-48, 51-56, 61-66, 69-74, 77-84.

[19]"Offhand, informally." Literally, "with a running pen."

OLIVER'S APPENDIX

Exhibiting a few, out of the many, very innocent Frolicks of Rebellion, especially in the Province of *Massachusetts Bay*.[1]

1774 August —

A Mob in *Berkshire* assembled, & forced the Justices of the Court of common Pleas from their Seats on the Bench, and shut up the Court House, preventing any Proceedings at Law. At the same Time driving one of his Majesty's Justices of the Peace from his Dwelling House, so that he was obliged to repair to *Boston* for Protection by the Kings Troops.

At *Taunton* also, about 40 Miles from *Boston*, the Mob attacked the House of *Daniel Leonard* Esqr., one of his Majesty's Justices of the Peace; & a Barrister at Law. They fired Bullets into the House, & obliged him to fly from it to save his Life.

A Colo. *Gilbert*, a Man of Distinction & a firm Loyalist, living at *Freetown*, about 50 Miles from *Boston*, being absent about 20 Miles from his Home, was attacked by a Mob of above an 100 Men, at Midnight. But being a Man of great Bravery & Strength, he, by his single Arm, beat them all off. And on the same Night, & at the same Place, Brigadier *Ruggles*, a distinguished Friend of Government, & for many Years a Member of the general Assembly, was attacked by the same Mob; but by his firm Resolution he routed them all. They, in Revenge, cut his Horses Tail off & painted him all over. The Mob found that Paint was cheaper than Tar and Feathers.

September 1774.

The Attorny General, *Mr. Sewall*,[2] living at *Cambridge*, was obliged to repair to *Boston* under the Protection of the King's Troops. His House at *Cambridge* was attacked by a Mob, his Windows broke, & other Damage done; but by the Intrepidity of some young Gentlemen of the Family, the Mob were dispersed.

[1]Most of these reports of disasters were taken from the Boston *Weekly News-Letter*, Feb. 23, 1775.

[2]Jonathan Sewall was the nephew of Stephen Sewall, the chief justice of the Superior Court whom Thomas Hutchinson succeeded in 1760.

About the same Time *Thomas Oliver* Esqr. the Lieut. Govr. of *Massachusetts* Province, was attacked in his House at *Cambridge*, by a Mob of 4000 Men; & as he had lately been appointed, by his Majesty, one of the new Council, they forced him to resign that Office; but this Resignation did not pacify the Mob; he was soon forced to fly to *Boston* for Protection. This Mob was not mixed with tag, rag & Bobtail only, Persons of Distinction in the Country were in the Mass, & as the Lieut. Governor was a Man of Distinction, he surely ought to be waited upon by a large Cavalcade & by Persons of Note.

In this Month, also, a Mob of 5000 collected at *Worcester*, about 50 Miles from *Boston*, a thousand of whom were armed. It being at the Time when the Court of Common Pleas was about sitting, the Mob made a lane, & compelled ye. Judges, Sheriff, & Gentlemen of the Bar, to pass & repass them, Cap in Hand, in the most ignominious Manner; & read their Disavowall of holding Courts under the new Acts of Parliament, no less than Thirty Times in the Procession.

Brigadier *Ruggles*'s House at *Hardwicke*, about 70 Miles from *Boston*, was also plundered of his Guns, & one of his fine Horses poisoned.[3]

Colo. *Phips*, the high Sheriff of *Middlesex*, was obliged to promise not to serve any Processes of Courts; & retired to *Boston* for Protection.

A Committee, with a Justice *Aikin* at their Head, & a large Mob at their Heels, met at *Taunton* aforesaid, at Term Time, & forbid the Court of Common Pleas to sit.

Peter Oliver Esqr., a Justice of the Peace at *Middleborough*, was obliged by the Mob to sign an Obligation not to execute his Office under the new Acts. At the same Place, a Mr. *Silas Wood*, who had signed a Paper to disavow the riotous Proceedings of the Times, was dragged by a Mob of 2 or 300 Men about a Mile to a River, in Order to drown him; but one of his Children hanging around him with Cries & Tears, he was induced to recant, though, even then, very reluctantly.

The Mob at *Concord*, about 20 Miles from *Boston*, abused a Deputy Sheriff of *Middlesex*, & compelled him, on Pain of Death, not to

[3]Timothy Ruggles (1711-95) had risen as a soldier in the French and Indian War to the rank of brigadier general. As a Loyalist he was forced to leave Massachusetts in 1775 and spent his later life in Nova Scotia.

execute the Precepts for a new Assembly; they making him pass through a Lane of them, sometimes walking backwards, & sometimes forward, Cap in Hand, & they beating him.

Revd. Mr. *Peters*, of *Hebron* in *Connecticut*, an Episcopalian Clergyman, after having his House broke into by a Mob, & being most barbarously treated in it, was script of his Canonicals, & carried to one of their Liberty Poles, & afterwards drove from his Parish. He had applied to Governor *Trumble* & to some of the Magistrates, for Redress; but they were as relentless as the Mob; & he was obliged to go to *England* incognito, having been hunted after, to the Danger of his Life.

William Vassall Esqr., a Man of Fortune, and quite inoffensive in his publick Conduct, tho' a Loyalist, was travelling with his Lady from *Boston* to his Seat at *Bristol*, in *Rhode Island* Government, about 60 Miles from *Boston*, & were pelted by the Mob in *Bristol*, to the endangering of their Lives.

All the *Plimouth* Protestors against Riots, as also all the military Officers, were compelled by a Mob of 2000 Men collected from that County & the County of *Barnstable* to recant & resign their military Commissions. Although the Justices of the Peace were then sitting in the Town of *Plimouth*, yet the Mob ransack'd the House of a Mr. *Foster*, a Justice of the Court of Common Pleas, a Man of 70 Years of Age, which obliged him to fly into the Woods to secrete himself, where he was lost for some Time and was very near to the loosing of his Life. Afterwards, they deprived him of his Business, & would not suffer him to take the Acknowledgment of a Deed.

A Son of one of the *East India* Companies Agents being at *Plimouth* collecting Debts, a Mob roused him, in the Night, & he was obliged to fly out of the Town; but ye. Midnight favoured his Escape.

December 1774

A *Jesse Dunbar*, of *Hallifax*, in the County of *Plimouth*, an honest Drover, had bought a fat Ox of one of his Majesty's new Council, & carried it to *Plimouth* for sale. The Ox was hung up & skinned. He was just upon quartering it, when the Town's Committee came to the Slaughter House, & finding that the Ox was bought of one of the new Councellors, they ordered it into a Cart, & then put *Dunbar* into the Belly of the Ox and carted him 4 Miles, with a Mob around him, when they made him pay a Dollar after taking three other Cattle & an Horse from him. They then delivered him to another Mob, who carted him 4 Miles further, & forced another Dollar from him. The second Mob delivered him to a third Mob, who abused him by throwing Dirt at him, as also throwing the Offals, in his Face & endeavoring to cover him with it, to the endangering his Life, & after other Abuses, & carrying him 4 Miles further, made him pay another Sum of Mony. They urged the Councellors Lady, at whose House they stopped, to take the Ox; but she being a Lady of a firm Mind refused; upon which they tipped the Cart up & the Ox down into the Highway, & left it to take Care of it self. And in the Month of February following, this same *Dunbar* was selling Provisions at *Plimouth*, when the Mob seized him, tied him to his Horse's Tail, & in that Manner drove him through Dirt & mire out of the Town, & he falling down, his Horse hurt him.

In November 1774, *David Dunbar*[4] of *Hallifax* aforesaid, being an Ensign in the Militia, a Mob headed by some of the Select Men of the Town, demand[ed] his Colours of him. He refused, saying, that if his commanding Officer demanded them he should obey, otherwise he would not part with them: —upon which they broke into his House by Force & dragged him out. They had prepared a sharp Rail to set him upon; & in resisting them they seized him (by his private parts) & fixed him upon the Rail, & was held on it by his Legs & Arms, & tossed up with Violence & greatly bruised so that he did not recover for some Time. They beat him, & after abusing him about two Hours he was obliged, in Order to save his Life, to give up his Colours.

Quære—Whether it would not have been as strictly legal to have stolen the Colours from his House, without all this Parade?

The Mob Committee, of the County of *York*, where Sr. *William Pepperells* large Estate lay, ordered that no Person should hire any of his Estates of him, nor buy any Wood of him, nor pay any Debts to *him* that were due to him.

One of the Constables of *Hardwick*, for refusing to pay the Provincial Collection of Taxes which he had gathered, to the new Receiver General of the rebel Government, was confined & bound for 36 Hours, & not suffered to lie in a Bed, & threatened to be sent to

[4]According to the Boston *Weekly News-Letter*, Feb. 23, 1775, Dunbar's first name was Daniel.

Simsbury Mines in *Connecticut*. These Mines being converted into a Prison, 50 Feet under Ground, where it is said that many Loyalists have suffered. The Officers Wife being dangerously ill, they suffered him to see her, after he had complied.

The aforementioned Colo. *Gilbert* was so obnoxious for his Attachment to Government, that the Mobs being sometimes afraid to attack him openly, some of them secretly fired Balls at him in the Woods. And as he was driving a Number of Sheep to his Farm, he was attacked by 30 or 40 of them, who robbed him of part of the Flock, but he beat the Mob off. And this same Colo. *Gilbert* was, some Time after, travelling on his Business, when he stopped at an Inn to bait his Horse. Whilst he was in the House, some Person lift up the Saddle from his Horse & put a Piece of a broken Glass Bottle under the Saddle; & when the Colo. mounted, the Pressure run the Glass into the Horses back, which made him frantick. The Horse threw his rider, who was so much hurt as not to recover his Senses 'till he was carried & arrived at his own House, at 3 Miles distance.

In September 1774, when the Court of Common Pleas was assembled for the Business of the Term, at *Springfield*, a large Mob collected, & prevented the sitting of the Court; they would not suffer Bench or Bar to enter the Court House; but obliged Bench, Sheriffs & Bar, with their Hats off, in a most humiliating Manner, to desist.

February 1775

A Number of Ladies, at *Plimouth*, attempted to divert their selves at the publick Assembly Room; but not being connected with the rebel Faction, the Committee Men met, and the Mob collected who flung Stones & broke the Windows & Shutters of the Room, endangering the Lives of the Company, who were obliged to break up, & were abused to their Homes.

Soon after this, the Ladies diverted their selves by riding out of Town, but were followed & pelted by the Mob, & abused with the most indecent Language.

The Honble. *Israel Williams* Esqr., who was appointed one of his Majesty's new Council, but had refused the Office by Reason of bodily Infirmities, was taken from his House, by a Mob, in the Night, & carried several Miles; then carried home again, after being forced to sign a Paper which they drafted; & a guard set over him to prevent his going from Home.

A Parish Clerk of an Episcopal Church at *East Haddum* in *Connecticut*, a Man of 70 Years of Age, was taken out of his Bed in a Cold Night, & beat against his Hearth by Men who held him by his Arms & Legs. He was then laid across his Horse, without his Cloaths, & drove to a considerable Distance in that naked Condition. His Nephew Dr. *Abner Beebe*, a Physician, complained of the bad Usage of his Uncle, & spoke very freely in Favor of Government; for which he was assaulted by a Mob, stripped naked, & hot Pitch was poured upon him, which blistered his Skin. He was then carried to an Hog Sty & rubbed over with Hogs Dung. They threw the Hog's Dung in his Face, & rammed some of it down his Throat; & in that Condition exposed to a Company of Women. His House was attacked, his Windows broke, when one of his Children was sick, & a Child of his went into Distraction upon this Treatment. His Gristmill was broke, & Persons prevented from grinding at it, & from having any Connections with him.

All the foregoing Transactions were before the Battle of Lexington, when the Rebels say that the War began.

AN ADDRESS TO THE SOLDIERS

FOR THE *Massachusetts-Gazette*

AN ADDRESS

To the Soldiers of Massachusetts Bay who are now
in Arms against the Laws of their Country.[1]

MY FELLOW CITIZENS!

You have been addressed by the general officers of the continental
army as *fellow soldiers,* and with that insinuating art which was designed to move your passions: I would not draw your attention from
it, provided you will devote your cooler moments to a dispassionate
consideration of its subject matter.

Suffer me on my part to address you as *fellow citizens,* for I cannot have such dishonorable thoughts of you as to suppose that when
you put on the soldier that you then put off the citizen; citizens most
of you were, you enjoyed the comforts of domestic life, you lately
followed your different occupations and reaped the profits of a
quiet and peaceable industry, and I hope in *God* that you may yet do
it, without any disturbance to your innocent wives and children;
but in the late courses of your lives, you must not only have given
great uneasinesses to your families, but I dare to say, that all of you,
were not quite free from uneasiness in your own minds. I know my
dear countrymen! that many of you, have been drove to take up
arms against your Sovereign, and the laws of the happiest constitution that ever human beings were blest with; some through the necessities incident to human nature, and others by that compulsion
which the malevolent and ambitious arts of your leaders have made
necessary to deceive you with, in order to screen themselves from
that vengeance which the injured laws of society had devoted them
to. Many a tear of pity have I dropped for you and for the fate of
my country, and many more tears I fear that I shall be forced to shed
for that wrath which awaits you from an offended Heaven, and an

---

[1]Boston *Weekly News-Letter,* Jan. 11, 1776.

injured government. Many of your associates have already quitted the field of battle, to appear before that solemn tribunal where the plea of the united force of all the colonies will be of no avail to bribe the judgment or avert the sentence of an offended Deity. Some of them, in the agonies of death, sent messages to their friends to forbear proceeding any further, for they now found themselves in the wrong; others have repeatedly said, that an ambition of appearing something considerable and that only, led them into rebellion; and the unhappy leader, in the fatal action at Charlestown, (who from ambition only, had raised himself from a bare legged milk boy to a major general of an army) although the fatal ball gave him not a moment for reflection, yet had said in his life time, that *he was determined to mount over the heads of his coadjutors and get to the last round of the ladder or die in the attempt:* Unhappy man! his fate arrested him in his career, and he can now tell whether pride and ambition are pillars strong enough to support the tottering fabric of rebellion.

But not to divert you from an attention to the *address of your officers;* I would rather wish you to weigh it with exactness, and after you have so done, if you then should think that it is better to trample upon the laws of the mildest government upon earth, and throw off your allegiance to the most humane Sovereign that ever swayed a sceptre, and submit to a tyranny uncontrouled either by the laws of *God* or man, then blame none but yourselves, if the consequences should be fatally bad to you and to your families.

Your officers, my countrymen! have taken great pains to sooth and flatter you, that you may not quit your posts and forsake *them* until they have accomplished their ambitious and desperate schemes: Your leaders know that they have plunged themselves into the bowels of the most wanton and unnatural rebellion that ever existed; they think that by engaging numbers to partake in their guilt that they shall appear formidable, and that by so numerous an appearance the hand of justice will not dare to arrest them. Some of you know that this argument hath been frequently urged; but you must know, that much superior powers than this continent can boast of, have been conquered by that government which you are now at war with.

Your officers tell you, that they have reduced the regiments from *thirty eight* to *twenty six,* and assign as a reason, that *many officers from a puny habit of body found themselves incapable of fulfilling the duty of their station, have been obliged to absent themselves from their posts, and consequently the duty has fallen very heavily upon those who remained:* Whether this is a true reason or not, some of you can tell; be it so or not, why then not appoint others? are none of you fit for officers but those *who absented themselves from their posts?* You generally took up arms about the same time, and I dare to say that many of you were as well qualified for commissions as those who left their posts.

Another reason they sooth you with for disbanding *twelve* regiments is, that *the vast expence of attending the maintenance of so many regiments might have disabled the continent from persevering in its resolution of defending their liberties, if the contest should be of any continuance.* Surely my countrymen! you cannot be deluded with such trifling pleas: Can this continent, which undertakes to carry on a war with the power of Great Britain, be alarmed at a few millions of dollars? Their resources are boundless; the issuing of paper money is easily accomplished, and while you can be compelled to take it, the continent can never *be disabled from persevering in its resolutions.* Unhappily for them, they have discovered to you what will be much for your interest to know, viz That the vast expence of this civil war will be a burden too heavy for the shoulders of you or your posterity to bear: Consider, that already three millions of dollars have been emitted in paper, and that 434,000 dollars, equal to £976 000 O. T. is assessed on the province of the *Massachusetts Bay,* to redeem their part: and how much more must be raised to carry on this unnatural war, which was commenced to gratify the pride and desperation of many of your leaders, time alone will discover: You have just entred the lists, but there is much yet to be done; to finish the mighty independent empire, which they have planned for you, demands such resources as it will require one century to spunge away: Most of you have groaned under a tax of about 2 or 300 000 pounds old tenor, but when millions are thrown into the scale, they will press you down never to rise more.

Your officers tell you; that *men who are possessed of a vivacity of disposition, though brave and in all other respects unexceptionable, are totally unfit for service.* This is a new doctrine advanced to make good officers and soldiers: It is a mystery, which I leave to that dullness and stupidity which your officers have complimented you with to unravel; the meaning of it *you* are best acquainted with, but it puts *me* in mind of what I have heard from the mouth of an arch traiter, who was disappointed in his expectations of the promotions of his near relation, viz. *That the people were a set of d——d stupid asses and were fit only to be drove.*

You are further told, *that the present campaign is far from an hard one:* How hard you have worked and how much duty you have done, you yourselves can tell best. Many, who have seen your labours, have thought them great; and I am much inclined to believe, that you have gone through some difficulty, especially when your officers, having forgot the popularity of this harangue, almost in the next breath tell you, *that the post you at present occupy, was fortified and secured by infinite labour.* It is an old and just maxim, my countrymen! that *deceivers ought to have good memories.*

You are next addressed, in the invariable stile for years past, of news papers and popular harangues, with the abuses of ministers and generals: this may keep up your spirits for ought I know: Town meeting oratory I know has frequently had this effect, 'till the spirit of it was evaporated, and then it flattened so as to be quite insipid. They boast much of the attachment of *Nova Scotia* and *Canada*, to what they call your interest, as well as of the rest of the continent. I give you one word of advice, and as it is from a book which it is said you are fighting for, so I suppose that you will not totally disregard it; it is this, *let not him that putteth on the harness boast as he that putteth it off.* But as to the success of union, which you have met with, the same book says, that *rebellion is as the sin of witchcraft:* It is so my countrymen! in a double sense; for in the first place, no person but one who was bewitched, would run the risk of engaging in a rebellion; and in the next place, which is the true meaning of the words; as witchcraft is renouncing the authority of *God Almighty* and applying to the devil, so rebellion is withdrawing allegiance from a lawful sovereign, overturning his government and laws, and joining with a power inimical to him.[2]

[2]The same parallel of demon wizards bewitching the senses of the people was used in some popular poetry attributed to Jonathan Odell (*The American Times: A Satire. In Three Parts* [London, 1780], pp. 7-8):

> What groupe of Wizards next salutes my eyes,
> United comrades, quadruple allies?
> Bostonian Cooper, with his Hancock join'd,
> Adams with Adams, one in heart and mind;
> Sprung from the soil, where witches swarm'd of yore,
> They come well-skill'd in necromantic lore;
> Intent on mischief, busily they toil,
> The magic cauldron to prepare and boil;
> Array'd in sable vests, and caps of fur,
> With wands of ebony the mess they stir;
> See! the smoke rises from the cursed drench,
> And poisons all the air with horrid stench.

You are also told, that *as the southern provinces have ever placed the greatest confidence in your zeal and valor, they did not think it necessary to raise any bodies in the other provinces for this particular service.* Do you believe my countrymen! that any of the *Massachusett* officers were concerned in drawing this address to you? If so, beware of them, before it is too late. I will not believe it: It surely must be drawn by some of your foreign officers, whom you have disgraced yourselves by suffering them to command you, when you had men of your own province, who were at least equal to them and who would have more naturally cared for you: But you may have felt the ill consequence of it e'er now, and it may be too late for redress. The true English of it runs thus—*The Massachusetts have a different interest from the rest of the continent; they are a sett of brave hardy dogs, and are always encroaching upon their neighbours, and ought to be humbled; and when we have established our independency, we shall have much to fear from them: Let us therefore make them the mercenaries, they will sacrifice every thing for money, we can pay them in paper which they are so fond of: By engaging them for soldiers, they will get knocked in the head, their wives and children will be ruined; and when we have established our empire, we shall have nothing to fear from them; they will become an easy prey to the rest of the provinces, and we can parcel them out among us as we may think proper.*

The remainder of your officers address to you, I leave to your own remarks: It is so full of compliment and flattery, in order to reach your passions, that I cannot help blushing for you, and if you are caught by it I shall then pity you, and you will blush for yourselves.

That you may not plead ignorance, in justification of yourselves in case the fate of war should be against you, I will now let you into the origin and progress of the public disorders which for many years past have sickened the state of the province, and at last hath terminated in a most unnatural and ungrateful rebellion. I am persuaded, my countrymen! that you are ignorant of the true rise of your disorders; the aim of your leaders hath been to keep you in ignorance; they knew that your ignorance was their protection: Had you known their views, you would not only have spurned at the thought of overturning the constitution, but I venture to say that some of you would have dragged them to the bar of justice, there to have received that punishment which now awaits *them*, and I wish that you yourselves may not be involved in, as partakers in their crimes.—

The history runs thus, and every page of it is capable of ample proof. Know then, for many years past this province hath been deeply immersed in the *smuggling* business: Perhaps some of you are ignorant tho' I am sure all of you are not, of the meaning of *smuggling business:* I will tell you what it means: *it is an importation of goods, contrary to the laws of the society to which we belong; it is a defrauding the King of those dues which the law hath granted to him; which fraud is equal in criminality to the injuring of a private person; it is a violation of the laws of christianity; it is injuring and publickly ruining our neighbour; in short, when it is thoroughly engaged in, it naturally tends by degrees to the effacing every sentiment of virtue.* This is a description of the smuggling business, and it is here where I fix the sudden rise of the present rebellion.

In order to evade those laws against unlawful trade, those who were concerned in it exerted themselves to defeat them. Unluckily for the government, at that juncture, a person, who had a long while been hunting after preferment, was disappointed of his game: On which a friend of his who was versed in the law, vowed revenge, he swore that *he would set the province in a flame if he died in the attempt:* He fulfilled his oath and burnt his fingers to such a degree that he hath irrevocably lost the use of them. Remember my countrymen! that there is one sort of flame, that consumes not only a man's property, but also a man's understanding, and ruins, very often his posterity also.—This man's adroitness in law was thought necessary to be engaged in the cause of defeating acts of parliament: He was engaged, and he had shrewdness enough to start a thought, which, artfully pursued, hath generally its expected effect in all popular commotions; he said, that it was necessary to enlist a *black regiment* in their service; the bait was snapped at; and many ministers of the gospel, too, too many for the honor of the christian religion joined in the cry: The press then roared out its libels; the sacred desk, which ought to have been devoted to the doctrines and precepts of the Prince of peace, rang its changes on government and sounded the trumpet of sedition and rebellion: Boys who had just thrown away their satchels and who could scarcely read English mounted the pulpit and ventured to decide on matters which had puzzled the sages of the law. Nay, they could not be contented to decide controversies of law, in their harangues to their audience, but must shew their parts in their solemn addresses to the Supreme Being, telling him who had been guilty of murder where the law had pronounced the supposed crime to be only self-defence, and some of them even debased the sacred character, by setting on the rabble in the public street, to insult a person who was obnoxious to the leaders of the mob. At the same time, a notorious defaulter who had pocketed a large sum of the public monies, in order to screen himself, took it into his head to mouth it for patriotism; and by artful wiles and smooth demeanour he talked the people out of their understandings, and persuaded them to give him a discharge from the debt, on account of his patriotism. This man, whom but a day before hardly any one would have trusted with a shilling and whose honesty they were jealous of, now became the confidence of the people: With his oily tongue he duped a man whose brains were shallow and pockets deep, and ushered him to the public as a patriot too: He filled his head with importance and emptied his pockets, and as a reward hath kicked him up the ladder, where he now presides over the twelve united provinces, and where they both are at present plunging you, my countrymen, into the depths of distress. Libertinism, riot and robbery soon became the effects of this sort of public spirit; houses were plundered and demolished, persons were beat, abused, tarred and feathered; courts of justice were insulted; the pillars of government were destroyed; and no way to escape the torrent of savage barbarity but by paying obeisance to the sovereign mandates of a mob. Garrets were crowded with patriots; mechanicks and lawyers, porters and clergymen huddled promiscuously into them; their decisions were oracular, and from thence they poured out their midnight reveries: They soon determined to form an independent empire; yes, my countrymen! I assure you that this independent empire, which you are now assisting those pretented patriots to erect, was formed above seven years ago, though I dare say, that most of you are ignorant of the black design: and one of the patriots (peace be to his *manes*) openly avowed it, and declared that a valuation had been taken of the estates in the town of *Boston*, which he supposed would be destroyed by the naval power of *Great Britain*, and that all the friends of licentiousness were to be reimbursed out of the estates of the friends to government.

The patriots were determined to humble *Great Britain;* and, as a first step, they promoted a nonimportation agreement at the same time that the wealthy and artful among them had large quantities of goods by them by the advanced sale of which they made fortunes and ruined the small traders: They promised to send their new imported goods back to *England*, and instead thereof, their trunks were crowded with billets of wood shavings and brickbats, to the eternal disgrace of this province when they were opened in *England*. Some of the patriots carried about papers of subscription against importing goods from *England,* and washing women and porters, in order to swell the list, made their marks, for write they could not, that they would not import coaches or chariots from home: when they were told of the impropriety of such a conduct, and that the scheme would have no effect, they replied, that they were sensible of it, but *Great Britain* would be scared by it: they hired mercenaries in *England* to cabal and write for them and raise an insurrection: when they were told that *Great Britain* would be roused, they said that she was not to be dreaded; that she had neither men nor money; that there was more money in the Colonies than in England; that if she should resent it, that the Colonies would not pay them the millions that were due to her. Not content with this insult, the General Assembly disavowed any observance of Acts of Parliament. *Great Britain,* with her usual lenity, pitied our infatuation, tho' she was at last forced to send troops to support civil government; those troops we were then to destroy, and we did our best to destroy them; but felt the fatal consequence of the attempt: our violences at last rose to such an height, that injured sovereignty and an insulted government have been roused to assert their authority, in order to curb as wanton and wicked a rebellion as ever raged in any government upon earth.

Thus, my countrymen! I have very shortly stated to you the rise and progress of the present rebellion. I believe that many, if not most of you, were insensible of the ambitious views of your leaders: I do not think that you were so devoid of virtue as to rush into so horrid a crime at one leap; for let me tell you, that it is the highest crime that a member of society can be guilty of, and the punishment annexed to it is nothing less than a forfeiture of estate and life: your leaders have deceived you into what they do not believe themselves: they were desperate themselves, and they have involv'd you in their own just doom: they tell you your *properties* and *religion* are at stake: your ministers tell you so too; and I know you are too apt to take all that they say, for gospel; but pray, what danger is your religion in? why, it is said that popery is established in *Canada,* and will be established here: no, my countrymen! popery is not established in *Canada,* let your teachers and leaders assert it never so roundly: it is only indulged to the Roman Catholicks there: your continental congress says, that *God* and nature have given them a right to the enjoyment of their religion: it is what they capitulated for with *General Amherst:* it is what the just, the humane, *King George the third* confirmed to them: this is the King whom you so lately professed allegiance to, in opposition to the parliament; not considering that it was by acts of parliament that the crown was placed upon his head and on the heads of his predecessors: it seems indeed that your leaders have more lately found out that it is as necessary to deny the authority of the King as they have been daring in denying that of his Parliament; witness their late *Thanksgiving* Proclamation, which concludes with a *God save the People,* instead of the heretofore invariable, *God save the King.* Will it not suffice your leaders to mock the King but they must mock Heaven also? read it over, view the cloven foot of one of your spiritual guides peeping out, whose pen fabricated the mockery, and whose foot has many a time trod the recesses of rebellion with the *cabal*; and I dare to say, that had it not been made to oblige you to pay duties upon various articles: be it this, once over happy, but now miserably distracted province had not been so soon involved in distress.

I would ask also you my countrymen! how your *properties* are at stake? you will doubtless tell me, that acts of parliament have been made to oblige you to pay duties upon various articles: be it so; why then do you purchase articles that are to pay duties: why then do you not petition in a constitutional manner to have these acts repealed? the British parliament never assumed to themselves infallibility, and many a time have they repealed American acts when they have been convinced that the enforcement of them was incompatible with the mutual interest: it is true, your leaders did petition, but in such an unconstitutional manner, that it was below the dignity and contrary to the system of the English government to hear such petitions; and this your leaders knew must be the fate of them, and this method they planned in order to effect their independence and make themselves of that importance to you which they now appear in. But you can have no just plea for entring so deeply into opposition against the parent state: you may know, if you please, that *King Charles the first* granted to our ancestors a charter; you may call it a compact if you please too, and if it be so, the argument will be much against you, for in that you compacted to pay duties after a short term of years, and you have been fulfilling your compact, by paying duties, for above an hundred years past, till, of late, the scandalous *smuggling business* reared its front against the laws and brought the state into its present distraction—You have been told also that your land was to be taxed and that you were to be brought into lordships; this I know hath been artfully propagated among you,

[166]

and I dare assert it to be groundless: there is too much justice and benignity in the English government to advance such a scheme, and supposing that they had it in their idea to do it, so violent an opposition ought to have been suspended at lest, 'till the scheme had been brought into action: it is like one man's cutting another's throat, lest the other might possibly injure his grand children.

I am loth to detain you any longer, my countrymen! from sober reflection: for *God's* sake, for your own sakes, for your wives and childrens sake, pause a moment and weigh the event of this unnatural civil war. You have roused the British Lion; you have incensed that power which hath crushed much greater powers than you can boast of, and hath done it without your aid too. Great Britain is not so distressed for men, or money as some would make you believe: Your conduct hath raised the resentment of the greatest powers in *Europe,* and she may, if she pleases, accept of their proffered aid. But your priests and your leaders tell you otherwise; and I will just put the case, that supposing Heaven, in righteous judgment should suffer you to conquer: look forward then to the fatal consequences of your conquest: you will be conquered by an army of your own raising, and then your dreaded slavery is fixed; the ambition and desperation of your leaders will then demand the fruit of all their toils. Turn back a few pages of the English history; read the account of the civil wars of the last century; and view the triumphs and absolute sway of that tyrant *Cromwell:* he, like some of your leaders, began with humoring the enthusiasm of the times, and ended, the parricide of his country. Let me suppose again, as you vainly imagine, that this will not be the case, and that when you have conquered, you will then beat all your swords into plough shares; how long do you think it will be, before you are obliged to change sides, and beat your plough shares into swords again? you will then have twelve or fourteen colonies to form into an independent empire: where then is to be the seat of empire? surely the *Massachusetts-Bay* hath the best title to precedence; they begun the rebellion and they have the best title to reward. Do you think that the other colonies cannot furnish as artful demagogues as this province can? do not imagine that we are the men and that wisdom is to die with us: we shall be cantoned out into petty states, we shall be involved in perpetual wars for an inch or two of ground: our fertile fields will be deluged with blood, our wives & children be involved in the horrid scene: foreign powers will step in and share in the plunder that remains, and those who are left to tell the story will be reduced to a more abject slavery than that which you now dread. The colonies are too jealous of each other to remain long in a state of friendship.

I will now, my fellow citizens! change the scene to a more eligible view for your interest, and suppose it possible, tho' you don't think it so, that *Great Britain* can conquer you, and that instead of being victors you may be subjects again. You will then have the mildest government to live under, a government to be envied by the rest of mankind, and whose only unhappiness is, that it is too apt to abuse that liberty which *God* and the constitution hath blessed it with. She hath been loth to call you *conquered*; she hath, like an over fond parent indulged your pevishness, and witheld her resentment until she hath felt the smart of her indulgence: she is now roused, but her resentment is tempered with mildness. He whom you formerly acknowledged for your Sovereign drops the tear of pity for you, in his late speech, from the throne, a speech so attempered with paternal pity, royal firmness of mind and sentiment of dignity, as distinguishes the speaker as the father of his country and the orna- ment of human nature: clemency he is distinguished for; he is re- vered for his humanity; but his soul is impressed with too much magnanimity, to suffer his laws and the rights of his subjects to be trampled under the foot of rebellion; he holds out the sceptre of mercy, that bright gem of his royal dignity, for you to embrace; but if you chuse to kiss the rod of his justice, be you yourselves wit- nesses that it is not his choice: remember, that Heaven punishes but to save: the God of Heaven hath repeatedly checked rebellion, and our own history confirms its defeats. Rebellion is so odious in the eyes of all rational beings, that it is for the universal good that it should be suppressed; it saps the foundation of moral virtue, and therefore it is for the general interest that all nature should rise in arms against it; and I have not the lest doubt, that providence will arrest it in its carreer. When that time comes, complain not that you were not forewarned, and bear your own punishment without mur- muring.

That you may seriously reflect on your own impending fate, and the fate of your wives and innocent children, before you take the deadly plunge, and that you immediately retire from the precipice of ruin, is the friendly wish of

Your fellow Citizen.

Z. Z.

INDEX

INDEX

[171]